Lawyers, Law, and Social Change

STEVE BACHMANN

AUTHOR'S PREFACE
TO THE SECOND EDITION

The first edition of *Lawyers, Law and Social Change* (Unlimited Publishing LLC, 2001) was itself a retrospective collection of essays written over the previous 25 years. This new edition evolved in response to a series of circumstances nearly unimaginable at the time of its original publication.

The impetus to further reflect on the failures of the social change movement began in 2008. World capitalism crashed. The planet's most powerful nation, as rich in wealth as it was in a history of abusing people of color (whether black, brown, yellow or red of skin… or politically pink) elected to its highest office a person of African descent. Yet extremist elements of Congress later gained sway, resisting and even attempting to revoke virtually every effort to effect social change. By the year 2011, a nascent "Occupy" movement, grounded in protesting economic inequality, appeared first on the streets of American cities, then worldwide.

For the author, the dizzying events of 2008 and following included some personal diversions.

In the face of a right wing media onslaught, I worked with the Association of Communities Organized for Reform Now (ACORN) to mobilize citizens to vote for candidate Obama, who had once worked as a community organizer and litigated with me on the same side of an ACORN voting rights lawsuit cited in the 60 page addendum to this edition. [See addendum section pages 153-154]

ACORN could not resist capitulating to the right-wing media onslaught. [See addendum section page 159]

But the dismal events of 2008 and following sparked renewed interest in the social change movement.

The editors of the *New York University Review of Law and Social Change* contacted me about writing a 25-year update to my 1984 law review article that became the namesake for the first edition of this book, and about delivering the keynote address at their 40th anniversary celebration in 2010.

Meanwhile, the publisher of my first book, titled *U.S. Constitution for Beginners*, contacted me about writing a second edition, updated for 2012. It is expected out this year from For Beginners LLC, distributed by Random

House. Coincidentally, the first edition was edited by Danny O. Snow, the founder of Unlimited Publishing LLC, which is the co-publisher of this volume.

By the time I spoke at the New York University Law School, it seemed clear that if 2008 was a carnival, it was a circus which had come to town in the sense described by Bob Dylan in his song "Desolation Row."

In 2010, the world economy still sputtered, still run by people who believed in the neo-liberalism that caused the mess. [See addendum section page 164]

The former community organizer in the White House seemed more interested in drawing on his experiences as student president of the *Harvard Law Review*, where he had served as a trimmer between privileged liberals and relentless reactionaries.

Sadly, I was unable to advance the release date for the new edition of *U.S. Constitution for Beginners* in time for Michele Bachmann's 2011 seminars for the Congress elected in 2010. Or her doomed 2011 presidential campaign.

In light of, or in spite of, these developments, I am producing this second edition of *Lawyers, Law, and Social Change*. To the first edition, it adds a verbatim copy of the 2010 update which appeared in the 34th volume of *New York University Review of Law and Social Change*, preserving even the page numbering. Additionally, a copy of the keynote address I delivered at the NYURLSC's 40th anniversary celebration precedes the 2010 article.

The first edition ended with the sentences "It does seem clear that if a mobilization of people is going to occur, it will not happen without organizing. And the problem with the years since 1984 is that it seems that outside some exceptions, most of the organizing has been done by the Right."

My observation then, and now, is that those who seem to have been practicing what I have preached are the votaries of reaction. I suppose we can take some comfort in this, not because anyone on the Right has been reading what I say, but because what I say is so obvious that even the most obtuse can see what needs to be done to take and to hold power.

Yet I grieve equally at the sorry record on the Left. Some of the fault can be placed at the feet of the unscrupulous Right. But not all of it. [See addendum section pages 157-159 and 163]

Someday lay people – and lawyers – may effectively mobilize and organize against the plutocrats and mandarins, as well as their thugs and apologists. In the meantime, we can respect people like John L. Lewis, Daisy Bates, Jack Straw, Wat Tyler, John Ball, Thomas Rainsborough, Mary Wollstonecraft, Frederick Douglass, and William Blake; and when we join them in the grave, we can take hope in the notion that we have passed their legacy to those who follow us, through messages that we "bottled" in print

– and, better yet, historical praxis.

Désobéir d'abord: alors écris sur les murs (Loi du 10 Mai 1968.)

– SRB, February 2012.

TABLE OF CONTENTS

INTRODUCTION

The purpose of this anthology is to present an ACORN perspective on matters of lawyers, law and social change. ACORN's full name provides some description of itself, Association of Community Organizations for Reform Now. It is a grouping of low- and moderate-income neighborhood groups which have worked together for social change since 1970.

When one considers the relationship between lawyers, law, and social change, a number of questions arise. Not the least of them is "What constitutes 'good' social change?" If "pro bono" means "for the good," what is the good? If it involves law for the public interest, what is that? Is it a "poverty lawyer" who serves poor individual clients at legal aid? Is it the public defender who defends indigent individuals from accusations of criminal activity? Is it the public prosecutor who pursues criminals so that they cannot prey on members of the public? Is it the activist lawyer who represents environmental groups? Labor unions? Women's groups? Pro-choice groups? Pro-life groups? Civil Rights groups? The Ku Klux Klan? Harvard Law School has fellowships for lawyers practicing "public interest" law, and awards have gone to lawyers who fall into many of the preceding categories. Perhaps the HLS definition of the pro bono lawyer is one who doesn't get paid as well as the stereotypical moneybags lawyer who works for the big law firm or the enormous corporation.

Assuming one could ascertain what constitutes the social good, another critical question is what if anything lawyers have to do with implementing it. The joke in Anglo-American folklore is that they have nothing positive to contribute, and the best thing that they could do would be for all of them to go off and die. Other perspectives might see the lawyer's role as critical, marginal, irrelevant or essential.

While the ACORN perspective entertains reservations concerning the efficacy of lawyers, ACORN certainly has employed attorneys over the years to help it advance the interests of its low- and moderate-income constituency. Since 1976, I have been one of those attorneys. Over the years I have speculated and written on what roles lawyers might play in the implementation of meaningful social change; and sometimes how they might actually live those roles. Some of these writings are collected in this anthology. If they do not guide the reader to particular conclusions as to these matters, at the very least they will hopefully help to conceptualize his or her thinking on these matters.

The essays in this collection are ordered chronologically, but they do fall into some subject matter coherency.

The first two essays deal with living life as a social change lawyer. The first essay consists of an excerpt from my thesis paper at Harvard Law School which dealt with the ethics embodied in the Code of Professional Responsibility. Since it was written in 1976, much of it is dated beyond endurance. The part which I believe remains relevant marks two issues concerning lawyer life situations. The first issue relates to political oppression: the harassment that social change lawyers endured before the 1960s is a history that should not be forgotten, particularly if the present resurgence of the Right leads to new versions of harassment in the 21st century. The second relates to the phenomenon of proletarianization. In 1976 I argued that the Marxist conception of capitalist development (including proletarianization) seemed to apply both to Americans in general and lawyers in particular. The degree to which this Marxist approach remains useful and applicable to Americans and lawyers some 25 years later seems to me a question still worth raising. At this juncture I should acknowledge the assistance of my thesis advisor Prof. Diane Lund in grappling with these issues.

The second essay is a review of Arthur Kinoy's RIGHTS ON TRIAL, and was first published in 62 TEXAS LAW REVIEW 1601 (1984). I found Kinoy's book valuable not only as a record of the civil rights movement from one lawyer's perspective. The extent to which Kinoy conveyed the existential sense of living that record also made the book worth discussing.

A third essay which was never written but which the reader might wish to write on her own would be a review of Christopher H. Johnson's MAURICE SUGAR: LAW, LABOR AND THE LEFT IN DETROIT, 1912-1950 (Detroit: Wayne State University Press, 1988). It traces the career of a social change lawyer who now has a law center named after him in Detroit. The book provides not only a record of the U.S. labor movement during critical phases in its history. The lawyer around whom the narrative revolves experienced significant defeats as well as important victories during his career. (As background to this book the reviewer will want to ensure that she also reads Nelson Lichtenstein's THE MOST DANGEROUS MAN IN DETROIT: WALTER REUTHER AND THE FATE OF AMERICAN LABOR (N.Y: Basic Books, 1995).)

The third essay which actually appears in this book is that which gives this book its title, "Lawyers, Law and Social Change," which first appeared in 13 NEW YORK UNIVERSITY OF LAW AND SOCIAL CHANGE 1 (1984-1985). I would like to acknowledge a number of people who gave help in producing this article: my then law partner Andrew Weltchek; Bill Mascioli, Mark Risk, Eddie Hartnett, and Emily Ruben of the *New York*

University Review of Law & Social Change; and, finally, Derrick Bell who first exposed me to issues of "Law, Lawyers and Social Change" in his course of the same name at Harvard Law School in 1974. Since then, Prof. Bell has made his own mark in social commentary, see, e.g., AND WE ARE NOT SAVED (N.Y: Basic Books, 1989). Also, since then, a number of books have been published which I wish would have been available to me when I wrote this article in 1984. I refer to one of them in a postscript to the article. Two other sources which I would cite have cultivated theories and concepts of class in productive directions. The first is Pierre Bourdieu's DISTINCTION: A SOCIAL CRITIQUE OF THE JUDGMENT OF TASTE (trans. R. Nice) (Cambridge, MA: Harvard University Press, 1998). First published in France in 1979, this study investigates the role that culture plays in class formation and class hegemony. The second is Sven Beckert's THE MONEYED METROPOLIS: NEW YORK CITY AND THE CONSOLIDATION OF THE AMERICAN BOURGEOISIE, 1850-1896 (Cambridge, UK: Cambridge University Press, 2001), which provides an excellent elaboration on class formation (i.e., the processes by which a class-in-itself becomes organized into a class-for-itself) in the concrete historical context of 19th century New York City.

The fourth essay is something of a postscript to the "Lawyers Law and Social Change" article. It is a review of Gerald Rosenberg's THE HOLLOW HOPE: CAN COURTS BRING ABOUT SOCIAL CHANGE? The review was first published in 19 NEW YORK UNIVERSITY OF LAW AND SOCIAL CHANGE 391 (1991-1992), with the editorial assistance of Mike Bowen and the staff of the *New York University Review of Law & Social Change.*

The existence and oppression of poor people has been considered an indication of societal sickness meriting rectification since at least the writing of the Old Testament. The next two essays deal with the matter of attorneys attempting to participate in that rectification. Essay Number Five approaches the topic from the perspective of "poverty law." Comments and encouragement from Prof. Bill Quigley, Director of the Gillis Long Poverty Law Center at Loyola Law School, played a significant role in the production of this article.

Essay Number Six considers the topic from the religious perspective of Prof. Robert Rodes of Notre Dame Law School, as articulated in his book PILGRIM LAW.

The last essay in the book plays the role of an "epilogue." It reviews various of the arguments raised in the 1984 "Lawyers Law and Social Change" article, and discusses what the years since then might have to say concerning them.

CHAPTER ONE
LAWYERS AND THEIR
PROFESSIONAL HAZARDS

THE CONCRETE WORLDS BEHIND
THEORETICAL WORLDVIEWS

The story of American society up to the present is the story of the process of capitalism–a system based on private ownership of societal resources, which means that some individuals begin with rights to those resources while others do not. The system's motor is profit, which means that those who do have exclusionary rights to various aspects of society's resources will try to get more; and they do this by exploiting the source of value in the society–viz., living labor–which is to say that try extract as much free labor as possible for those who work for them.[1] (I.e., they pay their workers less than what the workers create for them, which is also to say–they make a profit!)

What this process involves in the long run is a grand polarization: on the one side, society's resources become more and more concentrated into fewer and fewer hands.[2] On the other side, those who become dispossessed become proletarianized, and thus more and more people must get permission from controllers of the society's productive forces in order to live. Moreover, the quality of life for the proletarians tends to deteriorate further and further, because the process of the capitalists' trying to appropriate for free as much of the proletarians' labor as possible continues and intensifies. This immiseration assumes two forms: the wage cut is the obvious form. Alienation[3] is the more subtle and probably the more cruel.[4]

The trend towards proletarianization in the United States is clear. On the side of accumulation, the concentrations of wealth have become so vast that they have transcended the "limited and limiting personal form" and begin to assume the institutional form.[5] And so it is that at present 1.6% of all businesses in the United States account for ¾ of all sales, and 1/10 of all firms employ nearly half of the paid labor force.[6] On the side of proletarianization, the percentage of self-employed in the American population has declined from 4/5 in the early 19th century to 1/3 in 1870 to 1/10 in 1970.[7] Those who work on farms have declined from half the population in 1880 to less than 4% in 1970.[8] Where did all these people go? Mostly into the ranks of the working class, which in 1900 comprised some 50% of the population.[9] When we recall that presently only some 10% of the population is now self-employed, we realize that many of the remaining 30-35% who are not clear-cut proletarians are not much better off. These people (lower level managers and technocrats) too "bear the marks of the proletarian condition" although they do enjoy a "petty share in the prerogatives and rewards of capital."[10]

And the immiseration intensifies. If wages have gone up the worth of money has gone down. The unequal national distribution of wealth has remained constant over the course of the century and shows no sign of tending towards more equality.[11] And more and more jobs in America are becoming "rationalized" which is to say more and more jobs are becoming routinized so they can be better controlled by the managers. "On balance it is probably proper to say that the technical knowledge required to operate the various industries of the United States is concentrated in a grouping in the neighborhood of only 3 percent of the entire working population."[12] The privilege of decision making, as we have seen, seems to have been distributed in varying amounts to some 15-20% of the work force, with more ultimate powers of management limited to a privileged 10%.

From the above we can deduce that capitalist American society has been developing two radically different life experiences, two objective sets of circumstances that any given subjective ego might experience–the one, a bourgeois experience, the other, a proletarian. Given these two differing circumstances, two differing world views develop: the bourgeois, and the proletarian. The bourgeois view is atomistic because his socioeconomic life experience is atomistic. He lives in a market competing against other ego-centric atoms. Individual autonomy makes sense to him because in his work the bourgeois is isolated, and he does make his own decisions regarding how to cope with the world of the market.[13] By contrast, the proletarian tends to find her/himself responding more deeply to a collective world view, and this is also due to her/his objective socio-economic life experience. The proletarian is not autonomous. S/he is subjected to the direction of the capitalist, and is normally a member of a mass group consisting of many individuals sharing situations, interests and concerns identical to her/his own (at the very least in relation to the capitalist). Conceiving of her/himself as a unique autonomous atom, arrayed against a society consisting of equally disparate atoms thus makes little sense to the proletarian.

We should note here that the bourgeoisie adopts and promulgates its world view (paradigm) not only because it rings with the truth of its life experience. It also espouses these views of the sake of maintaining its hegemony over the proletariat–because as long as the proletarian is induced to conceive of her/his socio-economic situation in atomistic terms, the road to effective combination with other proletarians (and immediate overthrow of bourgeois rule) is blocked. The proletariat's ability to cultivate itself into a conscious class-for-itself, in the full Marxist sense of the word, is impeded.

In order to achieve its concrete liberation, the proletariat must first liberate its own vision. The theory is that as history develops, reality will ultimately pressure the proletariat into looking at reality through the most appropriate paradigm.[14] That historical reality will provide–indeed, *has* provided–the pressure is hard to dispute. Even commentators beginning with the bourgeois paradigm have come to acknowledge the *crucial* importance of collective action in society if the individual is ever to wrought any practical effect in society.[15] The Supreme Court has not been blind to the point, either.[16]

ETHOI AS FUNCTIONS OF CLASS STRUGGLE

Given the insights that the preceding Marxist analysis has provided us, we can now provide a more worthy explanation for the existence and conflict of the two ethical views heretofore cited. One ethic is based upon a proletarian paradigm, the aim of which is contrary to the bourgeois order. By contrast, the Establishmentarian ethic derives from the experience of the bourgeois class: it responds to its sense of socio-economic reality, and it promotes its class interests against that of the proletariat.

How the Code of Professional Responsibility and its predecessors express and implement these class interests is the subject to which we now turn.

The Code of Professional Responsibility derives from and accordingly reflects the bourgeois socio-economic life experience.[17] The present Code derives from the old Canons which in their turn "drew heavily upon George Sharswood's ESSAY ON PROFESSIONAL ETHICS, published in 1854."[18] Sharswood's world, of course, was an America which had yet to be subjected to general proletarianization of the majority of the population.[19] [20] In Sharswood's America, most of the adults who "counted" (i.e., white males) could be counted as bourgeois, albeit petty bourgeois.[21] Yet Sharswood's 1854 vision could nevertheless ring true to a group of (legal) professionals whose socio-economic situation has yet been spared significant proletarianization, in that the lawyer's work situation resembles the bourgeois' in terms of the autonomy and opportunities for individual expression that his/her occupation entails–as opposed to the regimentation of more proletarian occupations.[22] And thus it was that in 1938 Karl Llewellyn could cite the Canons for being appropriate to a small town of 25,000 people.[23] And more recently, in 1967, Justice Douglas could brand the legal profession for being "middle class in its assumptions."[24]

But in addition to expressing a bourgeois life situation, the Establishmentarian ethic also serves a political function, viz., the promulgation of bourgeois class interests in the face of popular upsurges. The original Canon rules regarding solicitation and stirring up litigation helped to close off lower class access to legal assistance.[25] Contingent fee arrangements were subject to close scrutiny, given their potential for motivating attacks upon corporations' profits.[26] This pattern of checking the lower classes' use of the courts to improve their lots vis a vis corporate interests continued into the 1960s. We have seen how the Canons were used to attack the activity of the NACCP and various unions.[27] It is of interest to note that the Association of American Railroads spent $325,000 annually to finance offices in New York, Atlanta, St. Louis, Chicago and Los Angeles to look for possible ethical violations on the part of lawyers retained by union members for workmen's compensation claims.[28] As a result, over 1500 investigations were instituted,[29] some of which provided the basis for Bar Association proceedings against union counsels in Iowa, Nebraska, Oklahoma, Montana, Michigan, Ohio and Virginia.[30][31] Finally, nascent OEO offices were greeted with a number of lawsuits challenging their legitimacy on "ethical" grounds.[32]

And, of course, if one wishes to check the hoi polloi's access to the power of the state possessed by the Courts, what more effective way than to hit at their mediums, the lawyers? It has been suggested that the original Canons were promulgated so as to keep under control the number of aspiring lower class Jews and Catholics who were trying to break into the profession during the early part of the 20th century.[33] But one need not rely on innuendo to be aware of the attacks on people's lawyers from Brandeis to Kunstler, and every quasi-Commie in between.[34]

The politics underlying the Establishmentarian ethics become blatantly obvious when we note who have NOT been subject to ethical sanctions. In 1934, a group of right-wing lawyers organized the National Lawyers Committee of the American Liberty League to attack the New Deal. Among other things, these lawyers issued elaborate press releases, declared a law unconstitutional while a case was pending, and finally offered free legal services for anyone whose rights had been abridged. Instead of calling this solicitation, or stirring up litigation, ABA Opinion 148 exonerated these lawyers.[35] With regard to soliciting by law intermediary organizations, Justice Carter of California found it unusual if not unfair to apply ethical sanctions against unions, and not against "contractors' associations, merchants' associations, cattlemen's associations, etc." all of whom did essentially the same thing as did the union with its legal referral service.[36] Justice Traynor reached the same conclusion, and to Justice Carter's list he added bankers associations.[37] Finally, we might note that though the Canons could be used to impede bourgeois class interests, they are not designed to create any unnecessary trouble. Commentators have remarked as to the lack of ethical injunctions which deal with "solicitation" of clients through the use of entertainment, eating clubs, country clubs, etc.[38]

Thus, the Canons engender support not only for their intellectual appeal, but also for their appeal to the bourgeois' sense of socioeconomic reality, and also his political interest. However, there is one other sort of appeal which these Establishmentarian ethics and bourgeois paradigms inspire, and that is their emotive appeal. We have noted the legal profession's sensitivity to the issue of autonomy when we enumerated the grounds that were cited to justify the considerations which censured lay intermediary organizations. This solicitude for autonomy can be traced to the lawyer's historical roots in the (petty) bourgeoisie; and to the lawyer's humanity (recall our points regarding human nature). But we might also suggest that lawyers are presently hyper-sensitive over the issue of autonomy because the "rationalizing" process of capitalism threatens to proletarianize their occupation too. And this terrifies not only on grounds of loss of status, but also on grounds of loss of humanity. Lawyers who already are integrated into lay intermediary organizations, or who work for legal services, are especially irritating to the normal lawyer because they present him with a completed version of the proletarianized lawyer (i.e., their professional trappings are shed, their autonomy is limited, they work for a wage, etc.) But the process towards proletarianization has already begun within the confines of the regular "profession." The legal profession is witnessing concentration just like any other profit-making industry under capitalism. In the competition for profits, law firms have grown enormously in size, and have intensified markedly in specialization. The labor process here too becomes fragmented, with paralegals participating in much of the legal work. Suddenly, clerk, associates and junior partners find their labor being directed by another authority figure. Given our analysis, we can express this process to continue.[39] As will the negative reactions to it.[40]

CHAPTER TWO

BOOK REVIEW

RIGHTS ON TRIAL: THE ODYSSEY OF A PEOPLE'S LAWYER

By Arthur Kinoy. Cambridge: Harvard University Press,
1983. Pp. 340. $20.00.

By Arthur Kinoy. Cambridge: Harvard University Press, 1983. Pp. 340. $20.00.

Arthur Kinoy's legal career reads like a history of the recent American Left from the lawyer's box. *In Rights on Trial: The Odyssey of a People's Lawyer*,[41] Kinoy discusses his involvement with the Rosenbergs, the Mississippi Freedom Democratic Party, the House Un-American Activities Committee, Adam Clayton Powell, Dombrowsky v. Pfister,[42] the Chicago Seven, and many other people, groups, and cases. This list indicates that Kinoy has the capacity to deliver a left wing equivalent of *My Life in Court* by Louis Nizer,[43] or *The Defense Never Rests* by F. Lee Bailey,[44] but we might hope for something more from a "people's lawyer" than simply a compilation of self-centered war stories or the inside poop in famous cases. We might hope, for instance, for some insights on the theory and practice of legal work.[45] Happily, Professor Kinoy grapples with these matters as he writes of his remarkable encounters with our legal and political past. Overall, however, *In Rights on Trial* is more a witness to history than an exercise in jurisprudence.

* * *

"The natural rights of man" represents, of course, an erroneous line of thought. Is there such a thing as rights bestowed by nature? Isn't it man who bestows rights on man? Were the rights we enjoy bestowed by nature? Our rights were bestowed by the common people, and primarily by the working class and the poor and lower-middle peasants.[46]

–Mao Tse-Tung

* * *

In discussing the theory of progressive law, Kinoy emphasizes that law is subordinate to politics. Kinoy repeatedly stresses that the key to changing laws and society is to cultivate mass popular movements that can impel such change. He recalls that in 1964, when he defended Jim Dombrowski in Louisiana,

> [t]he fundamental conviction underlying the developing movement in Mississippi ... was the recognition that its substantive goals could be achieved only through direct massive activity of the southern Black people themselves. There was a growing realization that the 1954 decision in *Brown*, the national reaffirmation of the century-old constitutional promise of freedom and equality, was not self-enforcing in any respect.[47]

Kinoy similarly appraises *COFO v. Rainey*[48] and his efforts to appoint federal commissioners in Mississippi to protect civil rights:

> Only to the degree that the lawsuit provided an arena in which people could learn to work together and to experience the possibility of fighting back did it serve a valuable purpose. And only to the degree that it said to people, in terms they could understand, that they had to rely on their own action, no one else's, did it play an important role in sharpening people's understanding of how to move ahead.[49]

In 1965 Kinoy began to struggle against the House Un-American Activities Committee. He witnessed once again "one of the underlying precepts of the functioning of a people's lawyer, that the legal activity must stimulate and be totally interrelated with the development of mass action by the people themselves."[50]

In the eight-year legal and political battle against HUAC, Kinoy and others sought support from tens of thousands of people, by "holding meetings, leafleting, filing petitions, lobbying, and fundraising in every sort of way." Kinoy's position is clear: legal progress can best be achieved by mass mobilization.[51]

Kinoy's experiences conform to those of other progressives. For example, labor's seminal victory in *NLRB v. Jones & Laughlin Steel Corp.*[52] was won in the factories before the Supreme Court rendered its decision on April 12, 1937.[53] As Kinoy suggests, the "rights" "established" by *Brown v. Board of Education*[54] were not really secured until after the mass movements of the early 1960s.[55] Joel Handler studied thirty-five cases from four major areas of social change and came to the following conclusion about the value of public interest legal work:

> Social-reform groups have turned to law reformers and the legal system because they are weak. The powerful rarely need

the courts; they can exert their influence in politics, administration, and the private market … [B]y turning to the legal system, social reform groups have appealed to traditional institutions, and their claims for social justice have been based on traditional American constitutional values. It should come as no surprise, then, that law-reform activity by social-reform groups will not result in any great transformation in American society. Instead, it is, at its most successful level, incremental, gradualist, and moderate. It will not disturb the basic political and economic organization of modern American society.[56]

Despite the remarkable victories achieved in the courts,[57] we should not be overly optimistic about the worth of purely legal struggles.

Kinoy has done well to remind us that a law reform strategy based primarily on change by judicial process is both ill-conceived[58] and ahistorical.[59]

* * *

We reach, then, not a simple conclusion (law = class power) but a complex and contradictory one. On the one hand, it is true that the law did mediate existent class relations to the advantage of the rulers … On the other hand, the law mediated these class relations through legal forms, which imposed, again and again, inhibitions upon the actions of the rulers. For there is a very large difference, which twentieth-century experience ought to have made clear even to the most exalted thinker, between arbitrary extra-legal power and the rule of law …

…

The rhetoric and the rules of a society are something a great deal more than sham. In the same moment they may modify, in profound ways, the behaviour of the powerful, and mystify the powerless. They may disguise the true realities of power, but, at the same time, they may curb that power and check its intrusions…

…

…I am insisting only upon the obvious point, which some modern Marxists have overlooked, that there is a difference between arbitrary power and the rule of law. We ought to expose the shams and inequities which may be concealed beneath this law. But the rule of law itself, the imposing of effective inhibitions upon power and the defence of the citizen from power's all-intrusive claims, seems to me to be an unqualified human good.[60]

-E. P. Thompson

* * *

Ironically, Professor Kinoy must bear some responsibility if any undue patina of hope glimmers around the strategy of achieving reform through the courts. The noted first amendment scholar Thomas Emerson praised his efforts: "[Kinoy's] success in persuading the courts to afford judicial relief to his 'movement' clients, despite tradition and precedents pointing the other way, is little short of miraculous."[61] Indeed, Kinoy's accomplishment in *Dombrowski*[62] was nothing short of miraculous. It is especially noteworthy that Kinoy often "won" for clients who, according to vulgar Marxist theory, should have expected little or no success at the bench and bar. In fact, Kinoy's remarkable success leads to a consideration of the central issues of his book: Should one bother with court encounters at all in a social change movement? If so, how does one win?

The first question is answered easily. Although involvement in legal process might exhaust the movement's money and resources,[63] lawsuits serve a number of useful functions. For example, "[e]ven the most limited victory [can] ... build morale tremendously" in times of frustration.[64] At the very least, an aggressive suit might place the movement's enemies in a defensive posture.[65] The complaint might be used as an organizing tool if distributed as a leaflet.[66] Establishment figures might be hauled to a public deposition, thereby attenuating their authority.[67] The lawsuit itself might be used as bargaining leverage in a particular campaign.[68] Most importantly,

> The ultimate test of the appropriateness of a given legal strategy could not be solely the likelihood of success within the court structure. The wisdom of bringing a lawsuit, of opening up a certain line of legal strategy, had to be judged in a wholly different way. The crucial question was what role it would play at that moment in protecting or advancing the people's struggle. If it helped the fight, then it was done, even if the chances of immediate legal success were virtually nonexistent.[69]

Thus, legal tactics do play a role in the implementation of social change. Kinoy suggests that how one plays the game ultimately matters more than whether one wins or loses. Nevertheless, winning is important, and any conscientious lawyer–populist or otherwise–must wonder about Kinoy's "secret" for his impressive victories. Thus, we turn to the second question: How did Kinoy win?

If Kinoy has any "secrets" that can be articulated, perhaps they are intimated in passages like the following:

> Yet no matter the odds against us, we had to proceed as though we expected to win. For if we did not act as if we believed we could win, no one else would believe it either.[70]

He adds:

> We, the advocates for a movement that they were seeking to brand as "subversive to America," would be exposing the power structure and their lawyers as betraying the very principles upon which the constitutional structure was supposed to rest. *They* were the real subversives. This sense of the reversal of roles was to become a source of strength and confidence for me in the battles ahead.
>
> …I recalled Chuck Conley's words of several years before in Montgomery that it was best to "lay it all out." Buttressed by the recent experiences in Danville, we decided to follow this approach and be completely blunt.[71]

Speaking of the Willie Seals case, Kinoy states:

> [H]ere in Alabama I thought I was discovering the truth about the role of the legal profession throughout one huge section of the country, that it was the conscious instrument whereby the basic rights of millions of Americans were totally erased.
>
> This became the key for us that evening. This was the approach to the federal judge … We had to argue reality.[72]

And in his discussion of the House Un-American Activities Committee, he observes: "We needed an approach that could reach out and speak to the Court, in concepts that touched on its own perception of its duty as an institution…"[73]

In these and similar passages,[74] Kinoy suggests that law at its best represents the triumph of value and principle over oppression and domination. When law becomes perverted to serve arbitrary power instead of principle, then the strategy of the progressive attorney must be to call the institutions of law to order; he must expose how legal doctrine is serving oppression instead of justice and must guide the court to new doctrines that will transform law into a tool of justice.

Thus, in the face of governmental outrage Kinoy chose to "lay it all out" and to overthrow established doctrines[75]–and he convinced the judges that their responsibilities lay in responding to reality and implementing justice rather than in sustaining old doctrines that had grown sterile and vicious in the hands of scheming men. His primary strategy was to appeal to principle and reality. He also undertook conscientious historical research to clear the verbal rubbish off various legal doctrines and to recover the valid principles of justice buried underneath. For example, when Roy Cohn tried to use the grand jury to probe union officials without indicting them, Kinoy appealed to the grand jury's role as a shield against groundless accusation and smear.[76] When McCarthy and the HUAC attempted to circumvent the fifth amendment protections, Kinoy again appealed to history, principle and reality:

> The Fifth Amendment privilege was an institution constructed for the very purpose for which Emspak and Quinn had invoked it–to protect citizens from inquisitorial power run amok. At a critical moment in the Court's history, we were saying to it ... that the Cold War McCarthy hysteria had begun to undermine the very institutions which the Court itself was designed to protect: the elementary institutions of constitutional democracy, of which the Fifth Amendment was a fundamental part.[77]

In a sense, Kinoy stands for some of the best notions of law as articulated by E. P. Thompson.[78] Kinoy resists the "sophisticated" view that "the legal system was really 'owned' by the establishment"[79] and asserts that the rule of law is a treasure to be possessed by every citizen. Justice may triumph if we believe it may.

But at the risk of being dismissed as "sophisticated," we must ask: Can the discussion stop here? If we simply agree with Thompson and Kinoy that we must believe in and advocate a system based on principle instead of power, do we completely understand the role of law in social change? Simple appeals to principle do not always move judges. Kinoy reports at length how Congress abused the doctrine of standing to rebuff his challenge to the seating of the Mississippi congressional delegation.[80] Similarly, to note simply that electoral due process has been emasculated in the context of labor campaigns will not secure a fairer labor election procedure.[81] In *Dred Scott v. Sandford*[82] and *Plessy v. Ferguson*,[83] lawyers unsuccessfully appealed to the courts for justice.

Ultimately, therefore, mere appeal to principle is not enough.[84] Factors other than institutional integrity, justice, and common decency must have some relevance. One key factor in Kinoy's calculus is political mobilization. He notes that one spate of Supreme Court decisions "directly reflected ... [an earlier] Senate vote."[85] Kinoy alludes to additional social factors:

> [U]nderlying divisions within the power elite ... had begun to develop in the mid-1950s ... which were to shape many of the events to come. For certain of the long-range planners in the State Department, the White House, and the new United States worldwide multinational corporations, an embarrassing conflict was beginning to emerge. This was the contradiction between the United States' assumed role as the "leader of the free world" and the spectacular lack of freedom inside the United States, as evidenced by the unchecked McCarthyism in every area of life and the total segregation and enforced inferior status of Black people in the South, affecting every

other section of the country as well.

With this embarrassing situation at home, it was becoming difficult to parade as the champion of a "free world" in the international competition for leadership of the third world peoples.[86]

In sum, political balances of power, social unrest, and international considerations all affect a judge's receptiveness to a lawyer's plea for principle. The progress of America's two most successful social movements in the twentieth century demonstrates the effects of such factors. Labor, which had been shot at with guns for years,[87] won some recognition by Congress and the Supreme Court only after unprecedented socioeconomic change,[88] dislocation,[89] and, more specifically, aggressive militancy by the unions.[90] These developments forced settlements in major industries even before the Supreme Court approved such settlements in principle.[91] Blacks had suffered even longer than labor,[92] but mass black militancy, coupled with changes in the national and international spheres, were necessary to end apartheid in the United States.[93]

The conclusion is inescapable: principle requires something more than purity to succeed. Yet, how a people's lawyer can make use of social factors to create a strategy remains opaque. Kinoy does not translate his rich experience into a formula for progressive law practice.

* * *

> Now all you gentlemen who wish to lead us
> Who teach us to desist from mortal sin
> Your prior obligation is to feed us:
> When we've had lunch, your preaching can begin.
> All you who love your paunch and our propriety
> Talk not of this one thing (for it is late):
> You may proclaim, good sirs, your fine philosophy
> But till you feed us, right and wrong can wait!
> Or is it only those who have the money
> Can enter in the land of milk and honey?[94]
>
> –Bertolt Brecht

* * *

It is clear that political, economic, and other forces must implement and protect principles. Just as clearly, the bodies behind these forces require various forms of sustenance. Kinoy's efforts on behalf of social justice must have exacted their toll on behalf of his personal life.[95] We may have no right to prurient details that might titillate readers of the *National Enquirer*. Nevertheless, those readers who contemplate following Professors Kinoy's inspiring but difficult trail might benefit from more discussion of the telling personal sacrifices that accompany social struggle. A frank evaluation of such sacrifices might dissuade the wary from pursuing Kinoy's rigorous course, but it also could sustain future people's lawyers who might derive lessons as well as comfort from Kinoy's experiences.

Beyond the emotional and psychological strain, an equally important problem remains: How did Kinoy eat? Who paid his legal fees? At one point, he states that "foundation funding and substantial material resources were openly tied to eliminating the influence of 'Guild lawyers.'"[96] When Kinoy initially went into private practice, he learned about "theatrical law," because "each of us had to develop at least one area of private practice, plain ordinary legal cases without political implications, which would bring in sufficient fees to carry our other work."[97] Walter Gellhorn was instrumental in securing Kinoy a teaching position at Rutgers.[98] Beyond these comments, Kinoy rarely explains what sustained his stomach and legal costs. Again, such concerns are critical to those who would follow Kinoy's footsteps—more important than the concerns of personal life. Without loved ones, one grows depressed or insane. Without income, one starves; one never gets to court or enjoys depression. Perhaps disclosing his financial sources would jeopardize some of Kinoy's friends, allies and supporters.[99] But Kinoy could have shared the techniques of private practice, the mysteries of the academic teaching network, the science of grantsmanship, or some other practical experiences. His unfortunate silence on these issues leaves those who would follow his inspirational example to books like *How to Go Directly into Solo Practice Without Missing a Meal*,[100] *Dress for Success*,[101] *How to Manage Your Law Office*,[102] *How to Start and Build a Law Practice*,[103] and *The Grassroots Fundraising Book*.[104]

* * *

Only we, who are now living, can give a "meaning" to the past. But that past has always been, among other things, the result of an argument about values. In recovering that process, in showing how causation actually eventuated, we must, insofar as the discipline can enforce, hold our own values in abeyance. But once history has been recovered, we are at liberty to offer our judgment on it.

Such judgment must itself be under historical controls. The judgment must be appropriate to the materials. It is pointless to complain that the bourgeoisie have not been communitarians, or that the Levellers did not introduce an anarcho-syndicalist society. What we may do, rather, is identify with certain values which past actors upheld, and reject others. We may give our vote for Winstanley and for Swift; we may vote against Walpole and Sir Edwin Chadwick.

Our vote will change nothing. And yet, in another sense, it may change everything. For we are saying that these values, and not those other values, are the ones which make this history meaningful *to us*, and that these are the values which we intend to enlarge and sustain in our own present. If we succeed, then we reach back into history and endow it with our own meanings: we shake Swift by the hand. We endorse in our present the values of Winstanley, and ensure that the low and ruthless kind of opportunism which distinguished the politics of Walpole is abhorred.

In the end we also will be dead, and our own lives will lie inert within the finished process, our intentions assimilated within a past event which we never intended. What we may hope is that the men and women of the future will reach back to us, will affirm and renew our meanings, and make our history intelligible within their own present tense. They alone will have the power to select from the many meanings offered by our quarrelling present, and to transmute some part of our process into their progress.[105]

–E. P. Thompson

* * *

Perhaps my complaints about Kinoy's book reveal that I am looking for a book that never was intended. *Rights on Trial* is about the practice of law by particular individuals in a concrete, particular historical period. Rigorous jurisprudence and personal advice simply are not part of his agenda. Throughout his book Kinoy consistently and honestly reveals his tensions and elations, his "gut" judgment calls, and his confusions and insights. He describes how he looked to Justice White for reassurance during a Supreme Court argument.[106] He portrays backroom confrontations with balking southern judges.[107] There are sudden quiets, temperamental outbursts, and hours of frenetic work.[108]

In short, *Rights on Trial* relates a lawyer's passionate attachment to justice, law, and equality. The reader learns that the principles that law embodies do not drop from the sky like rain from Heaven. Rather, those principles are implemented because people like Arthur Kinoy get hot and bothered over them.

The book is further enriched by Kinoy's various existential models (both positive and negative). Among them are:

–Erwin Griswold, Solicitor General for the United States, who refused to argue to the Supreme Court Nixon's position that the President, through his inherent power, could ignore the fourth amendment in the interests of "domestic security."[109] Moreover,

> [S]omething even stranger happened. Griswold walked into the courtroom and sat down in the seat reserved for the Solicitor

19

General, as though to make it clear to the Court that he had not withdrawn because of illness of scheduling conflicts, but for some other reason. He sat there quietly throughout the argument, as if he were constantly saying to the Court through his physical presence, "I am not arguing this case. Just remember that."[110]

–Jerome Frank, "leading liberal judge [and] ... the intellectual leader of the New Deal and architect of its most progressive legislation,"[111] who, approached by Kinoy for a stay of the Rosenbergs' execution, said:

"If I were as young as you are, I would be sitting where you are now and saying and arguing what you are arguing. You are right to do so. But when you are as old as I am, you will understand why I"–and he paused, and repeated–"why I cannot do what you ask. I cannot do it."[112]

–Judge John Minor Wisdom, who, while he completed his dissent in *Dombrowski*, asked Kinoy to wait in his office and thus aided Kinoy's appeal to the Supreme Court.[113]

–Judge Harold Cox, chief judge of the federal court for the Southern District of Mississippi, who, "[d]uring a voter registration suit early in March 1964 ... had openly attached a group of Black would-be registrants as 'a bunch of niggers.'"[114]

–Civil rights activities Jeanette and Ed King, who persisted in their work even after Mississippi Klansmen shot bullets through their windows.[115]

–Jack Greenberg, director of the NAACP Legal Defense and Education Fund, who Kinoy consulted about the use of Reconstruction removal statutes. Kinoy reports: "The response was disturbing. Greenberg completed rejected all use of the Reconstruction statute, calling it a crazy idea amounting to 'playing with the courts.'"[116]

–Albert Jenner, "senior partner in an illustrious Chicago law firm," who joined Kinoy in attacking the legitimacy of HUAC.[117]

–Jim Dombrowski, whose democratic chutzpah helped push Kinoy down his road to legal history: "When Dombrowski responded to my description of the legal hurdles that lay ahead [in suing a senator] by saying simply, 'Why can't we sue a senator? Who's he?' that decided us. Within three days we had filed a federal complaint in the District of Columbia and served it on Eastland...."[118]

We cannot read these pages without reconsidering our own roles and responsibilities in the development and maintenance of justice. Kinoy's discussion of two individuals, however–Justice William Rehnquist and Huey Long–lack his usual incisiveness.

Justice Rehnquist's name appears on almost every third page of Kinoy's opening chapter.[119] Kinoy portrays him as the mastermind behind Nixon's "inherent power" theories.[120] Perhaps Kinoy began the book with the chapter *Wiretapping and Watergate* because of its two "high drama" aspects. First, Kinoy stems the tide of inherent power and unlimited executive privilege. Second, and more important, Kinoy proffers his own unusual explanation for the Watergate break-in and the famous eighteen-minute gap on the Nixon tapes. Kinoy points out that the eighteen-minute gap occurred on June 19, 1972, the same day that the Supreme Court announced *United States v. United States District Court* [121] and two days after the Watergate break-in occurred on June 17. Kinoy proposes the following sequence of events:

> Suppose that sometime prior to the Watergate break-in, someone in a high position of responsibility, privy to the secret meetings at which the Watergate wiretapping operation was discussed and finally authorized, heard in some way that the decision in the Supreme Court had gone the other way–the wrong way–against the administration? Suppose this person, in panic and concern because the cover of legality was about the be blown, told whoever was in charge of the Watergate operation to get in there and clean it out, remove everything from the Democratic headquarters fast, *before* Monday, the day on which the decision was coming down. The whole team would then be needed for a swift, total removal job. Suppose they went into the Watergate late that evening to clean it out, only to be caught in the act.[122]

Kinoy suggests that the eighteen-minute gap "involved an explanation to the President of the real reasons for Saturday night's break-in, and its relation to Monday morning's Supreme Court decision."[123] If the explanation came from high quarters in the Supreme Court or alluded to leaks from the Court, then it obviously would have been politically embarrassing; it could even lead to the impeachment of a Justice.[124] Of course Kinoy does not–and cannot–explicitly accuse Rehnquist of leaking critical information or providing explanations to the White House. Kinoy may imply such an accusation, however, when he notes that Rehnquist "remains the only member of the inner Nixon power elite unscathed by the post-Watergate holocaust, still sitting in his position of power and influence on the Supreme Court."[125] The Burger Court on other occasions has been accused of unseemly leaking,[126] and Justice Rehnquist's political history is hardly boring.[127] But perhaps Kinoy has gone as far as he can to implicate Rehnquist.

Kinoy's position concerning Huey Long is much less ambiguous: Kinoy calls him "that master of American experimentation with the forms of repression."[128] Kinoy's perspective may have been shaped by his membership in the Young Communist League[129] during the heyday of the

Kingfish, but his discussion glosses over Long's deep and complex personality.[130] As anyone familiar with Louisiana history will attest, Long represented a strand of popular and progressive resurgence that had its roots in Louisiana populism and socialism.[131] More important, any consideration of the profound questions of American political analysis must include a careful study of Huey Long. What does a radical figure in American politics do when he happens to be elected to office–particularly when he faces a determined and vicious ruling class? Long's "repressions" were tame compared to those of the conservative ruling class, whose power he aspired to break.[132] Long faced problems of running a state government, problems with which the Young Communist never dealt.[133] Certainly their comrades in Moscow created nothing worth bragging about.[134] If the Young Communists can talk about "revolutionary necessity" in the movements of Cromwell, Robespierre, Lenin, Stalin, and Mao, then Long certainly deserves closer consideration, not only as a proto-fascist,[135] but also as a revolutionary figure working within the unique context of American political forms. This topic deserves more consideration than this review can give; the point is that Kinoy's dismissal of Long is inappropriate and wooden. Perhaps this insensitivity reflects unexamined party lines received in student days or a lack of appreciation of American–and particularly Southern–history. Although Kinoy was peculiarly adept at uncovering history and using it for the causes of his clients,[136] he suggests that he was occasionally surprised at the results of historical research. Such shocks might lead him to investigate further the historical, theoretical, and political implications of Huey Long.

* * *

> The weight of this sad time we must obey;
> Speak what we feel, not what we ought to say.
> The oldest hath borne most: we that are young
> Shall never so see much, nor live so long.[137]
>
> –William Shakespeare

* * *

Professor Kinoy is, in the words of Karl Marx, one of the philosophers who concerned himself with changing the world, not interpreting it.[138] He played a role in changing it for the better. Perhaps his detailed report of his efforts at change will lead others to deeper insights about how to interpret and improve the world. We can hope that the lessons of his experience will allow us to retain the above-cited epitaph from King Lear, as opposed to another that might be cited in this auspicious year of 1984:

> And worse I may be yet; The worst is not,
> So long as we can say "This is the worst."[139]

CHAPTER THREE
LAWYERS, LAW, AND SOCIAL CHANGE

I
INTRODUCTION

* * *

That [Auschwitz] could happen in the midst of the traditions of philosophy, of art, and of the enlightening sciences says more than that these traditions and their spirit lacked the power to take hold of men ad work a change in them. There is untruth in those fields themselves, in the autarky that is emphatically claimed for them. All post-Auschwitz culture, including its urgent critique, is garbage. In restoring itself after the things that happened without resistance in its own countryside, culture has turned entirely into the ideology it had been potentially–had been ever since it presumed, in opposition to material existence, to inspire that existence with the light denied it by the separation of the mind from manual labor.[140]

* * *

This article will investigate relations between lawyers, law, and social change. The question is of interest to lawyers who are concerned with whether or not their profession has any relation to the actual implementation of justice.[141] More importantly, though, the question is of critical interest to a broader audience of social activists. Its answer will inform fundamental approaches to strategies and tactics in the field of social change. If one desires social justice, should one bother with law and lawyers at all, and if so, to what extent and in what fashion?

In investigating these matters, I begin by setting out my own position on the issue. This includes an explication of what is desirable social change, how to achieve it, and what role law and lawyers might play in the process. An examination of the factors sustaining this position follows. This includes experiences in professional practice, theoretical vision, and conceptions of history. Having substantiated the position, I will turn to more specific elaborations of where lawyers and law fit into my vision. Practical activities which lawyers ought and ought not pursue will be noted. I then compare my position to those espoused by three alternative positions on the left side of the spectrum: the public interest/legal reform advocates; the "a-legal" leftists; and the group I identify as "fusionist" (many of whom explicitly identify themselves with the Critical Legal Studies movement). These comparisons should not only clarify my position, but also advance the debate in this area. After that I turn to a discussion of the implications that my position holds for a notion of law. I conclude by illustrating how practice can mesh with theory.

II

PROPOSED POSITION

* * *

"The final type... [of social interaction,] community, is least developed in modern sociological and political theory.[142]

* * *

A social goal is not easy to articulate. Use of labels can easily confuse or mislead. Moreover, desired social futures must be created by actual and imperfect human endeavor, and cannot be thoroughly blueprinted by theory in the present.[143]

The most appropriate labels for my vision would be "communitarian," "social democratic," "democratic socialist," or "populist."[144] The vision would include at least the following characteristics: (1) a respect for personhood ("individuality");[145] (2) an appreciation of community;[146] (3) a commitment to democracy (social, economic, and political);[147] (4) realizability.[148] In one sense Fred Dallmayr has articulated these same concerns. Since he raises various issues which will arise later in this article, he is worth citing at length:

> In contrast to association, community does not imply a simple juxtaposition of supposedly independent agents.... As opposed to the homogeneity deliberately fostered in [the sphere of movements, or, fused groups], the communitarian mode deliberately cultivates diversity—but without encouraging willful segregation or the repressive preponderance of one of the social subsectors.... [T]he pervasive outlook or behavioral mode might be described as anticipative–emancipatory practice or as an attitude dedicated to letting others be–a distinctive and peculiar mode since it is lodged at the intersection of activity and passivity. As a corollary of this outlook, community may be the only form of social aggregation which reflects upon, and makes room for, otherness or the reverse side of subjectivity

(and intersubjectivity) and thus for the play of difference–the difference between ego and Other and between man and nature.

As the terms anticipative-emancipatory care and ontological anticipation indicate, the type envisaged here does not coincide with an empirically given or presently existing (or historically recorded) aggregate; nor, due to its concern with Being, can it be equated with a regulative principle or abstract utopia. On the level of political theory, anticipation points toward the end of politics in a dual sense: namely, the dismantling of political domination and the goal of politics, traditionally formulated as the good life.[149]

The preceding values will be implemented only by organized masses of people. The term "masses" is emphasized because, from a power perspective, "revolutionary reform" will be resisted by the "faction" that presently controls the American polity.[150] The term "organized" is stressed because only conscientious, coordinated efforts of masses of people will prove able to dislodge the faction and create revolutionary reform. Finally, mass effort is emphasized because of concern with the quality of "revolutionary" transformation. As historical experience warns us, democratic ends are difficult to secure without the implementation of democratic means.[151]

The character of law in this process is that of articulated value. The values which enjoy articulation as law depend upon the outcome of struggles between various social groups.

The role that lawyers play in the development and articulation of value and law in society is rather marginal. Organized masses of people, not lawyers, play the critical roles, and the significant victories (or losses) occur outside of the sphere of law. The more that lawyers try to implement social change directly, the more inimical their impact. In noting this point, I am not calling for the abolition of the legal profession. Lawyers do have a role to play in implementing social change, but it is a limited one.[152]

III

JUSTIFYING THE PROPOSED POSITION

* * *

"We would fall into an error that we criticize in our adversaries if we imagined our conceptual activities as a substitute, even a substitute source of insight, for practical conflict and invention."[153]

* * *

A. Practical Considerations: ACORN

The position I am espousing derives from my experiences in professional practice, theoretical conceptions, and perspectives from history.

My professional experience includes working in the law firm of Bachmann & Weltchek, which has served as general counsel to the Association of Community Organizations for Reform Now (ACORN) since 1976. ACORN is a non-profit corporation comprised of more than 50,000 low and moderate income families organized into neighborhood groups in over 40 cities across the United States. ACORN avoids advocating any particular ideological viewpoint,[154] but its social vision and its methods for accomplishing such visions are evident in its publications:

> You can win stop-lights from here to eternity, which is what many community organizations around the country have excelled at, but unless your organization addresses the question of who has the power to control what happens in a neighborhood, a city, a county, or a state–and who should have the power to control what happens in these areas–then all your organization will achieve is a proliferation of stop-lights in low to moderate income neighborhoods. Obviously, ACORN's goal is much more.[155]

Such means and ends may be summarized as "participatory democracy."[156]

This perspective has definite implications for ACORN's conception of and approach to law and lawyers. (Indeed, it was ACORN's frustration with a lack of "organizing lawyers" that led it to help found the law firm that became Bachmann & Weltchek.) ACORN distinguishes between a "lawyer's perspective" and an "organizer's perspective." Lawyers and organizers tend to approach problems differently, with often marked implications. For example, consider an intersection where the lack of a stop sign is causing traffic hazards and threatening children. A lawyer would solve this problem by going to court to get the stop sign put into place. From this process people either do not know how the stop sign got there or learn that lawyers produce change. Both results aggravate people's perceptions of their powerlessness, which is disastrous from an organizer's perspective. In contrast to the lawyer, the organizer would knock on all the doors in the neighborhood, organize a meeting of interested people, and help them collectively deal with the problem. They would probably hold a mass demonstration, meet with a city official, and successfully pressure her to provide the stop sign. From this experience, people in the neighborhood would learn that they can have power if they organize, and coordinate their efforts. Because so many individuals participated in producing the sign, nearly everyone in the neighborhood would learn this lesson. Suddenly an aspect of the neighborhood is the product of the residents' personal actions. ACORN's preference for this kind of community participation colors its attitudes about litigation and leads it to avoid courts.

ACORN will generally go to court in only three situations. The first is when ACORN needs to affect the organizing environment. Many people only get involved in an organization if they believe governmental benefits will result. Securing such benefits frequently requires a lawsuit.[157] For example, my firm once aided an organizing drive among domestic workers by suing the U.S. Department of Labor to force it to respond to their demands. Such lawsuits may also affect the organizing environment by creating free advertising for the organizing effort. Potential recruits will then know that the organization is aggressively fighting for their rights by the time an organizer personally reaches them.

The second situation in which ACORN will resort to litigation is if it has no other choice, such as when it is sued, or on the infrequent occasions when people are arrested for participating in ACORN demonstrations. ACORN may also be forced to go to court when an attempt is made to legally prohibit ACORN from soliciting members, donations, or signatures from a neighborhood. Since such attempts cut to the heart of ACORN's organizing, any means must be used to uphold these quintessential first amendment rights. In other cases, however, a lawsuit involves a desperate attempt to regain initiative. In Springdale, Arkansas, for example, ACORN's efforts to bring Lifeline, a program of lowered utility rates for the elderly, was attacked by the mayor. He had the local paper publish a list of everyone who had signed a pro-Lifeline petition circulated by ACORN. This obvious hit list[158] intimidated Springdale's residents. In response, ACORN sued the Mayor for a million dollars. He resigned from his office, and ACORN was able to continue its campaign.

Finally, ACORN will go to court when it needs an exit from an unproductive campaign. As noted, ACORN's purpose is less to win issues than to win power. Accordingly, a hopeless campaign is usually handed over to a lawyer, so that the members can redirect their efforts. The removal of members from the activity may work to ACORN's advantage. In Denver, ACORN struggled for months to force the city to provide better parking facilities for Broncos football games (fans were parking their cars in members' yards). ACORN pressure had produced some concessions, but not enough to satisfy the neighborhood residents. Unfortunately, the city refused to budge any further. At this point, the case was given to the lawyers. Happily, the resulting lawsuit helped pressure Denver into resuming negotiations with the ACORN members, and the controversy was ultimately settled to their satisfaction.

ACORN's limited reliance on lawyers derives primarily from its political and moral concerns about the kind of movement that lawyer-dominated processes might create. These concerns are less about what victories a lawyer might win than about what sort of groups might be created through social struggle. What is "won" is secondary, if not irrelevant.[159] The group that is developed is of primary concern.

B. Philosophical Considerations

* * *

"The name of dialectics says no more, to begin with, than that objects do not go into their concepts without leaving a remainder, that they come to contradict the traditional norm of adequacy."[160]

* * *

ACORN's societal ideals, and strategies for the implementation of those ideals, are consistent with the philosophical premises of dialectical materialism,[161] which as a paradigm[162] asserts the following:

1. A thing consists not only of the objective material, but also of the subjective mind that conceives of it.
2. Things are many sided, and perhaps infinitely so.
3. Things change (i.e., to understand something one must know its past and future as well as its present).
4. Consciousness derives from matter (whether matter be biochemicals, concentrated energy, or clay).
5. Thought is affected by material conditions, e.g., social, political, economic, and biological.[163]

The first three propositions relate to the "dialectical" side of the paradigm, the latter two propositions relate to the "materialist" side. In proposition 1, dialectical materialism does not degenerate into materialistic determinism because it acknowledges the role that thought plays in the constitution of reality. Through propositions 2, 3 and 5 dialectical materialism resists becoming dogma.

It is beyond the scope of this paper to prove that this perspective of dialectical materialism automatically leads to a communitarian vision. In one sense, that was Dallmayr's project, and the reader should consider his effort.[164] However, dialectical materialism, as defined here, is consistent with other social democratic visions.[165]

Yet for our purposes what is more important is the perspective which dialectical materialism assumes regarding the mechanisms of social change. Though it must acknowledge the importance of individual minds (because individual experience constitutes actual reality),[166] dialectical materialism tends to pose issues in terms of classes. Classes are a productive way of viewing social reality because in a class society individuals are subjected to varying social, economic and political experiences which society filters into class categories.[167] Objective class experiences lead to similar intellectual conclusions on the part of individuals, resulting in class consciousness and class struggle.

Marx formulated the process as a class-in-itself becoming a class-for-itself. The class-in-itself is simply a mass of people experiencing similar amounts of social, economic, and political power. The members are unorganized because they are barely conscious of their situations and their commonality. In contrast, the members of the class-for-itself are conscious of their mutual interests, so they unite, and organize to protect their concerns. They develop the machinery of an organization to assert their class interests, promoting their interests with regard to one another–as well as with regard to their class enemies.[168]

Marx believed that self-conscious organization was the key to becoming a class-for-itself Indeed, Marx was reluctant to identify a "mass" as a "class" unless it created a class-conscious, class-based political party.[169] Factors that contributed to the metamorphosis of a class-in-itself into a class-for-itself included similar experiences of oppression (social, economic and political) and sufficient opportunities for mutual interaction (through work, through social media, and through self-developed associational activities).[170]

Marx's concept of class directly relates to his conception of what constitutes social transformation. The conversion of the proletariat into a class-for-itself provides not only the class's capacity to take power, but also provides the grounds for democratic socialism, and, ultimately, the accomplishment of the ideal state of communism. Theoretically, as class members become more conscious and learn to organize, they learn, appreciate, and practice democratic self-regulation. Democratic encounters during the phase of self-organization turns into democratic government when the democratic self-organizing creates sufficient power to challenge society's old ruling powers.

This was Marx's theory, and most subsequent left-wing theories of social transformation fit within this conceptual framework. These theories begin to elaborate on Marx and differ on: (1) the responses to a proletariat that does not expeditiously organize itself, and (2) the responses to a ruling class that suppresses proletarian self-organization. These differences have led to competing versions of Marxism such as Lenin's elite party,[171] Luxemburg's mass strikes,[172] Mao's cultural revolution,[173] and Sartre's "fused groups."[174]

Yet, whichever variation or combination of variations, the focus of left-wing theory remains on class and the ways in which class experiences are transformed. Any further revisions of Marxist theory, if any, would be these: (1) The paradigm need not restrict itself solely to "classes" per se. Other social groupings can be understood through this perspective, particularly those whose material situations subject them to experiences that differentiate them emphatically from other social groupings (e.g., American blacks). (2) Successful "revolutionary reform" requires something beyond the transformation of the class-in-itself into the class-for-itself. This additional pre-condition is some kind of rupture in the ruling class. As the Leninist challenge implies, ruling classes are loathe to allow the development of a "mass" into a "class." Even the conscientious Bolshevik tends to require a disruption of the ruling elite, such as war, or internal disagreement over means and ends if the class is to enjoy enough space to grow in puissance and ultimately seize power.

Once the paradigm is adjusted, the conception of social transformation still focuses on social relationships and the development of social forces. This analysis leads to the conclusion that the lawyer's role in social transformation is limited to the point of being marginal. From this perspective, the ACORN approach is ratified by theory.

Of course, theory must ultimately prove faithful to history, and it is to history that the contending versions of Marxism appeal. It would appear that history generally supports the above version of social transformation. What the lawyers do is less important than whether and how various social groups organize themselves. Despite mythologies that have developed, the lawyerly approach did not implement, in any significant way, the meaningful social changes that have occurred in the United States during the twentieth century.

C. Historical Considerations

* * *

"… it is not with ideas that history is made to move forward, but with a material force, that of people reunited in the streets."[175]

* * *

The two social upheavals which wrought major transformations in twentieth century American politics were the labor movement of the 1930's, and the civil rights movement of the 1960's. In both instances an oppressed group, which initially enjoyed only nominal rights of self-determination, won the acknowledgment that its members had a right to be respected as human beings. American workers won the right to collective bargaining, and American blacks ended institutionalized racism in the South. The achievements of both groups were due more to mass mobilization than to the work of lawyers. To establish this point, I will examine the experiences of both the American labor movement and American blacks.

1. *Labor*

The condition of American labor before 1930 was dismal. Historian Richard Hofstadter has written of the relationship between labor and capital in the United States:

> I believe that no student of labor history is likely to quarrel with the judgment of Philip Taft and Robert Ross: "The United States has had the bloodiest and most violent labor history of any industrial nation in the world." Taft and Ross have identified over 160 instances in which state and federal troops have intervened in labor disputes, and have recorded over 700 deaths and several thousands of serious injuries in labor disputes, but one can only underline their warning that this incomplete tally "grossly understates the casualties.... With a minimum of ideologically motivated class conflict, the United States has somehow had a maximum of industrial violence. And no doubt the answer to this must be sought more in those of American capitalists than in that of the workers."[176]

A labor reformer who advised that labor turn to law would have been ridiculed in the late 1920's. Up to that period labor had been subjected to a number of attacks by the legal system such as: restrictions on picketing, profligate use of court injunctions, twisting of the antitrust laws, broadening the law of damages to include unincorporated labor organizations, criminal prosecutions, and record amounts of invalidated legislation.[177] This process culminated in the anti-labor policy of Chief Justice Taft, who delighted in the shooting of strikers[178] and announced upon his accession to the bench that he had been chosen to "reverse a few decisions," and described labor as "that faction we have to hit every little while."[179]

Given the preceding, it is obvious that some kind of disruption in the balance of forces in society was required for a labor breakthrough. The Depression provided that disruption.[180] In 1932, Congress passed the National Industrial Recovery Act with its famous Section 7(a) which ostensibly gave workers the right to form unions.[181] Whether Section 7(a) gave anybody anything is open to serious question, as historian Irving Bernstein queried:

> Section 7(a), a short and seemingly clear declaration of policy in a statute otherwise marked by complexity, lifted the lid off Pandora's box. The haste and inexperience from which it derived were breeding grounds of ambiguity; it raised more questions than it provided answers. Latent antagonism between unions and employers gained a point of focus.... Section 7(a) was enabling legislation and nothing more.[182]

Section 7(a) resulted from political horse trading by various interest groups during President Roosevelt's first attempts to cope with the Depression. It seems that Roosevelt's objective was the creation of a corporate state,[183] its various sectors controlled and operated by actors within the sectors using industrial codes. In return for its cooperation, labor extracted, among other things, Section 7(a). Industry accepted Section 7(a) as a trade-off for exemption from the antitrust law;[184] and as a preferable substitute for a thirty-hour work week bill proposed by Senator Black.[185] However, the precise meaning of Section 7(a) had yet to be determined, and various segments of industry and labor had their own ideas as to what it ought to mean. Labor would determine the scope of its rights through social struggle.

When Roosevelt signed the National Industrial Recovery Act he thought he had established the structure for a coordinated, cooperative, corporate economy. Instead, economic conflict and labor strife ensued. A number of industrial concerns formed company unions and hired agencies that specialized in strikebreaking and industrial espionage.[186] Others simply ignored the National Labor Board altogether, and many refused to appear at its hearings.[187] In November of 1933, as the National Association of Manufacturers launched a public campaign against the Board, many thousands of workers across the country attempted to assert their Section 7 rights.[188] Bernstein records that "[m]an days lost due to strikes, which had not exceeded 603,000 in any month in the first half of 1933, spurted to 1,375,000 in July and to 2,378,000 in August."[189]

Section 7(a)'s ambiguity exacerbated the problem. The companies could claim that company unions and/or a system of proportional representation satisfied the requirements of the Section, although such co-opting and divide-and-conquer tactics actually undercut the effectiveness of any representation. The Board and labor advocated majority rule and exclusive representation, giving the bargaining rights of a unit to the agent that secured the votes of more than fifty percent of the unit's workers.

As conflict between labor and capital intensified, a major question developed over which side the Roosevelt administration would take. The first answer came on March 25, 1934, when Roosevelt facilitated a settlement in the auto industry that basically ratified the anti-union principle of proportional representation.[190] Bernstein writes that after March 25, 1934:

> ...determined unionists in the unorganized industries recognized that they would win bargaining rights not by invoking law but by showing their own strength. The automobile settlement was to be a major cause of the great wave of strikes that engulfed the nation in the spring and summer of 1934.... In 1934 labor erupted. There were 1,856 work stoppages involving 1,470,000 workers, by far the highest

count in both categories in many years. A number of these strikes were of unusual importance.... Four were social upheavals–those of auto parts workers at the Electric Auto-Lite Company in Toledo, of truck drivers in Minneapolis, of longshoremen and then virtually the whole labor movement on the shores of San Francisco Bay, and of cotton-textile workers in New England and the South.[191]

The social upheavals to which Bernstein refers involved, among other things, general strikes, martial law, court injunctions (obeyed and ignored), and the killing and wounding of a number of people. "All in all, a minimum of fifteen strikers were killed in 1933, and at least forty more were killed in 1934. In a period of eighteen months, troops had been called out in sixteen states."[192]

On May 27, 1935, the Supreme Court invalidated Section 7(a) along with the rest of the National Industrial Recovery Act,[193] but by then the Section had become substantially irrelevant. Senator Wagner had already been pushing for passage of a new National Labor Relations Act since February (it was finally signed into law July 5, 1935), and the massive movements of 1935 were about to come under the conscientious organizing efforts of the Congress of Industrial Organizations. In late 1935 John L. Lewis and other industrial unionists walked out of the American Federation of Labor, and in 1936, the initiation of massive organizing efforts in a number of industries began.

Legally, labor's right to organize into unions was "won" on April 12, 1937, when the Supreme Court declared the National Labor Relations Act constitutional.[194] But, as Karl Klare has pointed out, by April 1937, labor had all but mooted the issue.[195] In February 1937, C.I.O. organizing had already forced settlements from General Motors, Chrysler, General Electric, and U.S. Steel.[196] The leaders of the nation's leading industries had accepted the principle of collective bargaining without waiting for the Supreme Court.

It is possible to speculate about the chain of cause and effect that precipitated the historical April 12 ruling. Roosevelt had first announced his court-packing scheme on February 5, 1937.[197] The initial Supreme Court "shift" had occurred on March 29, 1937,[198] and Justice Douglas has claimed that *West Coast Hotel* had been decided as early as December of 1936.[199] Whether the series of company/union settlements that occurred between the oral argument on February 9 and April 12 affected the Court directly is open to dispute, but two things are not open to dispute: first, the settlements had occurred, and the Supreme Court's ruling would not affect them;[200] second, Justice Roberts, the major swing vote that precipitated the shift in the *West Coast Hotel* and *Jones* cases, confirmed that he felt that the Supreme Court must shift–or else risk irrelevancy as a factor in U.S. life. He later admitted:

> Looking back, it is difficult to see how the Court could have resisted the popular urge for uniform standards throughout the country and for what in effect was a unified economy.... An insistence by the Court on holding federal power to what seemed its appropriate orbit when the constitution was adopted might have resulted in even more radical changes in our dual structure than those which have been gradually accomplished through the extension of the limited jurisdiction conferred on the federal government.[201]

Labor, of course, won no absolute victory in April or February, 1937. In May of 1937, for example, the Memorial Day Massacre occurred;[202] in 1939 the Supreme Court declared labor's highly effective "sit-in" tactic illegal;[203] and in 1948 Congress passed the Taft-Hartley Act which further restrained the array of legal tactics to which labor might resort.[204] Since World War Two labor's stance has changed from aggressiveness to accommodation. While in 1945 35.5% of the labor force was unionized, by 1983 this figure had dwindled to 17%.[205]

1937 did mark a social shift in the United States. Prior to 1937, the workers' right to organize was tenuous, while subsequent to 1937 the three branches of the federal government acknowledged that the policy of the United States was to "encourage the practice and procedure of collective bargaining."[206] A substantial number of important employers also accepted the practice and procedure of collective bargaining. Three main factors facilitated labor's victory: (1) labor militancy; (2) increased industrialization in the American economy;[207] and (3) the social and political dislocations precipitated by the trauma of the Depression. The work of lawyers was incidental to these primary causes.

2. Civil Rights

* * *

> You see, what the [Montgomery] bus thing did was simply more than withholding patronage from the bus; it was restoring a sense of dignity to the patrons, as best expressed by an oft-quoted black woman in Montgomery who said, "Since I been walking, my feet are tired, but my soul's rested." So that it was also, at the same time and a part of that, the beginning of self-determination. See, self-determination's some new phraseology, but, prior to the bus boycotts, the determination of our freedom rested with the court. With the bus boycott, WE determined it. It didn't make any difference what the court said. The court could say what it liked, we weren't gon' ride in

the back of the bus. We'd walk.[208]

* * *

Just as the victory of the U.S. labor movement involved more than collective bargaining, the issue of *Brown v. Board of Education*[209] was more than just a lawsuit about school desegregation. At bottom both movements involved changes that were subtle and humble, yet fundamental. The "victory" of the labor movement was that after 1937, a significant portion of the U.S. power elite was no longer prepared to attack unions with troops.[210] The "victory" of the civil rights movement was that sometime during the 1960's the caste system in the South fell, as a significant portion of the U.S. power elite was no longer prepared to sanction institutionalized racism. As labor and minorities are only less victimized than they have been in the past, their victories are negative. The essence of their victories is that labor and minorities finally achieved the right to be respected as something more than cattle by the people with the guns.[211]

The turning point for the civil rights movement occurred between 1962 and 1966. Until 1962, the Southern caste system remained intact, the black masses had not yet been mobilized, and the Bourbon faction of the white power elite continued to enjoy its dictatorial powers. Moreover, the federal government's efforts on behalf of oppressed blacks were sporadic and ineffective. By 1966, however, the shift had essentially occurred. The Southern caste system had been declared illegal, and the federal government and black masses had moved to ensure that the southern system of institutionalized racism would yield to "mere" discrimination, if not ultimately equality.

The factors that forced this shift included: (1) the mobilization of the black masses into the streets and into the registrars' offices, and (2) the willingness of the federal government to respond to the outrages perpetrated by the Bourbon racists after black mobilization.

The story of the 1950's is one of limited black mobilization, and massive white reaction. The statistics concerning school desegregation reveal the limited effects of *Brown*[212] and the Montgomery boycott (1955-1956), though initially successful, ultimately witnessed a lapse into the segregated custom of blacks sitting in the back of the bus–the Supreme Court notwithstanding.[213] The outrages at Little Rock produced some response from the Eisenhower administration, but the caste system survived. Following 1955, southern states passed a number of laws designed to reinforce institutionalized racism.[214] As the experiences of the Freedom Riders indicate, the laws of the Supreme Court were consistently, blatantly, and violently ignored.[215]

The 1960 Greensboro sit-ins signaled the beginning of various protests against the caste system across the South. However, it was not until the 1962 Albany demonstrations that these protests moved from the efforts of students and intellectuals to include masses of black people[216] In fact, some argue that the National Association for the Advancement of Colored People (NAACP) made but limited progress in the area of school desegregation because it was not an issue which mobilized lower-class blacks[217] Others note that, unlike the Student Nonviolent Coordinating Committee (SNCC), they relied too much on lawyers;[218] and, unlike SNCC, they did not concentrate on sending organizers into the field to mobilize people.[219]

The experiences of the Albany campaign encouraged civil rights activists to pursue a series of mass confrontations in Birmingham, Alabama. Kennedy's hand was forced,[220] and in June of 1963 he submitted a sweeping civil rights bill to Congress. After a similar summer of mobilization in Mississippi, Lyndon Johnson induced the Congress to pass the Civil Rights Act of 1964,

> [the] most penetrating civil rights legislation in the country's history
>
> ....
>
> The new act outlawed the exclusion of blacks from restaurants, hotels, theatres, and other public accommodation; empowered the Justice Department to bring school desegregation suits; denied federal aid to any program or service which practiced racial discrimination; and forbade racial bias in employment and union membership policies."[221]

The year 1964 also saw the adoption of the 24th Amendment to the Constitution which outlawed the poll tax.

In 1963, the Voting Rights project had been instituted, with the federal government and private foundations providing support, and SNCC, the Congress of Racial Equality (CORE), and the NAACP doing the legwork.[222] In 1965, the confrontation moved to Selma, Alabama, and Congress passed the Voting Rights Act during the same period that two hundred and fifty thousand people converged on Washington, D.C., for the passage of civil rights measures. Results began to appear in 1966:

> ...[T]he black vote accounted for the winning margin for a United States Senator in South Carolina, a governor in Arkansas, and two members of the House of Representatives. Project records show that in Arkansas approximately 85,000 of a total 115,000 to 120,000 registered blacks voted in the November 1966 elections; in South Carolina, 100,000 of 191,000 and in Georgia, 150,000 of 300,000.[223]

Though civil rights battles have been no more successful than those of labor, like labor in the 1930's, the civil rights activists did achieve a new level of social participation through their struggles.

Similar to the labor struggles, the role of the legal process in the civil rights movement was marginal. Even the highly celebrated *Brown* decision was rendered more with an eye to political than legal matters.[224] Subsequent to *Brown,* nothing substantial happened until masses of black people forced the executive branch to move. As the labor reforms were a political response to an economic depression, here the primary factors related to internal and external political considerations. Internally the black voters were beginning to make differences in traditional Democratic strongholds in major urban centers. Democrats had to choose between the Dixiecrats in the South, and the moderates in the North. Kennedy, perhaps brought to power through the black vote,[225] chose the North. Externally, during the 1950's, and especially the 1960's, Third World political power grew in world affairs. In the ideological war against communism, an America that practiced institutionalized racism stood at a disadvantage to Soviet Russia[226] in competing for the affiliation of the Third World countries.

IV

THE LAWYER'S ROLE

* * *

"The ultimate test of the appropriateness of a given legal strategy could not be solely the likelihood of success within the court structure. The wisdom of bringing a lawsuit, of opening up a certain line of legal strategy, had to be judged in a wholly different way. The crucial question was what role it would play at that moment in protecting or advancing the people's struggle. If it helped the fight, then it was done, even if the chances of immediate legal success were virtually nonexistent."[227]

* * *

The primary motor of social change is social struggle, not legal struggle. The question thus becomes: to what extent can lawyers and the law have an impact in this "extra-legal" area? The answer is that lawyers can play meaningful roles in actual social struggles, though their role relates more to the preconditions for social mobilization than to substantive issues. The lawyer's role is more the oiler of the social change machine than its motor; the motor of the machine remains masses of people. From a democratic perspective, this is how it should be, and from an historical perspective, the only way it can be.

The lawyer's facilitative role is most obvious and significant in three substantive areas of law: the first amendment, corporations and taxes, and criminal law. Additionally, to be effective, a progressive lawyer should be aware of the rules of civil procedure and ethics.

A. First Amendment

If a lawyer's role is facilitating mobilization, then a primary focus should be placed on first amendment law concerning the right to demonstrate, the right to organize and associate in groups, the right to petition and confront government officials, the right to proselytize, argue, and convince, and the right to secure members and to raise funds. In order to facilitate mobilizations, social reformers must reach their fellow citizens wherever they may be. They need access to public forums like streets, sidewalks, parks, shopping centers, mailboxes, and the mass media, to places where people live and play, and where people work.

The rights of American citizens today falls short of the needs enumerated above. Though Americans do have the right to solicit funds,[228] to handbill,[229] to speak in public,[230] and so on, the right of access to shopping malls,[231] mailboxes,[232] newspapers,[233] and to the electronic media could be improved.[234]

The social change attorney must be prepared to protect and sustain the rights that have so far been secured, and see if they can be extended.[235] Ultimately her goal is to realize the ideal expressed by John Hart Ely, that of a society wherein the political process (where values are identified, weighed, and accommodated) "is open to those of all viewpoints on something approaching an equal basis."[236]

Promulgating Ely's vision is not necessarily a droll enterprise. Though it might appear that with a few adjustments the viability of the free marketplace of ideas is secured, it could be read to call for a fundamental transformation of society. If all individuals in society are to enjoy an equal opportunity to affect their society, then all must have rights of access to social resources and liberation from various social constraints. Access to various resources, such as wealth, information, and education, would require drastic revision. In a fundamental sense, then, Ely's vision dovetails with the vision espoused by the social reformer.[237]

B. Corporations and Taxes

Mobilization is facilitated best by people organized into groups, and the importance of the right of association is now accepted.[238] The various forms of association in American law, however, present numerous advantages and disadvantages most familiar to attorneys. For example, an incorporated organization enjoys limited liability and clearly defined channels of authority but must fulfill various formal obligations to the state before it can enjoy such benefits. The lawyer must be able to advise her client appreciating her client's practical situations. In addition, the lawyer should know that an organization enjoying 501(c)(3) status from the IRS can improve its fundraising program because contributions could be deducted on the contributor's income taxes,[239] while realizing that IRS tax-exempt status can limit the sort of activities in which the organization might engage (e.g., lobbying, social action, etc.).[240] The lawyer must, again, be able to evaluate her clients' situations and present them with alternatives that will respond to their needs. The organizational structure that social mobilization adopts can significantly affect it, and so the attorney can perform valuable services for social reform groups in these areas of the law.

C. Criminal Law

Though the relation of the criminal law to mobilization facilitation is obvious (people in jail cannot mobilize), our perception of the role of the criminal law in social change must be elucidated to contrast it to the "traditional" notion of the radical lawyer and the criminal law. The traditional notion focuses on criminal trials, usually political show trials such as the Panther 21 and the Chicago Eight.

I do not wish to denigrate the significance and courage of those defendants and attorneys who have experienced the snake pit of the American political trial. However, I am less concerned with criminal trials, in part because of the decline in the number of such trials that punctuated the 1965-1975 period. Moreover, my diminished concern results from alternative foci: first, I tend to focus on events prior to the "circus" of the trial; second, I question whether the outcome of the trial really makes that much difference.

There are two central points concerning pre-trial activity. First, there is the issue of the client's situation: is she in or out of jail? Since out of jail she can more effectively mobilize,[241] it is crucial for progressive attorneys to master the laws dealing with arrest and bail. Law schools teach much about definitions of murder and the prerequisites of due process, but not about how quickly you can expect to get a client back onto the streets after an arrest, how to bargain with an arresting officer, or where to get the money for bail. The attorney must know the pre-conditions for release on one's own recognizance and other ways of securing a client's release, such as contacting a locally elected official who might have the authority to release a person without a bond requirement. These questions are critically important in the contexts of demonstrations and organizing drives, as demonstrations often involve ordinary citizens who would be less likely to mobilize after a long stay in jail,[242] professional agitators who would be reluctant to participate if their jobs involve jail time, and others who would be unable to serve their movement while incarcerated. In short, a lawyer associated with social change must be adept at keeping people out of jail as much as possible.

Since social change cases normally involve minor "crimes" which seldom precipitate jail terms, the most critical period will usually involve the period between arrest and bail. My experience indicates that the most frequent result is either a fine or successful bargaining with officials to drop the charges.[243] Thus, the primary opportunity for jailing occurs during the arrest phase and its immediate aftermath, and it is then that the lawyer's criminal law expertise is most needed.

The other question relating to pre-trial events concerns the focus of activity of the social reform movement. Agitating for social change is more important than the prison-term fates of particular individuals. Setting up criminal defense committees for particular groups of people, especially the leaders, diverts energies from the central struggle. History suggests that energies of all concerned, including the lawyers, should focus on the task of political mobilization, not criminal defense work. Martin Luther King's release from jail resulted from the upsurge of activities on the part of his peers in the streets rather than from trial motions. When the Chicago Eight, who enjoyed limited mass support, had to rely on lawyers, the state had, in a sense, already won. This realization leads directly to the question of whether or not the outcome of the criminal trial ultimately makes that much difference. If the state can force the movement to divert its resources to questions of criminal prosecution as opposed to political mobilization, then it has achieved its primary purpose. Whether the individual defendants go to jail or not, the movement has been quelled.

A witness for this position is Hosea Williams, once a director of the Southern Christian Leadership Conference (SCLC field staff, and later elected to the Georgia House of Representatives. After being jailed when organizing a march of young people in Savannah, he encouraged his supporters to continue demonstrating instead of helping him make bond and setting up a defense committee.

> [T]hem kids marched every night. They burnt Sears and Roebuck down. They burnt Firestone. Savannah was really in trouble. [In jail he received a call from Savannah's leading white citizen, Mills B. Lane, who said:] I wanna make a deal with you. Savannah is my home and I don't want to see that city burned down. They say you are running that movement from the jailhouse. I want you to stop those demonstrations, and if you stop those demonstrations, I'll make it possible for you to get out.[244]

The judge had set bond for Williams beyond $100,000, and Lane put up his own property. In the end, Williams moved his "class," and Lane moved his.[245]

There is one other area of criminal law relevant to the social change attorney. This is the situation of criminal investigations, particularly grand jury investigations, when the state has not yet jailed the clients, but intends to do so. The grand jury, originally instituted as a tool of liberty,[246] has long been abused. Courts have only recently begun to employ sanctions against abusive use of grand juries.[247] Whether the criminal investigation is conducted by the local police, the F.B.I., or a grand jury, the social change attorney must be able to judge whether or not her clients are being investigated for reasonable and legitimate purposes, and advise her clients accordingly.[248]

D. Procedure

The social change lawyer must also consider how procedural elements of the case can be used to magnify its impact. For example, since legal documents are public, one could duplicate the complaint and use it with a leaflet.[249] Additionally, the press frequently quotes from complaints, and so attorneys must ensure their accuracy. Social change lawyers can also use the discovery process to their advantage by publicizing facts and conducting public depositions of adversaries.[250]

E. Ethics

The progressive lawyer must be familiar with professional rules of ethics as they have conscientiously been used by elite groups to crush progressive movements.[251] From 1963 to 1978, the Supreme Court provided guidance in distinguishing legitimate first amendment recourse to the courts[252] from champerty.[253] History suggests that the social change attorney note these differences closely.[254]

Among the standards that the attorney should remember is that she may not represent parties with potentially conflicting interests unless all clients have been adequately advised of the situation.[255] The social change lawyer should pay attention to this rule when she is asked to represent a number of clients to prevent potential conflicts that might arise later. For example, in a case in which I participated, when our discovery motions produced an order from the court requiring the defendants to release the name of a police informant, our clients were offered a settlement involving thousands of dollars. Some clients wanted to settle while others wanted the name of the agent. In the end, the minority acceded to the majority. The progressive lawyer facing such a situation may wish to establish a system (in writing) for settling potential differences before the suit is filed.

Disciplinary Rules 2-109[256] and 7-102(A)[257] prohibit the attorney from pursuing legal actions in bad faith. Whether these rules will directly affect the social change attorney more often than her more establishmentarian peer is open to doubt, but the line may be too close when the suit is being filed for one or more of the ACORN reasons noted above, rather than based on its actual potential for success. Disciplinary Rules 7-106(C)(5), (6), and (7)[258] prevent the attorney from deliberately offending tribunals. This rule should be given additional consideration by any attorney considering adopting the postures of political defendants who would make a mockery of the courts.

Disciplinary Rule 7-106[259] prohibits the attorney from disregarding, or advising his client to disregard, a standing rule of a tribunal. The question here is what the lawyer is to do in advising her clients who wish to engage in civil disobedience. The rule suggests that she can play no role in aiding civil disobedience strategies. However, this undercuts the lawyer's capacity to assist her clients in an important mode of social change. At least one Supreme Court Justice has written:

> In my judgment civil disobedience–the deliberate violation of the law–is never justified in our nation where the law being violated is not itself the focus or target of the protest. So long as our governments obey the mandate of the Constitution and assure facilities and protection for the powerful expression of individual and mass dissent, the disobedience of laws which are not themselves the target of the protest–the violation of law merely as a technique of demonstration–constitutes an act of rebellion, not merely dissent.
>
> ....
>
> At the beginning of this discussion, I presented the dilemma of obedience to law and the need that sometimes may arise to disobey profoundly immoral or unconstitutional laws. This is another kind of civil disobedience, and the only kind that, in my view, is ever truly defensible as a matter of social morality.[260]

Whether Justice Fortas adequately cared for this issue is doubtful. His distinction between the two types of civil disobedience is next to worthless once one starts questioning the real openness of the political processes in this country.[261] On the other hand, however, once one argues that civil disobedience does entail a moral basis, the remaining question is the extent to which the lawyer, as an officer of the court, as a citizen, or as a human being, has the right to associate himself with civil disobedience. Perhaps one is restricted to the role played by the lawyer of Martin Luther King. King had been enjoined from marching in Birmingham, and he knew that "if we obey this order we are out of business."

> The lawyer said, "Well, now I couldn't tell you to march, I couldn't tell you not to march, because as a lawyer that would be a conflict of interests and my license would be taken away from me. The only thing I can say in regard to the injunction, you can't beat it.... Now, if you are willing to pay the fine and whatever is involved, then that's up to you all."[262]

King violated the injunction, went to jail, became "once and for all" committed "to the philosophy that one had a positive moral duty to violate unjust laws," and wrote the famous "Letter from the Birmingham Jail." The Supreme Court sided with the Alabama judge.[263]

Disciplinary Rule 7-107[264] deals with trial publicity, and constitutes one of the more problematic rules for the social change attorney. On the one hand, one might view it as a helpful rule, in that it may be cited to the press to force them to speak not with elitist lawyers but with litigants trying to bring a specific issue before the public.[265] On the other hand, it is often true that if her lawyer cannot speak for a litigant, no one will. This is especially likely if the lawyer is representing an amorphous or inarticulate group. If cases are used to generate publicity and raise consciousness, then it seems that this rule has a repressive effect on those who use the courts to promulgate their concerns. At the very least, it raises significant questions about the first amendment rights of the individual attorney.

Hence my prescriptions for what the lawyer who would align herself with social change movements should do. Some critics might argue that I accord the lawyer too much of a role, while others might say I accord her too little. I now turn to some of those alternative perspectives.

V

ALTERNATIVE POSITION AND CRITIQUE

* * *

Chief Justice Warren Burger attacked the "young people who go into the law primarily on the theory that they can change the world by litigation in the courts."[266]

* * *

A. Public Interest

From the public interest perspective one might argue that my vision unduly ignores the efficacy of the legal process and profession. The public interest profession's view of society is based on a judicial model,[267] hence public interest advocate Charles Halpern can write that "public-interest law rests on the conviction that the public interest is more likely to emerge, and the legal process to function more effectively, if all sides to a dispute are represented."[268] The public interest movement defines litigating as the processes appropriate for attaining its goals. The nature and scope of the role of law and lawyers in such a vision is obvious, while the shortcomings of such a vision are equally apparent.

To begin with, the value of the goal is open to dispute. The end seems to be a polity where the primary political acting is done by judges, lawyers, and bureaucrats who, like Platonic philosopher kings, create justice from whatever esoteric processes they employ.[269] While this may be satisfying for frustrated upper-middle-class lawyers who want to enjoy the powers of real citizenship, it does little for the rest of the body politic, whose role seems to be one of funding and applauding genteel champions.[270]

Even if the public interest vision is accepted, a more primary question remains: Are the public interest advocates employing means that will in fact accomplish their ends? From both the short- and long-term perspective, this is doubtful.

From the short-term perspective, the courts seldom produce much. One public interest lawyer has conceded that "[w]hen you're talking about major social change... there are obvious limitations [to public interest litigation.]"[271] This observation has been empirically sustained by the work of Joel Handler.[272]

Cases like *Brown* helped to inspire many well-meaning lawyers to attempt public interest litigation,[273] yet, as noted, the accomplishments of *Brown* were delivered more through political action than judicial pronouncements. Even more significant is that focus on such cases involves an appalling lack of a sense of history. Since 1789, decisions of socially progressive impact have not consistently emanated from the Supreme Court. In many cases the decisions were of limited relevance,[274] and in others the decisions were positively reactionary.[275] The recent period of success has resulted from the contingencies of political struggle rather than from the nature of the court itself.[276] Recent pronouncements from the Burger court suggest that the aforementioned historical epoch of progressive decisions is coming to an end.[277]

Yet, if these short-term objections are not enough, there remains the more fundamental point that public interest litigation defeats itself in the long term.[278] Public interest lawyering takes power from people and gives it to attorneys.[279] It increases the sense of helplessness and frustration on the part of the many,[280] and disguises realities of political struggle and creates false consciousness. Postulating their work as "public interest" work, these attorneys imply that there is but one public interest which everyone should support.[281] This is a dubious proposition, because one's own perspective is frequently colored by one's class position, one's present situation with regard to the society's resources and power. As demonstrated, social change has historically resulted from shifts in balances of power in society rather than from persuasive arguing,[282] and so the belief that silver-tongued oration alone will implement social change is wrong. Public interest law should be seen for what it is: the expression of political[283] interests which will go nowhere without substantial backing that thrives outside the chambers of the courts.

At this point it might be fair to ask if any good at all can come from recourse to the courts for the sake of social change. Handler has observed:

Most law-reform activity serves multiple purposes. Even if the social-reform groups and the law reformers are counting on direct tangible benefits from litigation, the litigation usually will help publicize the organization and the law reformers, legitimize values and goals, stimulate purposive incentives, and hopefully result in obtaining outside resources from elites, foundations, other organizations (for example, labor unions), and public agencies.[284]

Handler notes three major areas of indirect benefits: "(a) Where litigation is used to clear the underbrush (subsidiary to nonlitigation strategies); (b) for leverage to enable the group to mobilize resources and increase the potency of its other tactics; and (c) for publicity, fund raising, mobilizing outside resources, consciousness raising, and legitimacy."[285]

But what Handler notes is no different from the points made above. Participation in the legal system does have its role to play in meaningful social change, but it is a subordinate role. Elevating it to a premier role creates problematic if not disastrous consequences.

B. A-Legal

* * *

[T]here is a difference between arbitrary power and the rule of law. We ought to expose the shams and inequities which may be concealed beneath this law. But the rule of law itself, the imposing of effective inhibitions upon power and the defence of the citizen from power's all-intrusive claims, seem to me to be an unqualified human good. To deny or belittle this good is, in this dangerous century when the resources and pretentions of power continue to enlarge, a desperate error of intellectual abstraction.[286]

* * *

This section critiques what I have chosen to call an "a-legal" perspective of social change.[287] Perhaps the most obvious proponents of this view are the "crude Marxists" who might assert something like the following: law is merely the reflection of the needs and desires of a given society's ruling class. It is created by the elite as a tool to maintain its domination over other social groups. Recourse to law is thus counter-productive for the conscientious revolutionary reformer, except, perhaps, to expose the scandalous contempt for justice held by hirelings participating in the judicial system where outcomes are pre-determined.[288]

The "crude Marxist," or "instrumentalist" point of view, which has continued to be attacked[289] since Engels' criticisms of the late nineteenth century,[290] should be evaluated lest it be dismissed too easily.

First, the ostensibly cynical view of the "crude Marxist" is not always totally wrong, as the instrumentalist employment of the canons of ethics, and the frank hostility of Chief Justice Taft towards organized labor demonstrates. Part of the "massive resistance" employed by Southern racists during the 1950's and 1960's included straightforward instrumentalist use of the law.[291] On a more abstract level, Professor Morton Horwitz has established that, during the first century of American jurisprudence, law was used openly to promote economic growth and entrepreneurial capitalism. Though such instrumentalism is less blatant than the squelching of a dissident, it does sustain a particular social order, to the benefit of specific social groups.[292] Thus law's role in social conflict is not consistently subtle.

Second, some cynicism concerning western "rule of law" is in fact well-founded considering the historical contingencies and conscientious terror/violence upon which "rule of law" thrived in particular and privileged comers of the world.[293] Merleau-Ponty's points concerning this matter may lead us to consider the ideals we are advocating, and how we intend to effectively implement them.

These two points lead to a consideration of a third: the extent to which the ruling orders dispense with the rule of law altogether, and rely on sheer terror. Potential social changers must, in fact, be prepared to face raw force with no pretense to legal forms. Concerning the history of American violence in general, Richard Hofstadter has written:

> [O]ne is impressed that most American violence—and this also illuminates its relationship to state power—has been initiated with a "conservative" bias. It has been unleashed against abolitionists, Catholics, radicals, workers and labor organizers, Negroes, Orientals, and other ethnic or racial or ideological minorities, and has been used ostensibly to protect the American, the Southern, the white Protestant, or simply the established middle-class way of life and morals. A high proportion of our violent actions has thus come from the top dogs or the middle dogs. Such has been the character of most mob and vigilante movements. This may help to explain why so little of it has been used against state authority, and why in turn it has been so easily and indulgently forgotten.[294]

Fourth, Piven and Cloward, after close scrutiny of the labor, civil rights, and welfare movements suggest:

> Whatever influence lower-class groups occasionally exert in American politics does not result from organization, but from mass protest and the disruptive consequences of protest.... The wiser course is to understand [the limitations imposed by historical considerations and social institutions], and to exploit

whatever latitude remains to enlarge the potential influence of the lower class. And if our conclusions are correct, what this means is that strategies must be pursued that escalate the momentum and impact of disruptive protest at each stage in its emergence and evolution.[295]

In effect, Piven and Cloward maintain that social progress results from disrupting the system. Their perspective suggests that the role of law and lawyers is even more marginal than that suggested by my analysis, which centers on the importance of the transformation of the class-in-itself into the class-for-itself. Piven and Cloward shift the focus to questions of disruptions within the prevailing system as the critical and primary motors of social change.[296]

Some instrumentalism inheres in the a-legal perspective as it views law as a consequence, if not of conscientious socio-economic policy, then of conscientious political compromise. Legal processes tend to be viewed as effects rather than causes, and so activity in the legal field appears eminently marginal.

There is a certain appeal to the humility evidenced in a perspective like that of Piven and Cloward. Too frequently left-wing thinkers dispute the details of utopia without considering how to initiate a challenge to oppression.[297] By contrast, the humbler point of view seems to concentrate on what concessions might be extracted from a tragic and uncooperative process of history.[298]

Ultimately, however, both the tragic and the utopian a-legal visions question the role that law plays in social relations. The utopian is likely to say, smash the ruling class and its instrumental laws, and the subsequent social relations will care for themselves. The problem here is that social relations do not always care for themselves. Smashing often continues far beyond what anyone may have anticipated originally. Thus E.P. Thompson has noted the need for an appreciation of rules, and the systems and circumstances by which people relate to one another.[299] The lawyer involved in social change must therefore watch the processes by which the class-in-itself becomes a class-for-itself. Will it be an authoritarian or democratic process? The lawyer, with her training in matters of justice, fairness, and procedures for implementing them, may have a contribution to make beyond diminishing lawyerly elitism.

The same considerations hold true for the humbler approach suggested by Piven and Cloward. If history teaches us that we must expand disruption, what happens when and if we finally "escalate" its "momentum and impact" to a point where we have to worry about the responsibilities of taking and exercising power? Sometimes ruling elites bend, sometimes they break. At such junctures the "lower" class movement will have need for some experience in modes of structuring social relationships beyond the mere ability to riot. At such a point, experiences similar to those cultivated by ACORN would be necessary. People must experience making decisions and exercising power collectively. They have to appreciate the complexities of democracy: where manipulation begins, and how to implement respect for personhood. Again, these insights derive from conscientious practices sustained before the "final" victory is won.[300] They do not drop from the skies. They do not result from dreaming about them as the utopian might. They do not result from a focus that concentrates exclusively on riot.

Thus, the a-legal perspective correctly points out that legal procedures are subject to instrumental abuse. However, as E.P. Thompson has suggested, law is as important a bourgeois contribution to human civilization as industrial production. The respect for individuals that law implies must be an integral component of any movement for social change, or real social change will never occur. The lawyer thus has a role to play in assuring the maintenance of a system of respect and fairness, by struggling against lawyerly elitism and by sustaining the rule of law. In trying to hold power accountable she sustains the heritage won by our revolutionary predecessors.[301]

C. Fusionist

* * *

> The attractive power of mass consumption is based not on the dictates of false needs, but on the falsification and exploitation of quite real and legitimate ones without which the parasitic process of advertising would be ineffective. A socialist movement ought not to denounce these needs, but take them seriously, investigate them, and make them politically productive.[302]

* * *

In a sense, my objections to the public interest advocates and a-legal partisans are Aristotelian. Each was too extreme in its position: the former relying too much on law and lawyers to better social conditions, and the latter ignoring them too thoroughly. There is a third perspective on the role of law and lawyers which is presently enjoying some currency.[303] I have chosen to label this perspective "fusionist," for reasons explicated below.

The fusionists espouse a more optimistic approach to radical law, claiming that "the very public and political character of the legal arena gives lawyers, acting together with clients and fellow legal workers, an important opportunity to reshape the way that people understand the existing social order and their place within it."[304] They argue for going "beyond rights-consciousness [to focus] upon expanding political consciousness through using the legal system to increase people's sense of personal and political power.[305] Gabel and Harris illustrate the means of achieving these various strategic goals, including: telling an aggrieved tenant what she might do for herself first,[306] standing by a prisoner in the prisoner's dock,[307] requesting that "standing rules" against children in the courtroom be waived while a client is being sentenced,[308] politicizing ostensibly neutral legal processes, citing sexual oppression to bolster a self-defense defense of a woman indicted for murdering a man who raped her, and transforming a police harassment prosecution into first amendment terms.[309]

I agree with much of this approach. Their focus on the way human beings relate to each other to create law, politics, and reality, is excellent. Particularly commendable are the instances where the authors advocate organizing approaches.[310] My objection to the fusionists may be more of emphasis than of kind. However, the objection is ultimately rooted in differing conceptions of social goals, and how to achieve them.

Gabel and Harris, for example, speak in terms of "the overcoming of alienation [as] a central political objective," and "the primacy of liberating human desire as the foundation of radical political theory."[311] They imply that part of their objection to a "rights-oriented" approach to legal practice is its implications concerning "the necessity of social antagonism (since rights are normally asserted against others)".[312] They call this "way of thinking about people":

> [A] bizarre abstracting away from one's true experience of others as here with us existing in the world. An alternative approach to politics based on resolving differences through compassion and empathy would presuppose that people can engage in political discussion and action, founded upon a felt recognition of one another as human beings, instead of conceiving of the political realm as a context where one abstract 'legal subject' confronts another.[313]

Such remarks display an optimistic perspective on the capacities of human beings to cooperate with and love one another. Human desire is viewed almost innocently, as if the human body is filled only with love. The fusionists imply that if people would only sit down together and talk, social antagonism would end.[314] The role of force in human affairs is viewed almost as an accident.[315]

The Gabel and Harris perspective becomes more comprehensible within the perspective of fusionism. Dallmayr introduced the fusionist perspective as a mode of being, explicated by Sartre.[316] For Sartre the group in fusion was a way of living to be contrasted to "seriality," where people encounter one another as strangers, as "others," and as a "plurality of isolations."[317] By contrast, the group in fusion involved a way of relating when individuals shared common projects, and could see themselves in others. This concept is important for a number of reasons. First, it implies a view of the nature of humanity: alienation is aberration,[318] fusion is normal. Second, it implies an alternative to Lenin's elite party as the appropriate vehicle for revolutionary change.[319] Third, the fusion concept implies that Marx's ideal state of communism might be achieved. The informing assumption is that humanity "naturally" unites, and all that it needs is appropriate stimulation to do so.[320] Given this explication of Sartre,[321] the remarks of Gabel and Harris, as explicators of a fusionist perspective, take on additional meaning.

The question at this point becomes the extent to which the fusionist perspective can be reconciled with my communitarian perspective. It is not clear to me that they can, because they entertain alternative conceptions of value and human nature.[322]

The value of community embraces the value of social interaction (which fusionists espouse) while nevertheless arguing for the sustenance of potentially antagonistic individualism. Fusionism is likely to view such individualism, and its attendant separations and alienation, as an aberration which ought to be transcended once the appropriate social conditions are implemented.[323] My version of community finds this hard to accept. That people differ is not necessarily bad, and experiences of solitude can entail their own rewards. More importantly, though, we may have no choice but to embrace our individual situations. The matter that produces individual consciousnesses is going to continually produce disparate aggregates of matter and consequently disparate consciousnesses.[324] Though these disparate bodies and minds may find it possible and rewarding to get along with, if not love, one another, still they will differ from one another. The potential for contradiction, antagonism, and aberrations—as well as diversity and stimulation and letting-be[325]—will remain.[326]

These differing perspectives on human diversity lead to a different perspective on law. While the ways in which law legitimates and masks alienation and hierarchy constitute a major contribution of recent critical legal thought, the issue does not end there. Fusionist thought has a tendency to view law as an unfortunate aberration. Law is viewed as a function of alienation, existing as an artificial barrier keeping people from natural harmony. This conception is sensible if one believes that the state of natural harmony is attainable. However, if one believes that some aspects of "antagonistic" individualism are likely to remain in an ideal society, then one is likely to view law in a positive, as well as a negative, light. Law not only obfuscates community by promulgating perverse social relations, it also intimates community by postulating an ideal of social relations where every person is respected and empowered. Many times the practical implementation of the law makes a mockery of this ideal. But as E.P. Thompson suggests, it is as revolutionary as the Christian notion that every person, slave or emperor, has a soul.[327] Law is certainly a social practice, but in addition to conditioning us for hierarchy, it also rehearses us for liberation.[328]

My conception of law vitiates my appreciation of the points that Gabel and Harris make concerning symbolic conduct in the courtroom. To begin with, from the mundane perspective of my professional practice, I would simply observe that not all of my clients are totally taken in by courtroom folderol. It is not as if real human beings are passive targets of ruling class hokus pocus.[329] They do have a sense of hokum.[330] The problem, however, is not only one of inadequately appreciating real people. It is also one of being insufficiently dialectical. Though real human beings do not necessarily buy in totally to law's symbolic conduct, to an extent they do buy in. Now their buying in might frequently involve a capitulation to authoritarian forms of social conduct. But as we indicated earlier, the symbolic behavior involves a rehearsal for liberation as well as capitulation to authoritarianism. Though persons in the courtroom are on the one hand participating in a community of domination and hierarchy, they are at the same time participating in a community where every person is equally entitled to respect.[331]

Additionally, one might intuitively conclude that minor disruptions of symbolic conduct are simply not going to make that much difference in the real world of social struggle. It is all too easy to view them as frustrated substitutes for meaningful social action.[332]

At this level, my differences with the fusionist perspective turns to the issue of means for accomplishing social good. Since my ultimate values possibly differ more in degree than in kind from those of the fusionists, questions of degree also affect conceptions of implementation of social change. For example, although I agree with the fusionist emphasis on developing decent human relations before the revolution, I disagree that nice approaches to other human beings will suffice to bring about social transformation. Fusionism tends to argue that the revolution will come when growing experiences of fusion overwhelm the ruling order. This position is not sensitive to the role that force plays in history. Ruling class violence has frequently been employed in history[333] against groups that might fuse,[334] and so the disenfranchised must be prepared to use force as a shield, if not as a sword.[335] Cultivating a class-in-itself should thus prove more effective than planting fusionary seeds throughout society in hopes that they will grow, spread, and by their own inertia prevail.

This point, though, must be qualified in two ways. First, the cultivation of decent human encounters is important in the context of the transformation of the class-in-itself into the class-for-itself. The appropriate revolutionary vehicle is not a contingent fusing group or a Leninist elite party, but rather a class or a group resembling a class. The emphasis such writers as Sparer[336] and Goodwyn[337] place on conscientious institutional cultivation is correct.

Secondly, I acknowledge the horrendous nature and complexity of the problem. It is the problem of terror, and of the ways in which means may corrupt ends, or become ends in themselves. As Merleau-Ponty has posed the question, "[I]s the violence [of communism] revolutionary and capable of creating human relations between men[?]"[338] One appeal of the fusionist theory is that it suggests an end to terror, and Poster has provided us with some tantalizing arguments to justify this conclusion.[339] Merleau-Ponty, however, entertains a more tragic perspective:

> [I]n advocating nonviolence one reinforces established violence, or a system of production which makes misery and war inevitable... Political action is of its nature impure, because it is the action of one person upon another and because it is collective action.... To govern, it has been said, is to foresee, and the politician cannot excuse himself for what he has not foreseen. Yet there is always the unforeseeable. There is the tragedy.... [Our critics] are trying to forget a problem which has troubled Europe since the Greeks, namely, that the human condition may be such that it has no happy solution.[340]

Perhaps the differences of opinions hinge upon an optimistic or pessimistic conception of human nature and history. Although we hope that Poster and his version of Sartre is correct, we may better hedge our historical bets by cultivating groups in fusion in the context of transforming the class-in-itself.

The rest of my disagreements with the fusionist prescriptions tie into factors already noted. We should worry more about force than we do about hegenomic practices.[341] I find the differentiation between empowerment and rights consciousness rather scholastic.[342] While politicizing defense in the courtroom may be preferred from a personal and professional standpoint, it seldom effectuates much meaningful social change. As in the Savannah experience,[343] what happens in the streets is more important than what happens in the courtroom. Reversing priorities can be positively retrograde, as in the situation of the Chicago Eight, where the courtroom behavior was perceived as unacceptable and immature, and produced insignificant mass mobilization.

A dialectical materialist might observe that the fusionist perspective grows out of the material conditions of academics, intellectuals, and lawyers who look to justify their societal practices.[344] While I do not deny that such work has significance in implementing social change, I think it is a mistake to overplay it, to the extent that one simply misunderstands how social change is accomplished. Perhaps the problem is clarified by reference to my other profession: painting.[345] There are a number of arguments one can cite to justify the production of art. For example, it constitutes a protest against the given,[346] its very "uselessness" constitutes a revolutionary rebuff to the utilitarian ethos which dominates capitalist (and bureaucratic socialist) social relationships.[347] As comforting as these arguments might be to the frustrated painter, it is hard to believe that any radical lawyer would agree that a bunch of paintings are going to create the revolution. The same is true for lawyering. The simple fact is that as a lawyer or a painter the individual can play but a limited role in implementing social change. Those who believe otherwise are falling into the error of "Auschwitz culture,"[348] that is, they accord primacy to occupations where one does not have to engage in boring, alienating, hands dirtying work. The solution for the conscientious lawyer is the solution for the conscientious artist: both must attempt to integrate their work in insurgent cultures,[349] and energize those cultures.[350] If those cultures do not exist, or have been destroyed, then they must do what they can, like Milton.[351] But they must try to relate their work to past and future insurgency, and let their work inspire correct apprehensions of value and value implementation.[352] They must not mislead themselves or others by misstating the dynamics of social change.

In the end I am reluctant to say that the fusionists are misleading. Though their points of emphasis are problematic, in this time of social reaction, we not only share a common project. We also share a number of areas of agreement in pursuing that project.

VI

THE NATURE OF LAW

* * *

I found that law did not keep politely to a "level" but was at every bloody level; it was imbricated within the mode of production and productive relations themselves (as property-rights, definitions of agrarian practice) and it was simultaneously present in the philosophy of Locke; it intruded brusquely within alien categories, re-appearing bewigged and gowned in the guise of ideology; it danced a cotillion with religion, moralising over the theatre of Tyburn; it was an arm of politics and politics was one of its arms; it was an academic discipline, subjected to the rigour of its own autonomous logic; it contributed to the definition of the self-identity both of rulers and of ruled; above all, it afforded an arena for class struggle, within which alternative notions of law were fought out.[353]

* * *

This discussion should be closed by elaborating on my conception of the nature of law. I agree with the fusionists that it has to be understood as a praxis that implements authoritarian obfuscation. Yet it also intimates

53

some values worthy of espousal: for example, that power should not be the final arbiter in human affairs and that every human being is entitled to respect. By its allusions to these better notions, law enjoys its legitimacy. Though legal discourse often attempts to pervert notions of legitimacy, when law deviates from the valid ideals that it intimates, it undermines itself, and lays the groundwork for its eventual transformation.[354]

Fundamentally, law involves human behavior and values. It implements notions concerning appropriate roles for violence, the importance of free expression, and the particulars of freedom of travel and safety. At an abstract level, law involves conceptions of human values, how a human being should ultimately be treated. Law is by no means an insignificant aspect of human affairs.

Since law is so important, we must know how to change its form to meet our goals, and the insight that law concerns value proves helpful. Laws reflect the struggles over values by individuals and groups within society and are the truces that varying factions and classes adopt. They constitute temporary compromises while one group tries to assert power over others. Examples of this are found in the struggle between capital and labor,[355] and further examples are provided concerning the roles that lawyers and pharmacists play within society.[356] Thus, society's laws can be viewed as reflecting various societal balances of power at various junctures through history.

Since law is the end result of struggles over value, any assertion of value affects the final form a law assumes, with the extreme being the application of force. Though revolutionary violence or white terror asserts certain values through coercion and intimidation, there are other levels at which the struggle over values expresses itself, with an impact on the ultimate form that law assumes. Hierarchical, alienating, social relationships practiced within the legal profession, and in society in general, promote values involving hierarchy and alienation. When a working class student attending law school learns he is a clod because he lets his T-shirt show underneath a polyester shirt, a whole value system is subtly enforced where working people are inferior because they are unaware or incapable of fulfilling certain ideals.[357] Law is, thus, not simply what goes into the statute books or the West Reporter system, but rather a result of a whole social context created by the minute practices of every man, woman and child, every day of every year.[358]

The preceding observations lead to conclusions concerning what must be done to change law and implement the values espoused. The legalistic approach of the public interest people should not be ignored, because it can affect the writings of judges and legislators. Nor can the mundane approach of the fusionists be ignored, because the values implemented in day-to-day interpersonal relationships create the social norms and expectations influencing legislators, and judges. Self-assertion and conscientious political development are also relevant because they defend and create good human relationships and confront the legal elitists with political force that the elitists ignore at their peril. There is, of course, no simple answer, as each position holds merit, but certain approaches are more productive. History will suggest which emphasis is most effective.

A final concern is that the "crude Marxist" differentiation between structure and superstructure should be adjusted, if not superceded. According to this paradigm, economic matters are the key to understanding everything, while fields of human endeavor like law, art, religion and philosophy are "superstructural" reflections of the economic system.[359]

In our understanding, rather than being a reflection of the economic system, law is a practice between individuals and groups in society. Though it is a collection of words which distill the truces between factions and classes in society at any given time, it also involves people's reactions to these articulated norms. The relationship between the factory worker and her foreman is a good example. The worker receives an order, and considers whether to obey it. Though society's norms as presently articulated in law say that she should obey the order, the worker might wonder whether she should have a say in the operation of the plant. She may think the law is unfair and think nothing of disobeying the foreman, or accept things as they are. Whatever her reaction, it will have an impact on the previously articulated norms. If she and her coworkers believe in the norms or acquiesce in them, she will reinforce them. If, however, she and her co-workers, reject and resist them, they will also affect the norms. The point is that law is words sustained or undermined by attitudes and actions adopted by everyone in society, as well as the institutions and cultures created through self-conscious organizing by contending social groups.

The relationship between law and production is more of core/periphery than of structure/superstructure. While the latter model emphasizes that a superstructure is a mere reflection on the structure, the core/periphery model emphasizes that there can be interplay between the two spheres. However, core concerns tend to be more influential. In the end, the core/periphery perspective may be the correct version of the structure/ superstructure theory.[360] Note, however that when the vision developed in this article addresses core concern "models of production and reproduction," it refers to the politics of human relationships sustaining the model and how to organize those politics, rather than to the technology underlying the model.[361]

Whether or not this conception of law fits the structure/superstructure model is academic because my concern here is how lawyers and law relate to social justice. Ultimately, lawyers, judges, and lawmakers play only a marginal role in social transformation. To affect law directly, one should become a politician in the broadest sense and deal with the way people relate to one another in every arena of the social drama. The attorney should realize that she does have a role to play in social transformation, but she should appreciate the extents and limits of this role.

VII

THE NATURE OF PRACTICE

* * *

"The philosophers have only *interpreted* the world, in various ways; the point, however, is to change it."[362]

* * *

The theory presented above must be proven by actual experience. While experience usually provides its lessons in fragmentary pieces, perhaps one personal experience will explicate, substantiate, and provide grounds for the notion that the theory can productively inform practice. Residue from the experience is provided in *Redfield Telephone v. Arkansas Public Service Commission*,[363] which involved the revocation of the franchise of a public utility.[364]

In 1975, popular frustration with state regulation of public utilities in Arkansas was growing. Advocacy before the Arkansas Public Service Commission (P.S.C.) had brought only limited results. In 1976, ACORN helped organize in six different cities initiative campaigns for the authority to regulate electric rates within their jurisdictions. (The legal grounds were in a turn-of-the-century statute.) Litigation took our initiative propositions off the ballot in four cities. Though election results led to victory in Little Rock and defeat in Pine Bluff, the Little Rock initiative was ultimately overturned in court by a judge from outside of the city. Two judges in Little Rock had disqualified themselves, causing some observers to wonder whether or not they were avoiding the political heat of the wealthy utilities on one side, while not alienating the popular vote on the other side.

With this turn of events, ACORN became convinced that, if at all possible, the courts as well as the P.S.C. would have to be bypassed in the rate setting process. Accordingly, ACORN began looking for alternatives. Direct bargaining with the utility was chosen. If enough consumers would withhold payments from the utility if it did not bargain, then perhaps a decent settlement could be reached. Thus in early 1977, ACORN's lawyer began searching for what rights consumers might have in a strike context. In the meantime, the ACORN organizing staff spent significant amounts of time among the constituents serviced by the Redfield Telephone Company (R.T.C.). R.T.C. was a small utility in the counties southeast of Little Rock, and had been chosen as the experiment for ACORN's collective bargaining notion in part because its customer base, a couple thousand, was small enough to organize. Additionally, ACORN had been receiving calls asking it to react to the company and its President Stancil Glasgow. People complained that not only was his service horrible, he was insensitive to the point of being rude, if not racist, to many of his customers.

One of the first mass meetings that ACORN held was a rally in an auto racing field near Redfield. We filled a small van with law books and a lawyer (myself) to bring a "people's law office" to the rally. Some who attended the rally were reassured to have an attorney tell them that they did indeed have certain rights.

While ACORN organized Redfield, the P.S.C. also sent personnel down to the area to investigate complaints they had been receiving concerning Glasgow's service. The agitation stimulated by ACORN may have played a role in the P.S.C.'s decision to assume jurisdiction over the situation and hold hearings on whether to rescind the franchise of the R.T.C. Since the purpose of the enterprise was to set rates without the P.S.C., the P.S.C.'s move ended the reason for ACORN's organizing efforts. Yet, the energy aroused by our efforts was too great to abandon. Moreover, something had to be done about Glasgow. Accordingly, ACORN intervened in the P.S.C. hearing as representative of a number of ACORN members in the Redfield jurisdiction.

This gave me, the lawyer, a greater role in the campaign. In addition to preparing pleadings, I made trips to Redfield to interview prospective witnesses for the P.S.C. hearing. Helping them prepare their testimony, we concentrated not only on what would help to build the record, but also on what would help them articulate their rage, and galvanize their determination to see the issue through. These objectives complimented one another.

One incident at the hearing illustrated how effective lawyering can also produce positive organizational repercussions. In a sense, the hearing was a trial of Stancil Glasgow. His obnoxious arrogance had offended not only his customers, but also the P.S.C. He had various character witnesses appear on his behalf, including the wife of an Arkansas Supreme Court Justice. When his turn came to testify there was a sense that this was the heart of the hearing: the "Baron of Redfield" coming to account for himself. On his first day of testimony, Glasgow made statements which involved some potentially embarrassing contradictions. The following morning he read a statement attempting to retract some of them. During my cross examination, I began to press him on the contradictions, and under the pressures of the hearing, he broke into sobs. That incident made the headlines of that afternoon's statewide daily newspaper, and as a result, a number of ACORN members began calling into our ACORN office. It meant much to these callers that ACORN could bring a phone company president to account for his policies and actions. A campaign which had become circumscribed because of the courtly forum of the P.S.C. now reached a new level of energy.

After the hearing more traditional lawyering processes began. ACORN submitted the only brief to the P.S.C. calling for the revocation of R.T.C.'s franchise. While the P.S.C. deliberated over the decision, ACORN members sustained public pressure through public demonstrations.

The most militant demonstration occurred the following January when the P.S.C. held public hearings to determine whether or not it should develop a consumer's bill of rights. Given the P.S.C.'s apparent lack of solicitude for victims of the R.T.C., such concern on the part of the P.S.C. was anomalous. ACORN was determined to bring these issues up at the P.S.C. public hearings and brought more than two hundred members, many of them from Redfield, to voice their opinions. The P.S.C. hearing room holds only about 100 people, and by the time ACORN people arrived, over half the hearing room had already been filled with various spokespersons for the public utilities who believed that customers had enough rights. As the ACORN members began to crowd into the room, their lawyer, Andrew Weltchek, began to speak on their behalf. He had not been able to shave that morning because a freeze in Little Rock had broken his pipes. As he apologized for his appearance, he made a quip about the efficiency of local utilities. The joke precipitated a fair amount of laughter.

The tone had thus been set for a hearing unconstrained by traditional notions of tribunal decorum. ACORN members who could not fit into the hearing room chanted outside. In the afternoon, the P.S.C. moved the hearing to the more spacious Arkansas Supreme Court hearing room, and the ACORN members had their say.

The militance of the ACORN members helped raise the controversy over the extent to which the P.S.C. was protecting the rights of the Arkansas consumer. Though no one is privy to the Commissioners' deliberations, ACORN believed that public pressure as well as lawyerly disquisition ultimately led the P.S.C. to revoke the franchise of the R.T.C. The R.T.C. subsequently appealed the P.S.C. decision. While ACORN members demonstrated and pursued other issues, ACORN lawyers intervened on behalf of the P.S.C. Ultimately, the Arkansas Supreme Court upheld the P.S.C. decision, and the first franchise in the history of Arkansas had been revoked.

This experience illustrates many of the points in this essay, particularly the point concerning the many-faceted (dialectical) nature of law. Law both abetted and frustrated people's aspirations. People accepted and repudiated legal processes. Law was developed inside and outside the tribunal sites. People consciously organized and played significant roles to affect their situations. The lawyers played a variety of roles in this process. The "peoples law office" in the racing field helped to reassure the uncertain that there was some legal support for their position, and that a lawyer could help them. As lawyers, both Weltchek and I demystified the legal process to the community and made sure that the appropriate legal arguments were made before the commission. Our aggressive insistence that the drastic alternative of revocation was appropriate must have had some impact.

In the end, of course, one might question what was gained. A small businessman was replaced by AT&T. Is that progress? For ACORN it was progress because the issue was not simply whether a decision by the P.S.C. should be sustained or whether people could bargain collectively with their utilities. Rather the issue was the sort of power which people could exercise over their own lives, and how they could do it. ACORN helped those people organize. Through their own efforts, they did redress grievances they had against their phone company. This is more than most readers of this article will ever be able to say—unfortunately. Yet the point to note too is that the people of Redfield, as well as the people of Arkansas, saw that people can change their lives through self-organization. This has led ACORN people to try for more than stop signs (and franchise revocations) in Arkansas and elsewhere. ACORN has worked for city-wide housing programs, revision of the Democratic Party's delegation rules (four years before Jesse Jackson), people's radio stations, employment programs, and more. The organization continues to win and lose. People continue to struggle.

POSTSCRIPT, 2001

Because this article was written in 1984, I failed to mention two details in my Redfield Campaign narrative which now, in 2001, appear to entail much more entertainment value:

> First, the Lifeline litigation in Little Rock in 1976 provided the author with his first introductions to Webb Hubbell and Hillary (then) Rodham (now) Clinton. In his FRIENDS IN HIGH PLACES (published in 1997 by William Morrow and Company, Inc.), Webb Hubbell on pages 60-62 presents his version of events as follows:
>
> The first case Hillary and I worked on together was a strange one for two people who had gravitated to law to "make a difference." Instead of defending poor people and righting wrongs, we found ourselves squarely on the side of corporate greed against the little people. In the late 1970s, a group called Arkansas Citizens Organization for Reform Now [sic] (ACORN) formed to become an advocate for the poor. Their first target was utility rates—they wanted residential rates reduced by one third and industrial rates *raised* by a like amount. At first the Little Rock business community didn't

take ACORN seriously. But through smart positioning and effective grassroots politicking (not to mention high utility rates), the group managed to pass an initiated measure for the change they wanted.

The business community was flabbergasted. Who *were* these upstarts? How would we ever attract another industry? The law firm that was the epitome of the Little Rock establishment was handed the task of quashing the ACORN measure. Herb Rule took the lead, dealing with the clients. I was to prepare the witnesses and get the case ready for trial. And the brilliant young lawyer Hillary Rodham would come up with the research and theories to combat this obvious "unconstitutional" bleeding of the wealth of the city's industries.

Because all local judges used Little Rock electricity, a judge was imported from out of town. He turned out to be Robert Dudley from the little northeast Arkansas hamlet of Pocahontas [who later served on the Arkansas Supreme Court]…

When I got back to the office, Hillary was up to her frizzy hair in law books. We ordered pizza for dinner, and then, as these two onetime idealists struggled for a legal theory to question the constitutionality of consumer-friendly electric rates, the combination of pizza and drinks apparently inspired me. Here was the scene: We were in the Rose firm library, Hillary sitting in a chair taking notes while I lay resting my aching back on the floor under the conference table, espousing stream-of-consciousness constitutional law.

In the context of this particular article, another irony to observe was that I found Ms. Rodham to be cordial; but her interest in talking to me seemed to decline when I indicated an interest in discussing with her an article that I had read and enjoyed in a recent edition of the HAVARD LAW REVIEW. It was a critical review of Ronald Dworkin's TAKING RIGHTS SERIOUSLY, by a fellow named Peter Gabel. (The reader may refer to 91 HARV. L.REV. 302-315 (1977).)

Second, my narrative emphasizes that during the legal proceedings before the P.S.C., only ACORN argued for the revocation of Glasgow's franchise. In part this was a criticism directed against the Arkansas P.S.C. for being too timorous. At the time of writing it, I did not feel it worthwhile to note that I was also implicitly criticizing the Arkansas Attorney General, who had intervened in the proceeding, but whose office had not pressed for franchise revocation as a penalty for the conduct of Glasgow and his utility. The Arkansas Attorney General during this period was an individual named

William Jefferson Clinton, who eventually went on to higher office (including Governor of the State of Arkansas).

CHAPTER FOUR

BOOK REVIEW

The Hollow Hope: Can Courts Bring About Social Change?

By Gerald N. Rosenberg. Chicago and London:
University of Chicago Press, 1991. Pp. xii, 425. $29.95.

* * *

As for public interest lawyers, perhaps they will all finally go
into politics–where they belong.

–Charles Fried[365]

* * *

PREJUDICES

Since 1976 1 have been working with the Association of Community
Organizations for Reform Now (ACORN) and various allied organizations.
These groups work to advance the interests of low and moderate income
people, which certainly implies significant social change. ACORN is based
on the idea that the interests of low and moderate income people are
advanced through their direct empowerment; the ACORN perspective[366]
firmly holds that litigating through the courts runs counter to this goal of
direct empowerment.

Litigation validates the perception that ordinary people of low and
moderate income have nothing to do with law reform and social change,
and that such reform and change result only from the efforts of well-heeled
attorneys and judges. Litigation perpetuates the notion that significant
change occurs "by magic," because ordinary people of low and moderate
income frequently do not know or care what happens in the court rooms.
When ordinary people perceive that they can change nothing or that they
have to rely on "experts" or "magic" to solve their problems, they come to
believe they are powerless, they do less, and they grow more and more
powerless; which is to say, their original condition of limited capability for
societal change is only exacerbated. The deplorable conditions of the status
quo are intensified, not ameliorated.

The ACORN perspective, of course, is not universally shared. The opposite perspective is that of Public Interest Through Litigation (PITL).[367] The PITL perspective holds that societal good can be accomplished through court-centered pursuits. Obviously, not all lawyers working in the public interest sector necessarily hold the PITL view. But most probably do believe that major reform can be accomplished through litigation, and some devote their lives to large so-called "public interest" litigation.[368] When adherents to PITL pay attention to the impact that such litigation has on ordinary citizens, they focus on the benefits that such litigation supposedly bestows on ordinary citizens, and downplay or deny the extent to which litigation makes ordinary people feel powerless or dependent.

My investment in the ACORN perspective over the PITL perspective involves more than mere philosophical disagreement. Fascination with the PITL perspective has cost myself and my clients access to a number of important resources over the years. We have lost access to attorneys, because they believe their time might be better spent accomplishing "real" change in exciting, "cutting edge" cases. We have lost the services of law students because they believe the same things that those attorneys believe. We have lost organizers because they believe that their energies would be better spent in law school classrooms rather than in the streets. We have lost money because some contributors have thought it was better to spend money on a court case instead of a mailing list or a phone bank or an organizer's salary.

After five years these costs proved so strenuous that I sat down to write an article to justify the ACORN perspective, entitled *Lawyers, Law, and Social Change*.[369] In that article, I advanced the various points concerning empowerment which ACORN espouses. To bolster the ACORN tenets, I cited historical facts, suggesting in effect that if the reader was not convinced by my political, philosophical, or ethical assertions, then she should at least acknowledge historical reality. My historical arguments spanned roughly ten pages and alluded to the civil rights struggles in the 1950s and 1960s, and the American labor wars in the 1930s.[370] Based on this historical data, I alleged that attempting to promote the public good through litigation is a waste of time at best; at worst it constitutes moral profligacy.

From a review of the bibliography of *The Hollow Hope*, it seems likely that Gerald Rosenberg has never read my ten pages. Nor does he seem to have read various ACORN related literature which also pertains to issues of social reform.[371] The most striking aspect about Rosenberg's book for people who share the ACORN perspective, however, is how magnificently the work independently substantiates the historical basis of the ACORN argument.

Entering into this old debate about the efficacy of using lawsuits to prompt significant societal changes, Gerald Rosenberg, an assistant professor of political science at the University of Chicago, examines the role that courts have played in bringing about "significant social reform."[372] Courts certainly can effect change for individual litigants, and Rosenberg is quick to point out that he is addressing a much more profound subject. He focuses on litigation in the areas of "civil rights, women's rights, and the like"[373] that aims to produce "policy changes with nationwide impact."[374] Rosenberg assembles and analyzes the available empirical data to assess what role courts have played in the momentous social changes that the country went through over the last couple of decades. Yet, he does not attempt to explain fully the causes of the social reform or to suggest what role courts ought to have.[375]

As a means of exploring the courts' role in social reform without offering a full causal theory about social change, Rosenberg asks: "When and under what conditions will U.S. courts be effective producers of significant social reform? When does it make sense for individuals and groups pressing for such change to litigate?"[376] Rosenberg acknowledges that the influence court decisions have on society may take many forms and identifies two general kinds. First, court decisions may effect societal changes through a "judicial path that relies on the authority of the court."[377] That is, institutional social change might be court-ordered. The effectiveness of this type of court influence is measured by whether the change required by the court was actually made. The second kind of influence occurs along an "*extra-judicial* path that invokes the court powers of persuasion, legitimacy, and the ability to give salience to issues."[378] This more subtle and complex notion of the causal effects of court decisions is harder to detect. Court decisions could play a significant role in bringing about social change if the decisions affect the opinions and behavior of other political actors, the intellectual climate, or even the opinions and perceptions of the general populace.

To frame the evidence, Rosenberg notes a tension in the way Americans view the role of courts in social change. Citizens of our society generally demand that courts "defer to elected officials," while expecting the "courts to protect minorities and defend liberties."[379] We want both a "robust political life" and a just society.[380] Rosenberg describes the two poles of this tension as loosely corresponding to the "Constrained Court view" and the "Dynamic Court view."[381]

The Constrained Court view regards courts as generally powerless in affecting broad national policies or institutions. The theoretical underpinnings of the role of the judiciary in our society and the structure of the judiciary itself provide some support for the Constrained Court view. The judiciary is, on the whole, a conservative institution, because legal rights cannot drop from thin air and have to be teased out from existing precedent.[382] Courts cannot diverge too far from the mainstream given the extent to which the legislative and executive branches appoint their members and define their jurisdictions.[383] Courts have little practical power to effectuate their decisions because they lack the "sword" and "purse," and they do not have the capacity to launch legions of enforcers who might move a recalcitrant populace or bureaucracy.[384]

The Dynamic Court view, on the other hand, depicts courts as powerful sources for significant social reform. From this perspective courts supposedly enjoy an independence which allows them to stand apart from the smelly fray of politics and inspire the hoi polloi with carefully cultivated articulations of reason and justice. This view is skeptical about the political process and political institutions. In contrast, courts, free from the electoral influences and the proclivity for entrenchment that plagues the other branches of government, can act in favor of unpopular causes, even when faced with strident opposition by a majority of the public. Since courts must provide written opinions for their decisions, they cannot easily avoid the difficult and sometimes unpleasant issues which politicians are notoriously skillful at ducking. Also, being independent, courts can dislodge self-entrenched governmental actors and ferret out corruption in the electoral branches. Most importantly, according to this view, the independence of the judiciary enables courts to provide a forum for the "poor, powerless, and unorganized groups, those most often seeking significant social reform."[385]

Rosenberg recognizes that both views are too extreme: the Constrained Court view understates court effectiveness while the Dynamic Court view overstates court effectiveness.[386] Rosenberg reconciles the two views by positing types of social conditions under which the constraints of the Constrained Court view may be overcome, to enable the courts to be effective in bringing about social change in the way predicted by the Dynamic Court view. By reconciling the two diametrically opposed views, Rosenberg generates a hypothesis that guides his analysis of the empirical evidence. However, given the necessity of certain social conditions for court effectiveness, Rosenberg posits that the Constrained Court view "more closely approximates the role of the courts in the American political system."[387] While acknowledging that under certain conditions the courts can be effective in furthering significant social reform, Rosenberg argues that court effectiveness "occurs only when a great deal of change has already been made."[388]

FACTS

* * *

One's task is not to turn the world upside-down, but to do what is necessary at the given place and with a due consideration of reality. At the same time one must ask what are the actual possibilities; it is not always feasible to take the final step at once. Responsible action must not try to be blind.

–Dietrich Bonhoeffer[389]

* * *

Since both the Constrained Court view and the Dynamic Court view entail some logic, the only way to test Rosenberg's hypothesis that the Constrained Court view is more accurate is to turn to evidence. Accordingly, Rosenberg moves to the most important part of his study: an examination of the historical record.

In the field of civil rights Rosenberg establishes that by any honest empirical measure, the highly touted *Brown v. Board of Education*[390] accomplished nothing:

> [A] closer examination reveals that before Congress and the executive branch acted, courts had virtually *no direct effect* on ending discrimination in the key fields of education, voting, transportation, accommodations and public places, and housing. Courageous and praiseworthy decisions were rendered, and nothing changed.[391]

Rosenberg argues that the watershed years were 1964 and 1965, during which were passed the Civil Rights Act of 1964 and the Voting Rights Act. Rosenberg's empirical findings substantiate this assertion. In education:

> The statistics from the Southern states are truly amazing. For ten years, 1954-1964, virtually *nothing happened.* Ten years after *Brown* only 1.2 percent of black school children in the South attended school with whites. Excluding Texas and Tennessee, the percent drops to less than one-half of one percent (.48 percent). Despite the unanimity and forcefulness of the *Brown* opinion, the Supreme Court's reiteration of its position, and its steadfast refusal to yield, its decree was flagrantly disobeyed. After ten years of Court-ordered desegregation, barely 1 out of every 100 black children attended school with whites. The Court ordered an end to segregation and segregation was not ended... The numbers show that the Supreme Court contributed virtually *nothing* to ending segregation of the public schools in the Southern states in the decade following *Brown.*
>
> The entrance of Congress and the executive branch into the battle changed this... [D]esegregation took off after 1964, reaching 91.3 percent in 1972... In the first year of the [civil rights] act, 1964-65, nearly as much desegregation was achieved as during all the preceding years of Supreme Court action.[392]

Similarly, in the field of voting:

> [S]triking is the large jump in the number and percentage of blacks registered to vote from just prior to the passage of the 1965 Act to just after it... Prior to 1957, when only the Court acted, only 1 out of every 4 blacks was registered to vote in the South where nearly 3 out of every 4 whites were. Nearly threequarters as many blacks registered to vote merely in the two years after the passage of the [1965 Voting Rights Act] as had been registered in all the years prior to 1957.[393]

In 1961 segregation still existed in transportation[394] and in that same year the FDIC still supported racist lending practices.[395] Rosenberg justifiably concludes that "[i]n terms of judicial effects, then, *Brown* and its progeny stand for the proposition that courts are impotent to produce significant social reform."[396]

Rosenberg arrives at similar conclusions in the field of women's rights. However, in contrast with the courts' role in the area of civil rights, the courts initiated very little in the field of women's rights. Rather, they participated in societal trends that had been developing since the 1960s and before. For example, in the controversial field of abortion:

> [T]he data... show that the largest numerical increases in legal abortions occurred in the years prior to initial Supreme Court action ... There was no steep or unusual increase in the number of legal abortions following *Roe*. While the increases were large and steady, they were smaller than those of previous years.[397]

Part of this was due to the fact that the federal and state governments had been increasingly liberalizing abortion laws prior to 1973, the year in which *Roe v. Wade*[398] was decided.[399]

The Supreme Court began to act in the area of women's rights around the same time Congress and the executive branch began to attack sexist practices.[400] While in the 1970s the Supreme Court struck down a number of gender-based discrimination statutes,[401] Rosenberg argues that no significant change resulted from these decisions.[402] One need not be a radical feminist to observe that the women's revolution remains incomplete–access to abortion remains limited,[403] and women still experience more violence, less leisure time, and less economic and employment opportunity than men.[404] The courts have proven ineffective in bringing about significant change in this area. Notwithstanding the Supreme Court's strong decisions in holding gender discrimination unconstitutional, "court-ordered change in women's rights has changed little."[405] The courts would not and could not effect greater change than that made by the Congress and the executive branch. Hence, almost immediately after *Roe v. Wade,* the Supreme Court began circumscribing women's access to abortion.[406] In the heady years of the early 1970s, the Court toyed with the notion of making gender classifications in legislation "inherently suspect" and therefore subject to "strict judicial scrutiny," just like race classifications; but that jurisprudential watershed never transpired. [407] The adage one learns in high school history class would seem to apply: the courts follow the polls, not vice versa.

Some proponents of the PITL perspective might argue that their position is not dependent on a belief that the courts resemble faucets, which, once they are opened, will automatically splash forth social change. The PITL advocate might offer a more sophisticated model, suggesting that litigation proves productive through more indirect means, such as educating social elites or inspiring the dormant masses. The Dynamic Court view elaborated by Rosenberg provides one such model. This view holds that courts have important indirect effects in furtherance of social reform, insofar as courts educate Americans, "dramatiz[e] issues," and provoke organized action by "invigorat[ing] and encourag[ing] groups to mobilize and take political action."[408] And, indirect causation is not necessarily insignificant causation.

Rosenberg deals with this version of the argument, too, with evidence that is equally thorough. He presents graphs and tables of compiled data to demonstrate that media coverage concerning civil rights issues increased, not after *Brown,* but rather after the demonstrations of the 1960s.[409] What moved the political elites to productive civil rights action was not *Brown*: "[T]he point is that civil rights action, especially in the 1960s, was based in large part on the elite belief that, unless there was federal action on civil rights, mass bloodshed would occur."[410] Regarding the issue of consciousness raising, Rosenberg observes that:

> In general, surveys have shown that only about 40 percent of the American public, at best, follows Supreme Court actions …[I]n 1966, despite important Supreme Court decisions on race, religion, criminal justice, and voting rights, 46 percent of a nationwide sample could not recall *anything at all* that the Court had recently done …
>
> Among Americans who have some awareness of what the Court does, there is little evidence that Court decisions legitimate action. That is, people aware of what the Court does may disagree with it. In fact, the more knowledgeable a person is about the Supreme Court, the more likely he or she is to disagree with it.[411]

These points were borne out for both white and black Americans during the civil rights period. For whites, awareness of civil rights issues seems to have come primarily "from the mass media's portrayal of the violence unleashed against peaceful protesters."[412] As for blacks, Rosenberg points out that "knowledge of, and support for, *Brown* do not appear to have been high."[413] *Brown* did not inspire the Montgomery bus boycott.[414] Moreover, the pivotal demonstrations of the 1960s were inspired by Montgomery,[415] the Freedom Rides,[416] African nationalism,[417] and the leadership of Dr. Martin Luther King, Jr., who seems to have had little use for litigation-based strategies for social change:

> Was King motivated to act by the Court? From an examination of King's thinking, the answer appears to be no. King rooted his beliefs in Christian theology and Ghandian non-violence, not constitutional doctrine. His attitude to the Court, far from a source of inspiration, was one of strategic disfavor. "Whenever it is possible," he told reporters in early 1957, "we want to avoid court cases in this integration struggle." He rejected litigation as a major tool of struggle for a number of reasons. He wrote of blacks' lack of faith in it, of its "unsuitability" to the civil rights struggle, and of its "hampering progress to this day." Further, he complained that to "accumulate resources for legal actions imposes intolerable hardships on the already overburdened." In addition to its expense, King saw the legal process as slow. Blacks, he warned, "must not get involved in legalism [and] needless fights in lower courts" because that is "exactly what the white man wants the Negro to do. Then he can draw out the fight." Perhaps most importantly, King believed that litigation was an elite strategy for change that did not involve ordinary people. He believed that when the NAACP was the principal civil rights organization, and court cases were relied on, "the ordinary Negro was involved [only] as a passive spectator" and "his energies were unemployed." Montgomery was particularly poignant, he told the 1957 NAACP annual convention, because, in Garrow's paraphrase, it demonstrated that "rank-and-file blacks themselves could act to advance the race's goals, rather than relying exclusively on lawyers and litigation to win incremental gains." And, as he told the NAACP Convention on July 5, 1962, "only when the people themselves begin to act are rights on paper given life blood."[418]

As *Brown* did little to "inspire" anyone in the field of civil rights, so too did the Supreme Court do little to "inspire" anyone in the field of women's rights. The reality, as Rosenberg demonstrates, is that the "tide" of the women's movement was already in motion before the Court first acted. Press coverage of women's issues jumped "in the years 1970 and 1971, before Court action."[419] As for the consciousness and actions of the political elite:

> [A] massive increase in the passage of women's rights
> legislation did take place in Congress but it was in the Ninety-
> second Congress, 1971-72, before the major Court cases. The
> Equal Rights Amendment was sponsored by 81 Senators and
> 273 members of the House, a majority in both bodies, in the
> Ninety-first Congress in 1970. It was passed in 1972.[420]

The greatest change in the public's attitude about abortion laws occurred before 1970.[421] And the groundswell of public support for women's rights in general "occurred in the late 1960s and early 1970s, before Court action."[422]

Perhaps most importantly, women themselves did not wait for the nine men then sitting on the Supreme Court to tell them when and how to act. Several groups were formed: the National Organization for Women (NOW), in 1966; the National Association for Repeal of Abortion Laws, in 1969; and the National Women's Political Caucus, in 1971, along with the Women's Rights Project and NOW's Legal Defense and Education Fund.[423] As early as 1968, women were engaged in militant and visible demonstrations.[424]

In sum, if Rosenberg's exhaustive analyses of the civil rights and women's movements have any message, it is that courts have little impact, directly or indirectly, on the progress of significant social change. In shorter surveys of change in the areas of the environment, reapportionment, and criminal law, Rosenberg unearths similar information and reaches similar conclusions.[425] If Rosenberg has not utterly refuted the arguments on behalf of a Dynamic Court view, he has, at the very least, shifted the burden of proof to the votaries of the PITL perspective.

WHAT IS TO BE DONE?

* * *

Someone once described characters in Hemingway's novels as people to whom things happen. In studying the American past, historians of the left in academia today tend to depict workers and even slaves as people who make things happen; not passive objects but active subjects engaged in organizing an industrial strike or forming a community dedicated to "moral economy." Yet when the current academic left studies the present rather than the past, an entirely different picture emerges, one in which nearly all possibility of human freedom and morality is gone.

–J. P. Diggins[426]

* * *

The Hollow Hope demolishes the Dynamic Court view. While I happily recommend this book to anyone who believes that lawyers can effect social change without the participation of the communities to be affected, I still note that it has two significant weaknesses. First, the book lacks an analysis of the sources of the PITL perspective and the resistance to accepting the ACORN perspective—at least among lawyers and their academic colleagues. To this query Rosenberg might reply that an answer requires a separate and involved empirical study. Nevertheless, we should not view the conflict between the ACORN and PITL perspectives as nothing more than a disinterested academic debate; the PITL perspective is rife with potential for intellectual laziness and self-centered thinking.

Intellectual laziness lurks in the PITL perspective because of the ease with which an historian can look at social change, match it against a chronology of Supreme Court decisions, and decide that a causal relationship exists. An interpretive analysis of the activities of masses of people who do not leave their histories behind in conveniently bound leather volumes is a more difficult undertaking.

Self-centered thinking may also tend to support the PITL perspective within the legal community. Like most people, lawyers believe that what they do is important. Given the money and time invested in their careers, it is not surprising that they want to believe that their investments pay off, not only in terms of money and prestige, but also in terms of historical significance. In lawyers, the human tendency to view one's own work as being of vital importance leads to a belief that the profession is the source of grand historical movement. Rosenberg does acknowledge that this tendency toward self-importance may lend unwarranted credence to the Dynamic Court view. The notion that courts play a central role in monumental and crucial social reform may be supported "because it offers psychological payoffs to key actors by confirming self-images, not because it is correct."[427]

Most importantly, however, the valorization of the PITL perspective may reflect a more fundamental and insidious tendency of Western culture itself: a tendency to set up hierarchies of human beings and their work so that some people (the bulk of us) are deemed to be less worthy, less valuable, than the rest (the elite few). Theodor Adorno has written of this horrible proclivity of Western society:

> That [Auschwitz] could happen in the midst of the traditions of philosophy, of art, and of the enlightening sciences says more than that these traditions and their spirit lacked the power to take hold of men and work a change in them. There is untruth in those fields themselves, in the autarky that is emphatically claimed for them. All post-Auschwitz culture, including its urgent critique, is garbage. In restoring itself after things that happened without resistance in its own countryside,

culture has turned entirely into the ideology it had been potentially–had been ever since it presumed, in opposition to material existence, to inspire that existence with the light denied it by the separation of the mind from manual labor.[428]

"Auschwitz culture elitism" is manifest in the celebration of the primacy of theoretical work over practical labor (whether it be in the factories, the fields, or the streets). For Adorno, those who celebrate the ranking of human beings and human work, have no right to criticize Auschwitz; their emphasis on theory over practice diverts resources from the kind of practical struggles which could have prevented the occurrence of Auschwitz;[429] and worse, such people contribute to the maintenance of a hierarchy of human beings. Once a ranking of human beings is considered palatable, the road to Auschwitz has been paved.[430] If thinkers can be ranked over laborers, why cannot thinkers employ workers as objects, or Germans treat Jews as things to be used and eliminated at their pleasure? Once we value one kind of human being, one kind of human labor, over another kind, we accept and perpetuate the most basic conditions for oppression; we set up the possibility that one kind of human being may be acceptably sacrificed for the sake of the other. The human stupidity of hatred and destruction aimed at entire groups of people is rampant in our society and throughout our history. Only by recognizing the savagery inherent in very basic structures of our "civilization" will we begin to reduce the potential for massive human oppression and slaughter.

Certainly, the PITL perspective is by no means solely responsible for such a fundamental flaw in Western society; nor does the PITL perspective alone stand accused of perpetuating the ominous characteristics of Western thought and society. Adorno meant to condemn all of the academic disciplines and the traditional social institutions in the perpetuation of oppressive conditions through self-aggrandizement. However, the PITL perspective is a prominent and stark example of this seemingly benign yet oppressive nature of human beings. Surely the simple irony makes the PITL perspective worth singling out: under the mantle of "public interest," the disciples of the PITL view may in reality be keeping the society, the "public," on its certain path toward large-scale manifest oppression.

It is understandable, given the broad and unpleasant implications of this kind of critique, that Rosenberg would not pursue these issues in his study. Exploring such morally charged and delicate topics is difficult, to say the least. Further, Rosenberg could have been dissuaded from drawing these kinds of conclusions from his work because of a moral reticence: that is, because any moral decision is potentially morally defective, it is hard to stand in judgment of others.[431] The moral complexity of the topic and the sheer magnitude of the issues involved are sufficient reasons not to pursue them tangentially. However, for these very same reasons, the issues demand mention. For, insofar as Adorno's radical assertion has merit, the reader must confront in her own soul the urgent issues it raises.

My second "complaint" concerning *The Hollow Hope is* that there is insufficient analysis of how one actually effectuates worthwhile social change. Perhaps it is unfair to press Rosenberg too vigorously on this second point. After all, the principal object of his book was to discern what role courts play in social reform, not to establish a new theory of social change. However, the question of causation cannot be totally avoided in a study like Rosenberg's. To some extent, Rosenberg recognizes this point. He does offer some analysis of other potential sources for massive social reforms. But he insists that, "strictly speaking," the question of the courts' influence on social reform "does not depend on developing a full-blown theory of change."[432] Yet, despite a claim that a particular change did not occur because of cause "A," the phenomenon of change remains. At that point, one must acknowledge either that the change is inexplicable, or that other causes hold better explanatory power than cause "A."

Rosenberg's investigation of alternative sources of change in the areas of civil rights and women's rights consists of a discussion of the socio-political and economic forces which may have precipitated the social institutional changes in these areas. In the civil rights field, he points to direct action,[433] the adverse impact that segregation was having on the American economy,[434] the growing strength of black voting blocs in pivotal states,[435] and the adverse impact that segregation had for the United States in the context of the Cold War.[436] In the area of women's rights, Rosenberg cites several factors that possibly explain transitions in women's status: women's employment during World War Two,[437] decreasing birth rates,[438] women's rising educational achievements,[439] and the growth of various women's organizations which these trends and the civil rights movement spawned.[440]

Thus Rosenberg does offer some explanation for the success of the civil rights and women's movements. However, it is not clear what, if anything, a human being might contribute to these or other movements in the future. Should she wait for "structural changes" to develop? Watch the election returns? Vote? Join an organization? March in the streets? Go to law school?

Presumably many of the people who read *The Hollow Hope* are interested in how social reform might best be effectuated, and in how they might make some minor contributions to bringing about change.[441] Rosenberg at least acknowledges the importance of these questions.

He identifies the strategic concerns with which I started this Review: "strategic choices have costs, and a strategy that produces little or no change drains resources that could be more effectively employed in other strategies"; litigation "steer[s] activists to an institution that is constrained from helping them... [and] siphons off crucial resources and talent...

run[ning] the risk of weakening political efforts."[442]

To return, then, to the ACORN perspective, fueled and strengthened by Rosenberg's study: Social change occurs through the direct actions of ordinary people. Rosenberg's book establishes not only that lawyers and judges do not make history, but also strongly suggests that "ordinary" people can contribute substantially to the making of their own history. This point gets obfuscated by Rosenberg's emphasis on structure. Undue attention to "structural" concerns can devolve into an excuse for historical inaction and moral default. Humans must always take existential leaps into historical action, for a number of practical and ethical reasons. First, existential leaps are an unavoidable feature of human life: One always makes choices, even when one chooses to abstain from choosing. Second, even when structural factors appear discouraging, moral acts are needed to inspire those who might follow and take advantage of favorable structural conditions in the future. Finally, evaluating structural conditions is an uncertain, imprecise exercise; thus, the "cash value" of any moral act ran never be fully evaluated until after the act.[443] Therefore, in making decisions to act morally, ordinary people should not give unwarranted consideration to structural conditions.[444] A wise and judicious analyst of structural conditions would have characterized as pathetic the efforts of a slave leader (e.g., Moses) to goad a gaggle of Semitic tribes to secede from the mighty Egyptian empire around 1500 B.C. A wise and judicious analyst of structural conditions would have characterized as contemptible the efforts of a hillbilly preacher (e.g., Jesus) to talk ethics on the peripheries of the Roman Empire around 30 A.D.[445] A wise and judicious analyst of structural conditions would have characterized as futile the efforts of some scribbler (e.g., Diderot) to advocate rationality in the middle of eighteenth century France. A wise and judicious analyst of structural conditions would have characterized as untimely the efforts of some "Negro" seamstress (e.g., Rosa Parks) to get a decent seat on a bus in Montgomery, Alabama, in the middle of the "Leave It To Beaver" years. A wise and judicious analyst of structural conditions—possibly a contemporary of Professor Rosenberg at the University of Chicago or Paris—would have characterized as irresponsible the efforts of some hippie-sympathizing playwright (e.g., Vaclav Havel) to secure freedom of expression rights for some second-rate rock group in Czechoslovakia in 1976.

From the ACORN perspective what is important is not only that people make history instead of judges and lawyers, but that *organized* people make history. This claim is supported by Rosenberg's work at a number of junctures. Rosenberg points to the Montgomery boycott (1956) and the demonstrations in Birmingham (1963) and Selma (1965) as critical events in the civil rights movement in that they mobilized blacks, moved white public opinion, and pressured the legislative and executive branches to accommodate the demands of the movement. Montgomery, Birmingham, and Selma were all products of conscientious organizing efforts, specifically on the part of Martin Luther King, Jr., who had little respect for the PITL sentiment.

The women's movement teaches similar lessons. Rosenberg discusses the founding of a number of self-consciously organized women's groups and the important demonstrations by these groups in the late 1960s and early 1970s.[446] Some of the results of this organizing include the impressive array of women's rights legislation passed by the Ninety Second Congress in 1971 and 1972, the passage of the Equal Rights Amendment by Congress in 1972,[447] and possibly, the Supreme Court decision in *Roe v. Wade* in 1973. Rosenberg also observes in the area of compensation in the workplace, that aggressive organizing, not court action, has brought results: "Despite litigation, where comparable worth policies have been instituted, they have been the result of collective bargaining and state government action, not litigation."[448]

Thus well-organized collective action helps to precipitate social change. Of course, the victories of the civil rights and the women's movements have not been total. Given the evidence, one might conclude that this is because these movements have limited their efforts to organize ordinary people, and have turned instead to litigation.

The final question to address is what an "activist" attorney or law student should do when faced with these findings. If the ACORN perspective is true, should she ditch her law degree and go organizing? In many cases the answer should be "yes." However, I would observe that some people–like myself, though I am not necessarily proud of this–make better lawyers than organizers. Moreover, lawyers do have a role to play in advancing social change organizations that attempt to survive and thrive in a complicated post-industrial society like these United States. But lawyers cannot and do not help social change by trying to accomplish it through a litigation-based approach. Their most meaningful contributions are to aid organizing efforts. Effective legal assistance may include corporate or tax work. It may involve First Amendment litigation and criminal defense work. Even the work of lawyers who participate in *Brown*-type cases can be justified, sometimes. For example, David Garrow reports that near the end of the Montgomery bus boycott, the viability of the Montgomery Improvement Association's car pool was threatened with an injunction on the theory that the blacks' car pool system constituted an infringement on the segregationist bus company's franchise. A Supreme Court ruling which invalidated Montgomery's segregationist transportation system[449] helped block the injunction and contributed to the victory of King's group.[450]

Yet, in citing the Montgomery experience, we must remember that the effectiveness of court action remains limited. Within a few days after the

Montgomery victory, racist snipers shot at King's home and at black riders.[451] A few years later, most blacks in Montgomery were still sitting in the back of Alabama buses.[452] Montgomery's ultimate meaning was realized by the efforts of those who found inspiration in its militant precedent, not in the jurisprudence which it generated. Montgomery helped to inspire the sit-in activists of the 1960s, who in turn inspired more social activists. Those civil rights activists–and the lawyers who helped keep them in the streets,[453] secured their treasuries' tax exempt status,[454] and made no more noise than necessary when their clients were determined to flaunt the courts[455] –contributed to social change and made history.

CHAPTER FIVE
COPPERS FOR ALBERT

The Poverty of Poverty Law Practice

INTRODUCTION

The purpose of this essay is to discuss the impoverished state of what has come to be known as poverty law, including the fields of law and approaches which are subsumed under that rubric in the law schools, and, moreover, the approach that is generally promulgated by the Bar in its "pro bono" and "legal aid" efforts outside the law schools.

In one sense the thesis of this essay is summarized in the following depiction of 19th century "poverty work" by Sweden's premier literary figure August Strindberg. Its length suggests its significance. In the scene that follows, the novel's protagonist Arvid Falk overhears his sister-in-law with a friend make an unannounced call on some of his neighbors in Vita Bergen, one of the poorer districts in Stockholm:[456]

> Falk … gave a start as, through the open window, he heard a carriage stopping in the street and two women's voices that he seemed to recognize.
>
> 'All right?' asked an older voice. 'I think it looks terrible.'
>
> 'I meant all right for our purpose. Do you know if there are any poor people in this house, driver?'
>
> 'I don't know, but I'd swear there are.'
>
> 'It's a sin to swear, so you needn't. Please wait for us while we go up and do our duty.'
>
> 'I say, Eugenie hadn't we better talk to the children down here first?' Mrs. Homan, the Auditor's wife, asked Mrs. Falk.
>
> 'Yes, we will. Come here, little boy! What's your name?'
>
> 'Albert,' replied a pale little six-year-old.
>
> 'Do you know Jesus, my little fellow?'
>
> 'No,' the child answered laughing and stuck his finger in his mouth.
>
> 'That's dreadful,' said Mrs. Falk, getting out her notebook.

'I will write: "Katrina parish, Vita Bergen. The young in complete spiritual darkness." Is darkness the right word? – Well, do you want to learn to know Him?' she went on.

'No.'

'Would you like a copper then, my lad?'

'Yes.'

'"If you please," you should say. "Utterly neglected. Succeeded through kindness in making them behave better."'

'What a horrible smell! Let us go in now, Eugenie,' said Mrs. Homan.

They went up the stairs and walked into the big room without knocking.

The carpenter took his plane and attacked a knotty board, so that the women had to shout to make themselves heard.

'Is anybody here thirsty for salvation?' shouted Mrs. Homan, while Mrs. Falk worked her scent spray over the children, who began to scream because their eyes were smarting.

'Are you ladies offering us salvation?' asked the carpenter, pausing in his work. 'Where did you get it? Perhaps there's charity too and humiliation. And pride, eh?'

'You're a coarse creature who will go to perdition,' Mrs. Homan replied, while Mrs. Falk wrote in her notebook and said she was quite right.

'Go on,' said the Auditor's wife.

'We know your kind. Perhaps you ladies would care to discuss religion with me. I can talk on any subject. Do you ladies know that a Council was held in Nicea in the year 829, when the Schmackalden articles were imbued with the holy spirit?'

'No, we don't know anything about that, my good man.'

'Why do you call me good? The Scriptures say only God is good. So you don't know about the Council in Nicea in the year 829, ladies? How can one want to go and teach others when one knows nothing oneself? Well, if there's to be any charity now, let it be while my back is turned, for true charity works secretly. Practice it on the children by all means – they can't defend themselves – but leave us alone! Give us some work if you like, and see that you pay us for the work, then you needn't go running round like this. A pinch of snuff, cobbler!'

'Shall I write this, Evelyn?' Mrs. Falk asked. '"Great lack of faith, hardened..."'

'"Obdurate" would be better, Eugenie dear.'

'What are you writing down, ladies? Is it our sins? In that
case your notebook is too small.'
"'The outcome of the so-called trade-unions…'"
'Very good,' said the Auditor's wife.
'Beware of the trades unions,' said the carpenter. 'Attacks
have been made on kings for years, but now we've discovered
that it's not their fault. The next attack will be on all idlers who
live off the work of others. Then you'll see the very devil.'

More than 100 years has passed since the publication of Strindberg's
novel, but the preceding passage seems all too relevant for contemporary
poverty law work today: The efforts of the well-to-do on behalf of the
impoverished do more for the self-esteem of the well-to-do than they do
anything concretely productive for the impoverished. And whatever the
well-to-do may accomplish through their efforts for the impoverished, what
the impoverished really need is organization. Accordingly, lawyers, law
students and law professors who want to try to help the impoverished
should help them in their efforts to build their own organizations. The rest
resembles tossing coppers to Albert: while the gesture involves a certain
poignant charm, so too it includes a promotion and indulgence of self, and
contempt for and an attack on the impoverished.

This essay will develop the preceding theses through the following lines
of argument. It will begin by developing an appropriate conception of
poverty. It will then discuss what might be viewed as effective solutions in
light of that conception of poverty. It will conclude by noting why these
solutions have not been put into effect, and why or why not one might
expect them to be put into effect for the future.

WHAT IS POVERTY?

The common sense conception of poverty defines poverty in terms of
an individual's access to or lack of money. This is not an unreasonable
approach, particularly if one believes that something like poverty exists, and
one would like to try to measure it. Indeed, this is the approach of the
Statistical Abstract of the United States: "poverty" is defined in terms of
access to income. In 1960 a non-farm family of four was considered poor if
its annual income level could not reach $3,022, while in 1990 the figure was
$13,359.[457]

Nevertheless there exist broader ways for conceptualizing poverty.
When the nation grappled with the issues in the 1960s, many of the
chieftains in the War On Poverty defined poverty in terms of helplessness
and dependency. The head of the Office of Economic Opportunity Sargent
Shriver stated that:

…poverty is not just an individual affair. It is also a condition,
a relationship to society, and to all the institutions which

comprise society. Poverty is need. It is lack of opportunity. But it is also helplessness to cope with hostile or uncaring or exploitative institutions. And it is vulnerability to injustice.[458]

Then Attorney General Robert Kennedy articulated the issues in a similar fashion:

> In the final analysis, poverty is a condition of helplessness—of inability to cope with the conditions of existence in our complex society. The inability of a poor and uneducated person to defend himself unaided by counsel in a court of criminal justice is both symbolic and symptomatic of his larger helplessness.[459]

Poverty, in short, involves helplessness and dependency. That the Shriver/Kennedy analysis enjoys validity is underlined by an etymological investigation of the word "poverty." It would note that the dictionary speaks of poverty in terms of a state of deficiency, where one lacks the means to provide materials needs or comforts.[460] It would follow the word to its roots, through the Old French to the Latin word "pauper." The Indo-European root is "pou" which, among other things refers to small items, children, and puerility.[461] Thus the essence of poverty becomes less a matter of money or means than it is a matter of powerlessness.

When one confronts the matter of powerlessness, one begins to appreciate why poverty can appear so hideous. Questions of power lead directly to questions of dignity and conceptions of individual worth. As a powerless person, the poor person is unusually subject to the whims and vagaries of fate, society, and other people. In a condition of being so vulnerable to manipulation by outside forces, the poor person becomes less an independent subject and more a de-humanized object. In such a position of dependency and defenselessness, one is to that extent less human.

Poverty, in short, gnaws at the humanity of its victims. And the more a society allows some of its members to be degraded into subhuman status, the more it contributes to the degradation and degradation potential of all of its members.

WHAT SHOULD/MIGHT BE DONE TO SOLVE POVERTY?
Maybe Nothing Should Be Done

From the preceding it would seem self-evident that a society should attempt to eradicate poverty as thoroughly as possible. Before discussing how that might be done, however, some of the arguments against attacking poverty might at least be acknowledged.

One capitulationist approach to poverty conceptualizes it in moral terms, suggesting that poverty is a state which the poor person deserves: to tamper with poverty would be to affront the wise providence of God; or at the very least, encourage sloth.

A utilitarian variation on the preceding perspective emphasizes the economic over the moral impact of sloth: this perspective argues that the terror of poverty is required to goad human beings into becoming productive members of the economy.

Another perspective is fond of quoting words inaccurately attributed to Jesus, viz., "there will always be poor around."[462] This perspective views poverty as something awful, but it despairs of coping with it in any efficacious fashion. It can conceptualize its despair either in individual or in group terms. In individual terms, poor people are seen as being generated by individualized disasters like illness or accidents or bad genes. From the group perceptive, poor people are seen as being generated because that is how God wills it, or that is how it always has been. A related perspective is that which blames poverty on some system or another (e.g., capitalism or racism); but because the cause is so enormous one recoils in despair from any notions of solving it.

Maybe Something Should Be Done

If any of the preceding objections to fighting poverty entail any merit, they relate to the futility of the task; for, as we shall see, poverty in the United States does manifest some intractable characteristics. Nevertheless, if the premier objection to poverty entails it assaults on human dignity, then the "futility" of fighting it becomes all but irrelevant; because any protest against degradation does in itself constitute a minor achievement for dignity. The efforts of the Greeks at Thermopylae or rebel slaves in 19th century North America or resisting Jews in 20th century concentration camps may have been doomed. But such refusals to accept lives of degrading servitude constitute worthy accomplishment. They have left the rest of humanity with visions and definitions of personhood which demonstrate that a human can be something more than a stomach, and instead involve a certain minimum of dignity and respect.

Thus a protest against human degradation involves its own moral justification, and the fact that protest against human degradation may ultimately prove futile is no argument against the protest.

While fighting poverty seems to entail its own rewards regardless of whether or not it is diminished, it might also be noted that some evidence does exist to suggest that conscientious attacks on poverty can in fact affect it. A review of United States poverty statistics from the past 30 years suggests that poverty is to a degree a contingent phenomenon. It can and does change, and its changes are to a degree subject to societal attack: While the statistics do indicate that poverty in the United States seldom if ever dips below 10%[463]–thus suggesting a certain eternal aspect to the phenomenon–they also indicate that the poverty rate can change, overall, and within groups. The rate has fluctuated over the past decades, starting at 22.4% in 1959, dipping to 11.4% in 1978, and reaching a rate of 14.2% in 1991.[464] As a group, fewer elderly suffer poverty now than they did 30 years ago: In 1959 the rate of poverty for the elderly approximated 35%, while in 1970 their rate had declined to 24.6%; and in 1991 they bettered the national average of 14.2% with a rate of 12.4%.[465] The meanwhile the lot of children in the United States had declined: while in 1970 the poverty rate for children stood at 14.9%, the rate had reached 21.1% in 1991, with more than one child in five suffering from poverty.[466]

The elderly, in short, have improved their position in a general and absolute sense over the years. It is not hard to attribute much of that improvement to various political choices made over the last 30 years as to allocations of societal resources. The elderly got Medicaid, Medicare, Social Security and so forth, and the young paid for it:

> Former Congressional Budget Office director Rudolf Penner acknowledged in 1987 that "the children have suffered a great deal as we have given more and more benefits to the elderly." ...Part of the explanation was the older voters were using political power to get more money.
>
> In 1982, by one calculation, the federal government spent ten times as much per capita on the elderly as on children.[467]

The recent historical experience of the elderly returns us to common sense notions and approaches to poverty: if people are poor, the solution is to give them more money. While this proposition has some attractions, it may also entail its limits. Andrew Hacker recently calculated what might happen if all Americans were taxed at a rate of 100% after their first $200,000:

> At first reading, this would give the government a fund of $187 billion. But since this group already pays taxes at the top bracket, even taking everything over $200,000 would yield only $103 billion in new money. Were this sum shared equally among the rest of the nation's households, each would receive a check in the amount of $1,081. Were the recipients to be confined to families having incomes of less than $35,000, each would get $2,173.[468]

Hacker's analysis, though, did not focus on two other means of reducing poverty, viz., in-kind benefits (e.g., food stamps) and social insurance (e.g., Medicare). In particular social insurance has had its impacts. And the ultimate point–implicit in Penner's point about how the nation has sacrificed its children for its elderly–is that political choices ultimately determine who gets how much:

> ...the bulk of all expenditures and of dollar growth [in public assistance and social insurance programs from 1960-1980] has been for the elderly...
>
> ...it is not very surprising that measured poverty improved little during the 1970s. The single most important correlate with poverty–median family income–did not change. On government's side of the ledger, expenditures for cash assistance directed to the poor started small and hardly increased at all. In-kind benefits increased much more dramatically but they are not counted as income and thus have no impact on measured poverty. The really dramatic growth came in the social insurance programs aimed at the middle class. Some of those benefits did reach people who would otherwise have been poor, but most went elsewhere.[469]

The previous citation suggests that the politics of poverty involve not only sacrificing children to the elderly. They also suggest the degree to which the poor are sacrificed to the middle classes. This may result from voting patterns, racism, sanctification of the market, or whatever; but the in the end the degree of poverty and inequality which a society tolerates results directly from political choice:

> The United States spends a smaller share of national income on redistribution than do most other Western industrialized nations. Not surprisingly, by devoting fewer resources to redistribution the United States also accomplished less redistribution, leaving a greater degree of inequality than found in other countries. [citation omitted]
>
> International statistics do not prove that generous redistribution has a high cost in terms of slower economic growth. The United States spends comparatively little on redistribution, yet its rate of economic growth has not been outstanding in comparison to that of other advanced industrialized nations. Germany redistributes an unusually high fraction of national output [18.0% in 1960 and 26.5% in 1980 compared to 7.3% and 13.8% for the United States], yet its growth has not been conspicuously low [3.1% for 1960-1981, compared to 2.1% for the United States]... Social expenditures also grew faster in Germany, France and Italy from a higher base, and each of these countries has enjoyed faster per capita economic growth then the United States...
>
> In sum, there is no evidence that the United States has enjoyed a growth dividend as a consequence of limiting redistributional outlays. Other advanced nations have done as well or even better since 1960, even though they have

redistributed a larger share of income in the tax transfer re-
shuffle...

The choice of redistribution policy is ultimately political
rather than purely economic.[470]

In short, if something might be done to alleviate poverty, political action
would seem to constitute a premier key.

Actually, Organizing Should Be Done

Yet once one's attention is focused on politics, one is forced to recall
the analyses of Robert Kennedy and Indo-European words like "pou." The
helpless situation of the poor is, perhaps, simply another way of expressing
political incapacity. In a position of incapacity one cannot articulate what
one would want politically (whether it be a redistribution of wealth, more
social insurance programs, more parks, more ice cream, or whatever). In a
position of incapacity one cannot move an agenda–assuming one could
articulate one to begin with. The question thus becomes how the poor
might transform themselves into an effective presence on the political
landscape; for it is at that point that they might be able to have some impact
on the phenomenon of poverty as it exists in the United States.

The thesis of this article is that if there is any way out of this frustrating
and hideous dilemma for the poor, it is to be found in organization; because
organization is the key to effective political presence. If there is any key to
solving the situation of poverty for the poor it is through efforts which
contribute to their own self-organizing. Only through organization do the
poor have some hope of alleviating their conditions of helplessness:
Through organization they can articulate their circumstances, and the
solutions they would pose to solve those circumstances. Through
organization they can form a political presence to force the rest of society
to take their articulations seriously. This is true not only for society in
general, but also society's courtrooms in particular.

D. Black's SOCIOLOGICAL JUSTICE[471] suggests the degree to which
it essential for any American–poor or not–to have organization if she is to
enjoy any prospects of success, in society's courtrooms in particular, but
also in more general areas of social endeavor.[472] Black's book is a
sociologist's study of law in terms of how it works, not in how law would
like to see itself work, and his observations are worth citing at length. Black
begins by making various embarrassing but empirically substantiated
sociological observations:

> Law is socially relative...Who kills whom is an important
> predictor of how a case will be handled. For example, people
> who kill vagrants and prison inmates are largely immune to
> law, but an unemployed black ex-convict who kills a wealthy

white businessman is another case altogether. Then the killer himself may even be killed by the state–a punishment rarely if ever seen when the social characteristics of offender and victim are reversed. …the decisiveness and severity of judges and jurors depend on their social status and their social distance from the adversaries and their partisans. … The linguistic style of testimony is important as well, since it reflects the social characteristics of the witnesses and influences their persuasiveness.[473]

Black then turns to the role that organization plays in litigating success or failure:

Organization is important in legal behavior everywhere. Like the social status of the adversaries or the intimacy between them … the organization of the adversaries predicts how their case will be handled. Unorganized people–individuals on their own–useless law and are more vulnerable to law. Individuals vastly outnumber organizations in modern societies such as the United States, but organizations initiate more legal cases. Most complaints filed in small-claims courts are brought on behalf of organizations, and nearly all are directed against an individual. In addition, public and private organizations initiate over half other civil cases pertaining to larger claims, and two-thirds of these are directed against an individual. When crimes such a burglaries or robberies occur, organizational victims are more likely than individual victims to notify the police. Local and national governmental also initiate a multitude of criminal cases: The police initiate nearly all vice and traffic case, for example, and every case of any kind that reaches a criminal court is prosecuted by the state. Moreover, nearly all criminal cases are directed against individuals rather than organizations.

Although lone individuals are the favorite targets of organizations that initiate legal proceedings, the reverse does not apply. Far from it. Individuals are generally reluctant to assert their legal rights against organizations. In modern America, they bring twice as many civil lawsuits against fellow individuals as against organizations, and in legal domains where organizations are the primary wrongdoers, such as consumer and environmental matters, aggrieved individuals typically refrain from legal action altogether. They just "lump."

THE ORGANIZATIONAL ADVANTAGE

Not merely more litigious than individuals, groups are also

more successful. For example, they win more often. As noted in Chapter 2, organizations bringing civil lawsuits in the United States are more likely to win than individuals, especially when the defendant is an individual rather than another organization. In cases of alleged racial discrimination, a complaint brought to a state commission by an organizations (such as the National Association for the Advancement of Colored People) is more likely to succeed than a complaint by an individual. An organization is particularly likely to succeed when the alleged discrimination involves an individual offender rather than another organization. And organizations are more successful when they appeal a lost case, civil or criminal, to a higher court…

> Societies such as modern America have, so to speak, two legal systems: one for individuals, another for organizations.[474]

Black concludes that in a legal contest the importance of organization is hard to underestimate:

> A lack of organization is one of the greatest disadvantages–possibly the greatest–anyone can experience in legal life. Nevertheless, in modern societies such as the United States, most people with legal problems are completely alone and unorganized, like bastards in a tribe.[475]

Black's sociological interest in tribal/organizational protection for the individual leads to him to elaborate on how it works in two traditional societies:

> Some tribal societies discourage or even prohibit lone individuals from bringing cases to court at all. The Shavante of central Brazil, for instance, require that every case be brought by a so-called "faction." Only men can belong to these factions, and so women effectively have no legal rights. And some societies handle particular grievances and liabilities collectively that others would handle individually. For example, when homicide is defined as an offense against the victim's family or clan, the killer's family or clan might be held liable to pay compensation or to suffer revenge.[476]…

> virtually everyone in northern Somalia belongs to an organization, called a dia-paying group, designed to handle conflicts in everyday life. Lone individuals never face organized adversaries except when refusing to cooperate with their own dia-paying group. These groups not only pursue grievances of members against non-members but also assume liability for injures inflicted by members on non-member In principle,

therefore, any injury is remediable with a payment of compensation, regardless of the wealth of the individual who is responsible.[477]

Black emphasizes that it is not only traditional societies which entertain a reluctance to send isolated individuals into legally charged contexts. He cites Japan as an instance of a modern and productive industrialized nation where the realities of organizational efficacies are acknowledged:

> ...Unable to rely heavily on law for protection and predictability, the Japanese draw together into tightly knit groups and enforce their own standards of conduct. A system of patronage and sponsorship, or "informal suretyship," facilitates transactions between people of different groups. Anyone wishing to deal with another group must be introduced and recommended by someone already known and trusted.[478]

Black's analysis suggests that the "tribal" orientations of the Shavante tribespeople in Brazil and the Arabian nomads in Somalia and the Japanese in Japan simply intimates a reality that American jurisprudence–infatuated with an ideology of individualism–refuses to acknowledge, viz., the importance of organization:

> Few if any societies have ever distributed organization as unequally as those of the modern world. ...The most fateful transactions in modern life increasingly occur between individuals and formally constituted organizations. And in nearly all these transactions, the organizations have the advantage. ... Conflict between individuals and organization is increasing as well, and the advantage of organizations is again conspicuous.
>
> Another feature of the proliferation of organizations is the growing tendency of individuals to band together formally to deal more effectively with the organizations in their environment. Individuals counter organization with organizations of their own. Specialized groups arise to represent otherwise atomized individuals such as employees, consumers, professionals, farmers, students, ethnic and racial minorities, women, and numerous others. Organization begats organization. But in legal life the pattern is different. Lone individuals continue to find themselves in conflict with organizations, and these organizations continue to be particularly successful under these circumstances. Here, for unknown reasons, the tendency of individuals to counter organization with organization has not materialized.

> The participation of lone individuals makes possible many of the social differentials–known as discrimination–that characterize modern law. …without organizational help in legal conflicts, they are less likely to get what they want. Many individuals are thus doubly disadvantaged in legal life: first, because they are lone individuals who may face organized adversaries and second, because they are socially disabled, regardless of whom they face. In both respects, legal individualism perpetuates discrimination. One strategy to reduce discrimination in legal life would therefore be to reduce the participation of lone individuals. This would bring law closer to the evolutionary stage already reached in many arenas of modern life, where the introduction of formal organization has revived some of the conditions of tribal life. The organization of individual litigants would dramatically alter the balance of advantage in legal affairs…[479]

The importance of organization for the individual has been made not only by sociologists with an anthropological and empirical bent like Black. For his part historian/sociologist G.M. Luebbert has suggested that lack of organization implies historical death as well:

> Countless monographs on everyday worker life and endless debates of purely antiquarian interest are possible about whether the revisionism of party and trade union leaders reflected the "true" values of the workers. Such debates are of strictly antiquarian interest because, in the fast-unfolding epoch of mass politics, *the only values of enduring consequence, of more than spasmodic importance were those that were organized.*[480] [emphasis added]

Luebbert's observation raises one final but essential moral point, viz., the morality of letting the poor articulate for themselves what they want. It is through organization that ideas can be articulated, refined, advocated and ultimately advanced in society and history. No organization, no agenda. No organization, and others define your agenda. One problem inhering in the Hacker discussion of "solving" poverty was the degree to which it was implicitly telling the poor that a redistribution of money would solve their problems. This may or may not be so. Perhaps the poor would rather have ice cream. Or maybe more parks. Or health care. Or government. Or a combination of the above. Or perhaps they do simply want more money. The point, though, is that too many discussions of solving the problems of poverty have been by nonpoor people who insist upon treating the poor as objects, like some pet who has not yet been house trained. This is not anything new. As Luebbert has observed concerning 19th Century England:

The "New Liberals" set out to produce a positive alternative to socialism that would be more acceptable to the growing number of working-class activists who could see no future in Gladstonian self-help. Most of the central figures of New Liberalism were professional men, journalists, writers and civil servants. If the old Liberal nexus of paternalist employer, responsible trade unionist, and nonconformist conscience was breaking down, the professional middle class, which was rapidly expanding in this period, could offer an alternative collectivist route to social harmony. Many of the New Liberals had been involved as young men in the settlement movement of the 1880s–middle-class observers of the East End of London or the poorer districts of provincial cities who had studied poverty on the spot and searched out its remedies. The New Liberals grounded their solutions to the problems of poverty in exhaustive attempts to establish the facts *independently of the demands or assertions of organized workers* and employers. In and around Rowntree in York, New Liberals wove an ideology of "social science." They believed they had discovered a significant diagnosis of poverty and scientific remedies for it. The confidence this belief gave them, as advocates of policy and, eventually, as the administrative architects of new state agencies, was no less important historically for being ill-founded. [emphasis added][481]

In other words, non-poor 19th century Englishmen attempted to posit "solutions" to "poverty" which had more to do with their conceptions of propriety than it did to conceptions developed by the working poor in their own organizations and struggles. Through their own historical experience the latter had determined that socialism provided a solution to their problems of deprivation. But socialism was anathema to the middle-class New Liberals. And so they ignored the working poor; and in the name of the working poor they advanced a middle class conception of social harmony.

The professional middle class, of course, has every right to try to advance any conception of appropriate social order. Whether such will precipitate any benefits for the poor is another matter altogether. The point of the preceding social and historical analyses is that it is the impoverished who might best be trusted to articulate their own self interests. This articulation can occur only through organization. These articulations can be advanced only through organization.

From the preceding it would seem clear that anyone who would want to rally help the poor should focus on giving aid to poor people's organizations, organizations which work not only for poor people, but which are of and by poor people to some meaningful degree. This might imply a different sort of work for the lawyer who would give service to the poor, because much of her work might become oriented more to the corporate concerns of the poor people's organization than it would be to the individual needs of an individual poor person.[482] If the lawyer's work might not become utterly abolished, at least her work would become curtailed or circumscribed, given the extent to which the lawyer/client relationship is of itself one of dependency. If poor people and their organizations would eradicate the dependency which constitutes the essence of poverty, they would presumably aspire to eliminates many relationships of dependency as possible, including those that include attorneys.

WHY HASN'T (WON'T) POVERTY BE SOLVED?
Organizing Is Not Happening

This essay might conclude by arguing that the legal profession needs to devote more resources to poor people's organizations and leave it at that. But that approach would fail to note two relatively significant points, viz., the extent to which the option of helping poor people's organizations is NOT being pursued presently in various legal arenas. Moreover, it would fail to discuss some of the reasons for why poor people's organizations are not likely to receive much help in this society, despite the fact that enlightened articles like this are pointing out alternative and preferable means for fighting poverty.

What follows is a list of projects which have been approved or cited as pro bono projects by legal organizations in Michigan, Louisiana and the District of Columbia. In Michigan, the State Bar listed the following programs as eligible for pro bono contributions[483]:

> American Civil Liberties Union Fund
> Berrien County Legal Services
> First Step Legal Advocacy Project (FLAP)
> Lakeshore Legal Services
> Legal Aid Bureau of Southwestern Michigan
> Legal Aid & Defender Association
> Legal Aid of Central Michigan
> Legal Aid of Western Michigan
> Legal Hotline for Older Michiganians
> Legal Services of Eastern Michigan
> Legal Services of Northern Michigan Legal Services of Southcentral Michigan Legal Services of Southeastern Michigan, Inc.
> Macomb County Department of Senior Citizens Services Legal Assistance Program
> Michigan Indian Legal Services
> Michigan Migrant Legal Assistance Project, Inc.

Oakland/Livingston Legal Aid
Prison Legal Services of Michigan, Inc. Sixty Plus Law Clinic
University of Michigan Law School Clinical Law Program
Wayne County Neighborhood Legal Services
Women's Justice Center
Women's Survival Center

In 1994 the Louisiana Bar Foundation qualified the following for the state IOLTA Grant Program[484]:

AIDSLAW of Louisiana, Inc.
Acadiana LSC for the Iberia Parish Pro Bono Project
Acadiana Legal Services Corporation (including the former Central La. LSC)
Advocacy Center for the Elderly and Disabled
Associated Catholic Charities/Immigration Legal Services Program
Associated Catholic Charities/Project S.A.V.E.
Baton Rouge Bar Foundation/Pro Bono and LRE Projects
Beauregard Community Concerns, Inc./June Jenkins Women's Shelter
CASA, New Orleans
Capital Area CASA Association Central Louisiana Pro Bono Project Faith House, Inc.
Kisatchie Legal Service Corporation
LSBA Committee on Substance Abuse
LSBA Young Lawyers Section/Law-Related Education Projects
Lafayette Parish Bar Foundation/Pro Bono Project Lafayette Teen Court, Inc.
Legal Aid Bureau
Louisiana Center for Law-Related Education
Loyola Death Penalty Resource Center
Loyola University Street Law Program
Mental Health Association in Louisiana Metropolitan Battered Women's Program, Inc.
New Orleans Legal Assistance Corporation
New Orleans Pro Bono Project
North Louisiana Legal Assistance Corporation Northwest Louisiana Legal Services, Inc.
Safe Harbor, Inc.
Safety Net for Abused Persons
Shreveport Bar Association/Pro Bono Project
Shreveport Juvenile Justice Program/CASA Program Southeast

Louisiana Legal Service Corporation
Southeast Spouse Abuse Program
Southwest Louisiana Legal Services Society Inc. St. Bernard Parish
Battered Women's Center Teen Court of Northeast Louisiana, Inc.
Teen Court of Winnsboro-Franklin, Inc.
22nd Judicial District Bar Foundation/Pro Bono Project
Vernon Community Action Council, Inc./Domestic
Violence Aid Program
Volunteer Lawyers Project (Monroe)
YWCA New Orleans/Rape Crisis Program
YWCA of Monroe/Project SAFE
YWCA of Northwest Louisiana, Inc./Family
Violence Program
Youth Service Bureau of St. Tammany/CASA & LRE Programs

Finally, The Washington Lawyer cited the following as instances of pro bono practice from the District of Columbia Bar[485]:

Attorneys from Proskauer, Rose, Goetz & Mendelsohn joined with Lipton Corporate Child Care Centers, Inc. to host a nourishing "power lunch" at the Palm for residents of one of the District's homeless shelters as participants in The Shelter Project. Over the holiday season members of Proskauer, Rose, Goetz & Mendelsohn also helped provide toys, clothes, toiletries, and blankets to city shelters, and hosted parties at which they served food and delivered gifts. "We do a lot of important things in our firm all year," said Joseph Casson, managing partner of the firm's Washington office, "but nothing is as gratifying as The Shelter Project."

Leo Fishman, a sole practitioner in the District, is working as a volunteer attorney with the Legal Resources Center for Nonprofit Housing Sponsors to provide pro bono assistance to Bethany Inc., an organization devoted to helping homeless families with children. Bethany Inc. is currently in the process of acquiring and renovating an apartment building in the District. "This is a unique program," said Melanie Gerber, executive director of the Legal Resources Center. "Bethany is geared to help homeless families where substance abuse is a contributing factor. The program not only provides transitional housing, but combines substance abuse treatment. So it's a very innovative approach."

Linda Schakel, an attorney with Ballard, Spahr, Andrews & Ingersoll, and Peter Mahoney, senior counsel to Freddie Mac, have teamed up to provide pro bono legal assistance to the Trust for Affordable Housing, which is sponsoring a program to develop housing for mentally ill low-income individuals. The Trust for Affordable Housing is working in collaboration with the D.C. Community Mental Health Services. Schakel and Mahoney are working as volunteer attorneys through the Legal Resources Center for Nonprofit Housing Sponsors.

In the world of academia, one poverty textbook's four main chapters covered consumer, housing, welfare and court access issues for the poor, while another dealt with "poverty, inequality, and equal protection," "financial barriers to participation in the legal and political processes," "inequality of educational opportunity," and "income redistribution programs and policies."[486] A recent Harvard Law School course catalogue has indicated that a course entitled "Law and the Low Income Household" would cover social security and public assistance cases; a course called "Poverty Law: Politics, Policy and Practice" would cover public benefit law (AFDC, Social Security, Unemployment), social service law (job training, compensatory education), housing law, anti-discrimination law, administrative law and procedure; and "Legal Services for Poor People: Critical History" would deal with family law issues.[487]

The preceding samples, of course, do not define totally the universe of anti-poverty practice as it is promulgated by the legal profession in the United States.[488] Without more rigor it might be too much to claim that they are representative. At the very least, though, the preceding might be postulated as indicative of anti-poverty practice as it is promulgated by the legal profession in the United States.

What seems to be a distressingly common thread amongst most if not all of the preceding projects is the degree to which they maintain the dependency–which is to say the poverty–of their clients. Many of the projects are typical "poverty practice" legal enterprises, in that they assume that there exists a certain set of problems which poor people tend to experience as a class (e.g., welfare, landlord tenant). They assume further that they can and should be solved through litigation. The ultimate assumption, of course is that the services of an attorney are useful if not necessary to accomplish the solution(s).

The problems inhering in such an approach have already been suggested. To the degree that lawyers are involved, to that degree the dependency relationship of lawyers and clients is retained, perpetuated and intensified. Indeed, given that these relationships tend to involve "free" legal services, this particular problem is exacerbated: the poor person lacks the financial ability to enforce some accountability which the "normal" paying client can exact.

Relying on lawyers tends to teach poor people that lawyers solve problems, not poor people. To the degree that litigation is involved, the lesson is exacerbated. Additionally, to that degree the efforts of poor people are steered from the arena of politics, where they might actually have more chance for success than in the constrained avenues of courtroom procedures.[489]

To the degree that individual poor people are served instead of poor people's organizations, to that degree poor people are prevented from solving their problems collectively. They lose the opportunity to create organized masses of people who can articulate their own interests, and then move them in the political arena.

Finally, there exists the degree to which the organizations which tend to be served are not in fact poor people's organizations. Even in the organizations where attorneys are not giving direct legal aid to poor persons they are giving aid to organizations which may be FOR poor people; but they are not OF poor people and/or BY poor people. In both cases the relationships of dependency is maintained. In the former the poor person is sent to some lawyer so the lawyer can solve his/her problem. In the latter the poor person goes to an organization in which s/he has limited or no power so that the organization can solve his/her problem. Since the poor person's position of dependency is perpetuated, so is his poverty–if it is not in fact intensified.

Thus, it is not clear that any of the mainstream "pro bono" activities are actually fighting poverty. To certain extents they in fact promote it.

A legal professional facing critiques along the preceding lines may repudiate them for various of the reasons intimated above: e.g., s/he likes being in a position of authority; or s/he believes that each little copper for Albert is at least better than a piece of air for Albert; or that the copper is for her own ego in the sense that it constitutes her small way of protesting an intractable wicked world. The point here, though, is less the reactions of lawyers who would repudiate the critique than the reactions for lawyers who would accept it, and embrace the proposition that lawyers need to help poor people form organizations which they control to advance their own interests. The point here is that there exist various instances of structural societal inertia that would work against those who would work for a new improved anti-poverty paradigm. Indeed, those instances of structural inertia have helped to create and perpetuate the old "pro bono" paradigm— in spite of its promises of failure intimated at its inception; and through time since then.

Societal inertia which works against the development of new antipoverty approaches derives from at least six different quarters, which we will note in turn.

The Ideology of Individualism

What constitutes the Ideology of Individualism has already been suggested by the analyses from Black previously quoted. The fiction is that

American people can and should live individually; that they do not need to affiliate with groups; indeed that they are better off without ties to groups. The word used to "prove" that individuality is a good thing is "freedom." Yet as Black's comments demonstrate, this freedom is a freedom to be weak. It is a freedom to be vulnerable to other individuals who trumpet individualism in theory yet practice organizationalism in practice. A classic instance of organizationalism in practice involves those who work in large corporate enterprises. These and other well-organized groups stand to gain power the more the rest of their fellows in society subscribe seriously to the ideology of individualism and remain outside of organizations. Hence the former fight the development of organizations like unions, even when the role that unions play in the collective bargaining process have been declared to be in the national interest.[490]

Hence when the poor must be palliated it will be through modes that will reinforce disassociation rather than association. It will be the mode of classic pro bono poverty law, focusing on individuals who supposedly have individualized problems. And as a result the short term problems of poor individuals may in fact be solved. Yet the long-term power of those who affiliate with large organizations will be maintained; hence perpetuating the long-term problems of those outside of organized strictures–like the poor.

The Ideology of Expertise

Another instance of structural societal inertia involves what might be labeled the Ideology of Expertise. The premise of the Ideology of Expertise is that normal American citizens require experts to solve their problems: contemporary society is too complex for an individual to handle, so s/he must resort to experts in almost every facet of his/her life. Today's American supposedly faces a panoply of problems, each of which is attended by a host of experts promising to solve each conundrum. Therapists promise to solve emotional problems. Psychiatrists promise to solve child rearing problems. Beauticians promise to solve pulchritude problems. Financial consultants promise to solve pocketbook problems. And so on and so on. Most if not all of the preceding "professions" cannot be practiced without some sort of sanctioning license from the state. While this might be thought to attest to the complexity of the profession and its importance for society, doubts begin to arise when one appreciates the extent to which the elevated statuses of many of the "professions" are historically recent, barely 100 years old. Surgeons, for example, doubled as barbers, while lawyers could hang out a shingle once they had decided they had apprenticed an adequate amount of time.[491]

Of course arguments might be cited to claim that the elevation of various of the professions has occurred "naturally" with the "natural" development and progress of science and civilization. Yet to cite such arguments would be to participate in the Ideology of Expertise.

> Recent studies of professionalization show that professionalism did not emerge, in the nineteenth and early twentieth centuries, in response to clearly defined social needs. Instead, the new professions themselves invented many of the needs they claimed to satisfy. They played on public fears of disorder and disease, adopted a deliberately mystifying jargon, ridiculed popular traditions of self-help as backward and unscientific, and in this way created or intensified (not without opposition) a demand for their own services. The evidence of professional self-promotion can no longer be dismissed by reasserting the sociological truism that "modern society involves the individual in relations ... that are vastly more complex than [those] his ancestors ... had to contend with.[492]

A critique of the Ideology of Expertise will note not only the Ideology's historical contingency. It also calls attention to the material interests which it serves.

At the economic level, the Ideology of Expertise helps to motor the economy. The Ideology of Expertise drums into the American consumer that she is a weak, helpless and stupid thing. This psychological attack not only encouragers the American consumer to buy services, it also bludgeons her into a state where she becomes ready also to buy things, which, like services, might care for the various deficiencies she has been convinced she possesses. (If you can't solve the kids through therapy, try a box of Chocolate Covered Sugar Bombs. And so on.)

The Ideology of Expertise also bolsters the class structure which attends the economy of consumption. Not every person in the economy of consumption can be a member of the top 0.5% of the population which controls over a quarter of the nation's wealth.[493] Yet not everyone needs to be consigned to the property-less pool of toilers and those who cannot even find a job. There exists at least one niche in the class structure between the proletarians and the wealthy, and that is the niche of the experts.[494] Barbara Ehrenreich has discussed the birth of this niche:

> The emerging professional middle class stepped into the fray in the role of peacemaker. Their message to the capitalists was that nonviolent social control would in the long run be more effective than bullet and billy clubs... ...the ultimate decision of American capitalists, as they moved into the twentieth century was—to put it somewhat crudely—that a cadre of professionals was cheaper than an army of Pinkertons.[495]

It might also be observed that those who are being paid by the owners to palliate the poor tend not to spend their time creating a social analysis or social situation that would end the privileged status of the owners. The "experts," in short, solve the socio-economic "problem" of themselves, and not just the masses. Their work at neutralizing the masses and incorporating them into the economy of consumption simultaneously neutralizes them and incorporates them into the economy of consumption (and inequality). It proves to be a great bargain for the wealthiest 0.5%.

The Ideology of Expertise, therefore, constitutes a fundamental organizing principle of contemporary U.S. society. The traditional pro bono poverty model participates in and reinforces this paradigm by suggesting that poverty–like everything else–needs a set of experts to resolve it. Thus anyone who would try to advance alternative modes of helping the poor (e.g., telling them through theory and practice that they are capable of helping themselves) will be running against a mode of thinking which every American is taught daily to embrace.

The Ideology of Patronage

A third instance of structural societal inertia involves what might be labeled the Ideology of Patronage. An elucidation on the Ideology of Patronage might begin with some comments on the iconography of William Gainsborough and his contemporaries, as explicated by Albert Boime.[496] In his study Boime points out how Gainsborough and others brought differing class perspectives to the human beings they painted. Gainsborough, for example, painted from an aristocrat's perspective, presenting the well-to-do in dignified lights. Gainsborough peasants, while not depicted as riff raff, were depicted as living out a life of easy toil and relative contentment; which fit the dreams of Gainsborough's aristocratic clientele just fine. In contrast Boime cites the paintings of the Italian artist Giacomo Ceruti, who rendered depictions of the Italian poor. These poor would have been less convenient for an aristocratic audience; they show suffering and self-awareness, and the capacity to act as independent political subjects. Boime's ultimate point is the extent to which an artist's iconography proves serviceable to various social visions, all of which have political implications. One vision depicts the rulers and the ruled according to a certain political vision. Anther depicts the rulers and the ruled according to another.[497]

The relevance of Boime's discussion to the Ideology of Patronage relates to the iconography implicit in an Ideology of Patronage. Such an icon would depict a powerful Patron rendering a generous behest to a grateful dependent client. It would not question or challenge the inequality inhering in the relationship. Rather, it would justify it and celebrate it. It allows the patron to go home feeling pleased with himself in a moral light. It suggests to the client that this is the way the world is, this is the way the world ought to be, and s/he should not think too hard about changing things.

The relevance of this Ideology of Patronage to traditional pro bono poverty law practice should be clear. The latter is an enactment of the former. Through its re-enactments it reinforces and celebrates relationships of inequality and dependency. Through this vision the lawyers providing "free" legal services can see themselves as people of generosity and honor, worthy of their privileges. Their confidence in the propriety of the system is enhanced, their sense of moral righteousness is strengthened. Moreover, the picture of a grateful and dependent poor is a soothing one; resentment and potential social conflict are absent from this picture. On the other side of the relationship this vision teaches the poor that they should be grateful for the benefices granted them by the well-to-do; and that moreover, that this relationship of dependency is natural and fair; and accordingly to resist it or resent it would be done only by a fool or a churl.

The role of the Ideology of Patronage, then, is to contain moral imaginations. It enhances the confidence and complacency of the well-to-do. It denies the existence of alternatives for the dependent poor.

The Ideology of the Isolated Poor

If the role of the Ideology of Patronage is to contain moral imaginations, the role of the fourth instance of structural societal inertia is to contain political imagination. I would label it the Ideology of the Isolated Poor. The point here is that the pro bono poverty law model postulates the poor as an isolated group with its own separate and unique problems, disjoint and divorced from adjacent social groupings. By focusing on THE POOR it tends to pose THE POOR as the anomaly. The poor are postulated as the problem society must solve.

An alternative perspective, of course, might suggest that THE RICH are the anomaly. Perhaps the rich constitute the social group which society must solve in order to become fair.

The Ideology of the Isolated Poor ignores the possibility that THE POOR might have more in common with the working and middle classes than those latter two classes have with the rich.

A perspective that tends to divide the poor from the rest of the population obviously impedes the ability of the poor to conceive of making political alliances with other segments of the population (e.g., the working classes and the middle classes). It obviously does little to enhance the political imagination of the working classes and the middle classes. These may find it even more difficult to conceive of an alliance with the poor in social struggle.

The political beneficiaries of the Ideology of the Isolated Poor would appear to be the well to do. Clearly, it is not the poor.[498]

The Poverty Industry

A fifth instance of structural societal inertia relates to what has been called The Poverty Industry. This focus in one sense takes the insights of the Ideology of Expertise and applies them to the bodies that have been "dealing" with poverty since the 1960s. The questions here being raised are: Is it really the problems of the poor that are being solved with the pro bono poverty model? Might it not in fact be the problems of would-be professionals who don't want to do the dirty work of capitalism? and the actual ruling class that would rather not cope with a morally dissatisfied professional class?

It is probably fair to suggest that the present pro bono poverty law model derives from the War on Poverty instituted in the 1960s by President Johnson and his Great Society minions.[499] Criticism directed against that War might prove applicable to the pro bono poverty law model which it helped to sire. Writing in 1967, Elinor Graham asserted:

> …the social service orientation of the War on Poverty is activity- and job-creating for the middle and upper classes. Provision of social service, as opposed to income payments, requires formation of new organizations and institutions which in turn are the source of activities and income-paying role for the nation's expanding number of college-educated individuals. The War on Poverty, its programs and ideology, are a response to the demands of an educated "new class." It provides a legitimated outlet for the energies of a group that poses a greater threat to the political system and moral fabric of the society than the inadequately educated poor who are the official objects of aid.[500]

Graham's comments, of course, derive from a critical leftward bent. Nevertheless, they were substantiated only two years later by a more centrist Democratic congressperson:

> In 1969 Edith Green of Oregon, ranking Democrat on the House Education and Labor Committee, observed that "probably our most enduring monument to the problem of poverty has been the creation of a poverty industry. There are more than 100 companies in Washington, D.C. along which specialize in studying and evaluating the poor and the programs that serve them."[501]

Perhaps more significant, Graham's analysis is substantiated by one of the architects of the War on Poverty, Daniel Patrick Moynihan.

> …War on poverty was not declared at the behest of the poor. Just the opposite. The poor were not only invisible, as Michael

Harrington described them, they were also for the most part silent. ...

Apart from the always faithful labor movement, the only major lobbies working for any of the programs that came together to form the War on Poverty were the conservationists supporting the youth conservation camps, and the National Committee on the Employment of Youth, an organization representing a variety of groups in the social welfare field. The essential fact is that the main pressure for a massive government assault on poverty developed within the Kennedy-Johnson Administration, among officials whose responsibilities were to think about just such matters. These men now exist, they are well paid, have competent staff, and have access to the President...[502]

Moynihan cited Nathan Glazer to bolster his argument:

When Congress argues these programs, the chief pressures upon it are not the people, but the organized professional interests that work within that segment of the problem, and those who will benefit from or be hurt by the legislation.[503]

In conclusion Moynihan suggested that the War on Poverty was simply a political reality that American society needed to accommodate, less for the sake of the poor than for the professionals.

As the number of professional increase, so also do the number of professions, or neo-professions. More and more, middle-class persons are attracted by the independence of judgment, esoteric knowledge, and immunity to outside criticism that characterize professionals...

There are now an extraordinary number of such persons in the America. Those Americans classified as professional and technical workers have just passed the nine million mark more than the number of "managers, officials, and proprietors," more than the craftsmen and foremen. And of this group, an enormous number is involved in various aspects of social welfare and reform. Through sheer numbers they would tend to have their way; but as professionals in a professionalizing society, they are increasingly entitled to have their way. That is how the system works.[504]

It would appear, in short, that the main difference between Graham's and Moynihan's perspective is that one deplored while the other applauded the same reality.

Thus the premier critique of the War on Poverty approach involved the extent to which it solved problems of social stability–rather than the problems of the poor. This critique noted that the War helped to neutralize certain potential problematic groups. For the alienated upper middle-class professional types, it gave them jobs in the poverty industry. They could oppose the problems of capitalism without really solving any of them while at the same time retaining the delights of the class privileges[505] to which they had become accustomed.

The War accorded similar rewards to potential leaders from impoverished groups in the cities. The critique suggests that part of the point of the War was to stabilize black populations which had recently grown in urban areas through the black migration of the 1950s. By giving certain black leaders positions in the poverty industry they might be co-opted with their efforts channeled into less dangerous directions.[506]

How the critique on the War on Poverty might be extended to pro bono poverty law should be clear. Instead of solving poverty, pro bono poverty law solves the problems of black and white people who want to be lawyers but who do not want to serve capitalism. Their work may do nothing to alleviate poverty, but at least it helps them live a life with a certain level of material comfort and a certain limit to existential alienation.

The Ideology of Failure

As has already been noted, the individualist focus on the problems of the poor enjoys certain ideological underpinnings. Beyond that, though (also noted above) is the fact that this non-collectivist approach seems doomed to failure, given the extent to which organization is required to give the poor the power they truly need in order to formulate, articulate and ultimately solve their problems. Yet one more incidence of social inertia suggests that the inherent failure of this method is, if not planned and applauded, certainly accepted; and, by default, promoted. To put it bluntly, the system of which traditional pro bono poverty law is a part benefits from the failure of its traditional pro bono poverty law programs. Earlier in this essay some of the arguments for NOT fighting poverty were noted. Those arguments lead to various reasons for why the present social system would benefit from the continuation of high rates of poverty. For example, it would provide a certain amount of work discipline for the population, on the theory that people without capital need the terror of poverty to induce them to work. Furthermore, the higher the poverty rate the higher the profit potential for certain enterprises, given that a rate of poverty can to a degree undercut the bargaining position of certain workers. Finally, to the degree that people see poverty as insoluble, to that degree poverty might not in fact be solved, and to that degree poverty will continue to terrorize the population into working for low wage rates. Moreover, to the degree that people see poverty as insoluble, to that degree they may despair of rearranging the distribution of wealth in society. The wealthy presumably would benefit from such political despair. Thus if the present system for dealing with poverty has its own built in system for failure, it should surprise no one—at least no one who appreciates the socio-economic interests which it serves. Failure is so endemic to the present poverty law system in the United States that Harvard Law School now includes in a course concerning "legal services for poor people" a discussion of "burnout."[507] Presumably this helps the would-be poverty lawyers deal with their failure, and helps steer them to more "productive" sectors of the economy. Presumably it does not deal with the impact that the system's failure has on the poor; but that may be the point.

CONCLUSION

Poverty is political. Poverty is an expression of powerlessness in society. Poverty, if it is to be solved, will be solved only by addressing the issues inhering in the powerlessness of the poor. If the poor are to achieve some progress and mitigate some of their poverty they must organization. Through organization power accrues, given that organization affords the capacity to articulate and move agendas in society.

Accordingly if the legal profession wants to help alleviate poverty it must be prepared to help the poor build independent organizations which can lead the poor to power. This implies that the legal profession must abandon its more traditional approaches to poverty which do little more than exchange certain experiences of suffering for exacerbated and maintained experiences of helplessness and dependency. This also implies that the legal profession must pursue activities which militate against various social forces, which happily maintain a status quo of power, wealth and privilege for about 0.5% of the U.S, population; and crumbs of power, wealth and privilege for another 10-20% of the population (which includes lawyers).

It is open to question whether the legal profession will take the difficult steps of opposing society's power orders and undercutting their own positions of privilege. Indeed, it is hard to see how the legal profession can or will even take the steps to engage in a modicum of honesty about the poverty practices they pursue and perpetuate.

CHAPTER SIX
BOOK REVIEW

Pilgrim Law

By ROBERT E. RODES, JR. Notre Dame, IN:
University of Notre Dame Press, 1998. Pp. 199.

"Behold, the days are coming," says the Lord God, "when I will send a famine on the land; not a famine of bread, nor a thirst for water, but of hearing the words of the Lord. They shall wander from sea to sea, and from north to east; they shall run to and fro, to seek the word of the Lord, but they shall not find it."

– Amos 8:11-12

INTRODUCTION

PILGRIM LAW is a book written by Robert Rodes, Jr., a Professor of Law at Notre Dame Law School. Rodes' expressed goal is to "present a coherent theory incorporating the principles of liberation theology into Anglo-American jurisprudence."[508] While Rodes' project enjoys a fair degree of success–and more on that below–perhaps the larger significance of this work is how this book may serve as a bridge from the Catholic Left to a more catholic (i.e., Protestant, Jewish, and non-religious) Left.

RELIGION, CON AND PRO

I have earlier postulated a definition of "Left" to mean the people in society who would support and accelerate trends towards more equal distributions of power between human beings; and the "Right" to mean those who would support and intensify unequal concentrations of power between human beings.[509] Because power distributions have been and remain so unequal and so detrimental to the dignity of human beings, I postulate that in the foreseeable past and foreseeable future, most impulses towards the Left should be considered progressive, humane, and/or good.

105

Hence I consider Rodes' book to be a good thing, because I think it makes a good case for supporting and accelerating trends towards more equal distributions of power between human beings.

Yet the problematic history from which this book arises must be acknowledged. Roman Catholicism can be criticized from a number of "Left" perspectives. A Protestant will grumble about its challenge to Luther's right to individual conscience. A Deist like Voltaire may simply cry *escrez l'infame*. More contemporary observers will look with sorrow and disgust on the dubious role played by the Catholic Church during the Spanish Civil War, the Holocaust, and other 20th century disasters.

Of course, a Left perspective need not stop its critique at the borders of Roman Catholicism. Mainline Protestantism has done rather badly during the 20th century with its inaction if not complicity in the face of Nazis in Germany and racists in the American South. Less mainline Protestants have managed to look like fools at best (e.g., the Scopes trial); or bigots and terrorists at worst (e.g., verbal and physical attacks on homosexuals and verbal and physical attacks at abortion clinics).

The allusion to fundamentalist Protestants calls to mind problems associated with other fundamentalisms, e.g., Jews in Israel who assassinate their leaders, and Arabs of Islam who blow up airplanes. Indeed, it can be observed that fundamentalist religion seems to oppose almost everything that a good leftist might espouse–e.g., respect for women, homosexuals, Charles Darwin, etc., etc.

When religion is defined in the preceding terms, it is easy for a leftist to join Nobel Prize winner Steven Weinberg and observe:

> …I really don't believe in a cosmic designer [and] the reason that I am taking the trouble to argue about it is that I think that on balance the moral influence of religion has been awful.
>
> …With or without religion, good people can behave well and bad people can do evil; but for good people to do evil– that takes religion.[510]

The question at this point becomes whether religion can have anything to do with that which is progressive, humane, and/or good.

While such a dour vision of religion does have validity, it remains one-sided. The religious obsessions of Presbyterians and Puritans brought an end to monarchy in England in 1649, which some historians consider the premier event of the 17th century.[511] It was the religious fervor of Quakers and others that led to the abolition of the slave trade first, and eventually to the end of slavery in the United States. Social gospel ministers preached the cause of labor during the early 20th century. In the middle of the 20th century during the American civil rights movement, it was African American Christian ministers with African American churches who provided the vision and the bodies to end the vestiges of slavery which white America had refused to eradicate.

On the international level, the churches in Eastern Europe provided havens for opposition to the domination of Soviet Russia. In Latin America, it was priests working with the poor who provided havens for opposition to the oppression of local ruling elites.

In short, if one comes from a dialectical philosophical tradition, one will appreciate the degree to which religion in general and Catholicism in particular are not one-sided phenomenon. They are not all good, nor are they all bad, they are multi-faceted. The person who would work for the progressive, humane and the good will simply work poorly if s/he misses the degree to which religion in general and Catholicism in particular may contribute to the progressive, humane and the good.[512]

THE POVERTY OF THEORY

In the year 2001 it should be observed that religion's positive contributions to Left endeavor may not necessarily prove restricted to practicing bodies. It may also have something to contribute to varying theories. Theory is significant to the Left practitioner because presumably she would want to be able to justify her support for accelerations of trends towards more equal distributions of power between human beings; because if she cannot justify her efforts on practical or moral grounds, she is simply wasting her time—or worse, perhaps perpetrating evil.

Up until recently the "embarrassing" thing about religious "theory" has been that it has justified certain of its key positions on various "irrational" "leaps of faith." Competing theories—e.g., Marxism, neoconservatism, or liberalism—have claimed to be less irrational and more scientific. According to these ideologies, if one is to justify one's support for accelerations of trends towards more equal distributions of power between human beings, one need not rely on any irrational leaps of faith. But these claims have come to appear problematic if not fallacious.

As for Marxism, its leap of faith had always rested with the legs of the proletariat. It had been the proletariat which had actually made things, and had its surplus ripped off by capitalists. Once capitalism's contradictions ripened into rupture, the proletariat would be able to assume control over the means of production which it was already operating in the first place.[513] For the longest time Marxism was able to have it both ways with its proletariat: The proletariat had the moral advantage not only because it was unfairly oppressed. It had the moral advantage because economics was on its side: the dictates of morality would correlate to the processes of history. The problem, of course, is that the processes of history have suggested that capitalism may prove more resilient than originally thought; that proletarians may prove more incompetent or selfish than originally thought;

that with advances in technology the proletarians would be scattered into small, hard-to-organize units; and, with advances in technology too many proletarians may prove too irrelevant. In short, at this juncture in history, it is not all clear how Marxism can "scientifically" justify support for accelerations of trends towards more equal distributions of power between human beings. One might pity the proletarians for being oppressed or irrelevant. But why one should throw one's lot in with (likely?) losers is not clear. Marxism presupposes that the throw will end in guaranteed victory.

The other major ideology of liberalism does little better, despite what pretensions it might try to lord over Marxism. Liberalism exists in two flavors. In the United States the harder side is called (neo) conservatism, and in Europe it is called (classical) liberalism. In the United States the softer side is called liberalism, and in Europe it is called social democracy. Liberalism (soft and hard) believes in the power of markets to solve human issues. Soft liberalism focuses on the idea market at the expense of the economic market, while hard liberalism focuses on the economic market at the expense of the idea market. Both liberalisms, however, end up making leaps of faith as irrational as Marx' jump with the proletariat.

Soft liberalism justifies support for accelerations of trends towards more equal distributions of power between human beings on the notion that such constitutes the precondition towards a purer apprehension of humanity and human destiny (which would, hopefully, lead to an insight that equality is indeed a good thing). Clearly this involves more assertion than proof. The counter-argument would be that such equality would constitute preconditions towards a more mediocre, stupid and/or limited apprehension of humanity and human destiny. Since society has not yet achieved any states approximating equality, the soft liberalism's assertions must be considered a leap of faith as lacking in proof as Marxism' faith in factory workers.

As for the harder versions of liberalism, it is not even clear that they advocate support for accelerations of trends towards more equal distributions of power between human beings. Hard liberalism often appears quite happy with unequal distributions of power and goods between people. Perhaps hard liberalism advocates support for equalized distributions of power between human beings at the beginning ("equality of opportunity"). The notion here is that equality of opportunity at the beginning might allow the market to work in cleaner fashion as it allocates goods and power according to talent and a willingness to work hard. Here again, though, hard liberalism's tenets involve more theoretical assertion than historical proof. Society has never placed people at equivalent starting points for the market to be able to do its wonderful work; and part of the explanation may be due to market theory which demands that parents be allowed to do with their power what they will (including giving undue advantage to their children). The other assumption which has not been tested, of course, is the degree to which the market will ever be allowed to work in free and pure fashion. The notion of a market unpolluted by monopoly, stupidity, collusion and/or unequal bargaining power is almost as fantastic a Utopia as the ideal State of Communism.

In the end one may argue that between the ideologies some might enjoy more credibility than others. Nevertheless, the point remains that Marxism and liberalism (hard and soft) each involve their own "leaps of faith." One may argue whether they are more or less rational than the "leaps of faith" entertained by religion. But religion, at least, appears to be one of the few honest players in the intellectual debate because at the very least it seems relatively honest about its reliance on leaps of faith. Accordingly, a votary of the Left will not want to turn her back on religion because it does above the table what others do below the table. Rather, a votary of the Left may wish to investigate what religion might have to say about approaching leaps of faith. A tradition which has been at work for some two to four thousand years might on occasion have produced something more than mere fantasy and folly. During the years it might also managed to have produced a few insights worth considering.

RODES AND POVERTY

So what does Prof. Rodes and his religious perspective have to contribute to the Left? At the most mundane level his PILGRIM LAW constitutes one of the better primers when it comes to explicating the relationship between law and the socio-economic orders from which it emanates. One can argue over whether or not law is flotsam superstructure and whether the more fundamental and generating structures consist of society, class, economy and/or means of production. The usefulness of Rodes' exposition is the degree to which he demonstrates law's correlation to at least three different socio-economic orders.

For example, the purpose of the feudal system was to try to deal with the anarchy that arose with the decline and fall of the Roman Empire. Order constitutes feudalism's paramount value. Accordingly, in a feudal system, legal issues center around matters of inheritance, land tenure, and the moral authority of the ruling class (hence, e.g., ruling class members enjoy special privileges which cannot be granted to members of the "lower" orders).[514]

The order of feudalism establishes a context in which people can begin to look beyond mere survival towards accumulation, surplus and profit. Feudal values of stability ultimately yield to capitalist values of productivity. Accordingly, in legal contexts dominated by capitalism, matters of market (i.e., the freedom to produce and price) assume paramount concern.[515]

Feudalism "solved" the problem of order, which gave way to capitalism which "solved" the problem of production. The next issue which human societies have been trying to solve involve matters of distribution. The new order(s) (whether "capitalist" or "communist") are dominated by managers. "Through [managerialism] technology, organization, and expertise are employed by managers to solve problems beyond the reach of the market."[516] Issues of process come to the fore in the legal sphere.

Under managerialism "... all ... reforms involve changing ... procedures. The idea of evaluating results independently of procedures continues to be strenuously resisted."[517]

Rodes notes that at least one recent school has challenged the contemporary managerial state, the Critical Legal Studies Movement. His critique of CLS suggests that CLS cannot transcend the boundaries of the managerialist society of which it is too much a part:

> [CLS] forms of skepticism reinforce the resistance of managers and professionals to accountability outside their class. If you cannot understand a law either by reading what it says or by referring to the moral insights that give rise to it, then neither a layperson nor an ordinary meat and potatoes lawyers will be able to apply it without calling in an expert. Thus it will be unlikely to pose a serious challenge to a class whose power is built on expertise.
>
> ...
>
> It is not surprising, therefore, that CLS agendas, when they are specific, tend to look like liberal agendas, relying heavily on freedom and equality, and generally, in my opinion, subject like other agendas of the kind to the false consciousness of the managerial class. Given their project of excluding transcendent values from the law by making them cancel each other out, it is hard to see where else the CLS writers could have gone for agendas.[518]

It is at this cul-de-sac that Rodes' religious contribution begins to make its contribution to Left theory and practice. The general problem with law—and society—over time has been how to call it to account. What are the terms by which a legal or social system may be considered good or bad, or satisfactory or insufficient? In these circumstances to label law as mere superstructure is simply irrelevant, because in one sense law is the constituted expression of the structure. Feudal law expresses and incarnates feudal society, capitalist law expresses and incarnates capitalist society, and managerial law expresses and incarnates managerial society. The question, though, is how each of these societies (and their laws) justify themselves. To what extent do they fall short, and how does one determine the criteria by which one decides that a society and (and the laws which constitute it) fall short?

The problems with Marxist and liberal evaluations have been intimated. Marxism employs an historical perspective grounded in economic development to evaluate societies. Evaluated by Marxism, feudalism could justify itself against the background of the disintegration of Roman Order; but at the point it constrained capitalist development, it became outmoded if not immoral. Ditto for capitalism, but for Marx, capitalism was to become doomed by a proletariat which had the will and competence to replace capitalists. As the viability of the proletariat comes into question, so does the viability of Marxism.

Liberalism fares little better than Marx. Soft and hard liberalism would defend feudalism because of the protections and freedoms it offers when compared to Roman society dissolving on its disintegrating base of slave labor. By the same token feudalism stands condemned by unnecessarily limiting the freedom and production promised by capitalism. After that, capitalism–and managerialism–tend to be evaluated in terms of their ability to promote freedom. But there they both falter, where hard and soft liberalism criticize each other for the shortcomings that their favorite markets generate. Soft liberalism tells hard liberalism that it is hypocritical to regulate idea markets, and that its "free" economic markets generate the slavery of inequality and environmental depredation. Hard liberalism responds by noting that freedom in the idea market leads to degradation of culture, women and children; and that to regulate economic markets also leads to degradation, and resource misallocation.

It is at this juncture that Rodes cites his religious perspective, with the goal of being able to evaluate a social system from beyond the contingencies of history. There exist, of course, a number of religious perspectives from which to judge a social system and the laws which constitute it: e.g., the degree to which they comport with the laws of Yahweh as set out in the Torah, or the dictates of Allah as set out in the Koran. The criterion may worry more whether there exists room to follow Jesus Christ than whether or not the society embodies his teachings (whatever they may be) in law.

The religious perspective from which Rodes chooses to evaluate society is that articulated by "liberation theology" which posits a preferential option for the poor.

> ...This term originated in Latin America in the 1970s. It was first officially used by the Latin American bishops at Puebla in 1979. Later, it was adopted by the bishops of the United States in their economics pastoral and by John Paul II in *Centesimus Annus*. The doctrine is basically that the church, while not ceasing to recognize God's universal love for the whole human race, should teach that He has a special love and concern for

the poor–for those deprived of the material necessities of life and condemned to live on the margins of society–simply because they need more from Him than other people do. Both the church and individual Christians should reflect this special concern in their life and witness.[519]

Competing religious authorities and interpretations, of course, might be cited to provide alternative religious criteria. The significance of the preferential option for the poor relates to the degree to which it provides a criterion for evaluating social systems and their laws; and, moreover, the degree to which a votary of Left politics could find that criterion to be conducive to his/her politics. For example, the Order of feudalism becomes called into question because of the degree to which it privileges the ruling classes and physically degrades the lower orders.[520] Capitalism's abundance becomes called into question because of the degree to which the abundance is not shared, and social and ecological disruption are not contained.[521] Managerialism's respect for process is called into question when its celebration of process loses sight of substance.[522]

Thus in PILGRIM LAW Rodes not only provides a good Left primer to understanding various social and legal systems. His particular religious vision affords a powerful criterion by which those social and legal systems might be critiqued from the Left. A person on the Left who would ignore Rodes' contributions is being dumb as a matter of practicality, and stupid as a matter of morality.

FRIENDLY AMENDMENTS

In PILGRIM LAW, Rodes' makes contributions to Left thinking which are significant. How much more a reader might expect him to say is open to question. However, since a review of this sort might be expected to discuss some reservations and/or "friendly amendments" to his project, I will proffer three:

1. The degree to which Rodes provides viable options/suggestions for a Left lawyer who would try to perpetrate a Left practice
2. The degree to which Rodes' vision must be grounded only in his Catholic vision
3. The degree to which Rodes vision must be grounded only in a religious vision

LEFT VISION, LEFT IMPLEMENTATION

The good news about Rodes is that he insists that lawyers pay attention to the plight of the poor. The less good news is his insistence on the limits that frustrate any attorney who would attempt to do something about the plight of the poor.

Part of Rodes' position derives from practical observations. He cites a number of unfortunate but insistent facts:

–e.g., the legal aid lawyer can do little, and the corporate lawyer can try what s/he can: "The burdens of the poor are being fashioned in the corporate law office downtown faster than they can be relieved by the legal aid officers or by the government. Lawyers who advocate the cause of the poor before their business clients will probably do the poor at least as much good as lawyers who represent them in court."[523]

–e.g., at best poor people's organizations have limited success. "Some of these [community organizations] were successful both in effectively representing constituencies of poor people and in confronting established power structures on their behalf... Success was sporadic, and highly dependent on the vicissitudes of local politics."[524]

–e.g., at worst poor people's organizations recapitulate the hierarchies that oppress the poor in the first place:

> "...those who care or profess to care about the poor are strongly tempted to believe that the next best thing to empowering them would be taking power on their behalf.
>
> ...appropriating particular constituencies among the poor has become quite common. For instance, it appears to be painfully easy for ruling class blacks to enhance their position within their own class by appropriating the well-publicized and well justified outrage of the numerous blacks in the underclass. Members of the ruling class with ties to other discrete sections of the underclass have gone the same route with varying degrees of success.
>
> Even within the favored constituency, it is not in the interest of the poor to provide this kind of power base for members of the ruling class. In the first place, the approach encourages an invidious comparison of victim status among different groups of the poor, with the position of each group's ruling class surrogates depending on how broadly and abjectly that group is victimized.... At the same time, other members of the ruling class are led to believe that conferring privileges on the surrogates is beneficial to their constituencies among the poor. The motivation to exercise a preferential option for the poor is thus turned to the support of a faction of the ruling class.[525]

However, another part of Rodes' position derives from his theoretical conceptions: Rodes defines the poor as those who involuntarily "lack the material conditions to lead a fully human existence in the particular circumstances in which they find themselves," those who are "marginalized, treated as irrelevant, or deprived of some condition for a fully human existence..."[526] While this may provide a valid criterion for locating a poor person, one problem with it is that the moment an attorney actually helps that person, in the areas where s/he is helped, s/he becomes no longer "poor":

> Empowering the poor in the sense of giving them a say in their own lives is of course a major goal of any decent legal system. But it carries with it a paradox: those who are effectively empowered with respect to a particular aspect of their lives are, at least in that respect, no longer poor.[527]

In the end a person is likely to find herself frustrated if s/he consults Rodes for guidance as to what s/he might actually do. What is to be done? What must s/he to do be saved? Convince the clients of Bourgeois Pork & Barrel to behave? Bother with working at Legal Aid? Bother with poor people's organizations? Mimic Robin Hood and move from poorest person, make her less poor, and then move on to the next poorest person? At one juncture in his book Rodes suggests attention to certain legal strategies which would enforce accountability upon the managerial ruling class.[528] The problem here, though, is that a conscientious lawyer might find this option to be as trivial and frustrating as some of the other options are trivial and frustrating.

Whether Rodes is required to provide satisfactory options to anyone is an open question, particularly if he is correct in asserting that they simply do not exist in this world. To a degree this is in fact his position, in that as a Catholic, Rodes believes that human problems will find no ultimate resolution within the confines of history. Ultimate resolutions occur outside history, after death, or at the parousia.[529]

Yet at this point it might be appropriate to suggest that if one wants to grapple directly with these issues inside the confines of history, then s/he might want to consider taking his/her cues from Jesus of Nazareth when he worked with the confines of history. There are a number of interpretations of the praxis of this "historical Jesus" and it lies beyond the scope of this review to discuss, let alone resolve, the various controversies. Dominic Crossan, however, leads one school which is particularly suggestive for our own concerns. Given the degree to which he risks raising particulars, he is worth quoting in detail:

> The heart of the original Jesus movement was sharing an open table and offering free healing. The combination of shared material resources (eating) and shared spiritual resources (healing) is absolutely at the core of Jesus' mission. That process involved a radically different spirituality. It sought to bring individuals together into a community which experienced God in that companionship, but not just through that

companionship. Instead of the hierarchy of patrons and brokers, mediators and intermediaries which structured Mediterranean society and religion, Jesus lived an open and direct relationship with God and invited others to do likewise. The Kingdom of God was not a program for isolated individuals; it was for communal life empowering participants into direct contact with God rather and becoming itself a substitute for that challenge…

…those who Jesus sent out were not from a specific closed group. But they were probably not so much those who had voluntarily given up everything as those who had recently lost everything. They were located along that terrible divide between poverty and destitution. It was there that the processes of Roman urbanization pressed most heavily on the peasantry. Not every peasant was destitute, but peasant life was becoming very insecure and unstable. I suggest, in other words, that Jesus created a network of shared healing just as John [the Baptist] had created a network of shared apocalyptic expectation.

Jesus' program attempted to rebuild peasant life from its grass roots upwards by bringing these two classes, the destitute and the poor, more even than the poor and the rich, into interaction with each other. The Kingdom of God appears in that interaction because it resides, not just with the itinerants, but with the relationship between itinerants and householders. One group, the itinerants, must move beyond envy and hate; the other group, the householders, must move beyond fear and terror. One needs eating, the other healing; and at a certain point, eating and healing become one.

Such is my picture of the historical Jesus. In his offer of free healing and common eating he announced and created a community that was his NO to the established hierarchical, patronal patterns of his society. Lest he himself be interpreted as simply the new broker of a new God, he moved on constantly, never settling down. He would not be a mediator, but rather that announcer that no mediator should exist between persons and God. He announced, in other words, the unmediated brokerless Kingdom of God.[530]

I would derive the following conclusions from the preceding picture of the practice of the historical Jesus:

- worry more about helping the poor, less that you might make them less poor

- one can work not only with the utterly poor (the destitute); one can also work with the partially poor (the poor)
- sometimes organizing the poor can prove worthwhile
- sometimes organizing work with the poor can include working against hierarchies that are liable to develop within the process of organizing the poor

IS THIS VISION SOLELY CATHOLIC?

As I have argued, for the sake of the Left it is a good thing that a vision such as Rodes' can be cultivated from a relatively orthodox area of Roman Catholicism. I would also argue that it would be a good thing for the Left if versions of Rodes' vision can be derived from areas beyond those of orthodox Catholicism.

Crossan, whose vision of Jesus has already been cited, provides one version of the vision from a perspective of lapsed Catholicism when he argues that God's Order involves justice:

> I think [Jesus] could have sat down with Amos in the Mediterranean sun, under an olive tree, surely with wine and bread, and they could have agreed that what Amos might have called the covenant of justice, Jesus called the Kingdom of God. They were talking about the same thing. Now what I find disturbing–indeed, terrifying–about that is I don't really think that what's being said here is, "You people run the world this way, and God has an idea for a better way; but if you don't do it, well, it's kind of all right, though you might get a bit punished." The Kingdom of God means for me the fabric of the universe, the only way it will work. It will not work any other way. Now behind that I begin to see something that terrifies me more than the Kingdom of God, which is the patience of God. I do not think that God intervenes in any sense, not because God could not; I make no such statement. God does not. And that frightens me more even that the radical justice of God. I am completely convinced that if we set out to destroy ourselves, God will not intervene to stop us, and God will settle eventually for the grass and the insects. That terrifies me.[531]

Dietrich Bonhoeffer provides another version from Lutheran Protestantism when he suggests that the divine is to be found with the marginal and disenfranchised:

> Here is the decisive difference between Christianity and all religions. Man's religiosity makes him look in his distress to the power of God in the world: God is the deus ex machina. The

Bible directs a person to God's powerlessness and suffering; only the suffering God can help. To that extent we may say that that the development towards the world's coming of age outlined above, which has done away with a false conception of God, opens up a way of seeing the God of the Bible, who wins power and space in the world by his weakness.[532]

This vision which correlates God to justice for the poor does not derive solely from Christianity. An individual embracing the Jewish tradition could note how the Lukan version of the beginning of Jesus' ministry anchors itself in the following words of Isaiah:

> The Spirit of the Lord is upon me,
> Because he has anointed me to preach good news to the poor
> He has sent me to proclaim release to the captives
> And recovering of sight to the blind,
> To set at liberty those who are oppressed,
> To proclaim a year acceptable to the Lord.[533]

After that s/he might allude to many other verses from the Old Testament which correlate divinity to justice and concern for the poor, e.g., Isaiah 1:10-13, 17, 23; 3:14-15; 5:20-23; 10:1-2; Jeremiah 22:13-19;

Hosea 6:6; Amos 2:6-7; 4:1-2; 5:10-13, 21-24; 8:4-6; Jonah 4:10-11; Micah 3:1-12; 6:8-13; Nahum 3:1; Habakkuk 1:2-12; Zephaniah 3:1-3; Malachi 4:1.[534]

Finally, Vaclav Havel provides a viewpoint which might be considered Deist, at the very least outside Judeo- Christian theology. He too implies that divinity correlates to some sort of egalitarian social order.

> ...I've always been in favor of democracy, and for a long time I considered myself a socialist [until] I realized that the word no longer meant anything at all...
>
> ...as soon as man began considering himself the source of the highest meaning in the world and the measure of everything, the world began to lose its human dimension, and man began to lose control of it.
>
> We are going through a great departure from God which has no parallel in history.... I feel that this arrogant anthropocentrism of modern man, who is convinced he can know everything and bring everything under his control, is somewhere in the background of the present crisis...
>
> Man... must discover again, within himself, a deeper sense of responsibility towards the world, which means responsibility towards something higher than himself. ... only through directing ourselves towards the moral and the spiritual, based on respect for some "extramundane" authority–for the order

of nature of the universe, for a moral order and its superpersonal origin, for the absolute–can we arrive at a state in which life on this earth is no longer threatened by some form of "megasuicide" and becomes bearable, has, in other words, a genuinely human dimension.[535]

In short, persons of varying religious persuasions could come to political conclusions similar to those of Rodes.

IS THIS VISION SOLELY RELIGIOUS?

I have said that one value of Rodes' book is the degree to which it makes a contribution to Left theory and practice, in that it provides a justification for those who would attempt to secure a more egalitarian distribution of power. As discussed above, the faltering if not the demise of Marxism makes one wonder what if any justification at all there can be for attempting to secure a more egalitarian distribution of power. Certainly, the worshippers of the market will query whether equality can be a good thing on the basis of some notion that the market allocates "just desserts." Aristocratic radicals like Nietzsche might raise an alternative protest, either to the effect that people are simply unequal and it is ridiculous to make them equal; and/or that concern over how power might be measured to allocate is an impossible question to answer; and/or that worry over power allocations is the wrong question to ask when searching for human Good.

Rodes, Crossan, Bonhoeffer, Heschel, and Havel, make it clear that some sectors of religious thinking can be cited to justify efforts towards more equal distributions of power between human beings. The question at this point is whether or not one must be "religious" in order to rationally embrace a Left vision.

In part the answer rests on how one defines "religion." Prof. Stephen Carter has defined religion as "belief in supernatural intervention in human affairs."[536] If this is accepted as a valid definition, then it probably would be appropriate to cite Jesus, Amos, and Prof. Rodes as "religious."

However, it is not at all clear that Crossan, Bonhoeffer, or Havel would fit within Carter's definition. They believe in some order within the universe which, if violated, will lead to humankind's diminution if not destruction. Presumably they would characterize this order as "divine." Yet this divinity is less something that is going to intervene in human affairs, it is more the structure of Being.

Yet Bonhoeffer, presumably–if not Crossan or Havel–would argue that some sort of personal relationship can be effectuated with this Structuring Principle, even though it has nothing to do with religion:

> Our relation to God is not a "religious" relationship to the highest, most powerful, and best Being imaginable–that is not authentic transcendence–but our relation to God is a new life

in "existence for others," through participating in the being of Jesus. The transcendental is not infinite and unattainable tasks, but the neighbor who is within reach in any given situation. God in human form.[537]

At this juncture it might be appropriate to note not only how Bonhoeffer explicitly characterizes his position as non-religious. It would also be appropriate to note the degree to which this stance might be considered scientific. This "Bonhoefferian" perspective takes seriously the notion of God. Yet it rejects the notion that any definition of God should include any magical elements beyond ordinary human experience.[538] Its attitude involves the humility of the experimental scientist, in that it suggests that the divine is something to be learned through experience.[539] If this "Bonhoefferian" perspective is "non-scientific" in any fashion, it lies in the fact that it begins with the unproven postulate that Christ and the Bible provide the premier guides for intuiting God.[540]

Nevertheless, it should be noted that this "Bonhoefferian" perspective does not lie that far from the scientific attitude as defined by Thomas Kuhn, in that Kuhn has noted that science involves experimental investigation guided by paradigms.[541] The paradigm tells where to look and what questions to ask in order to garner knowledge. A scientist can never finally establish that her paradigm is the best key towards guiding her investigations. Nevertheless s/he retains it as long as it appears to be more productive than the other alternatives out there–and to determine whether something is "productive" or not is almost an aesthetic judgment, something which is never finally determined: scientists simply tend to abandon one paradigm over time in favor of another.[542] In this Kuhnian context the "Bonhoefferian" perspective would point out that its investigations of God through encounter with suffering has proven as instructive as any other paradigm; and it will not abandon it until something better comes along.[543]

Of course, one can balk at whether Prof. Carter's definition of "religious" should be accepted as dispositive. For better or worse Bonhoeffer's "science" grounds itself in a particular (Lutheran) creed. Some who find this to be too "religious" might wish to note the groundings of Crossan (quasi-Catholic) or Havel (Deist) who ground their "science" in a divine Structuring Principle. Yet some might find even these approaches to involve too much "religion," and want to dispense with any kind of attempt to attribute divine status to any sort of Structuring Principles. They might simply argue that their "paradigm" consists of a notion that equality in general is a good thing. They look to history as an experiment which will ultimately prove that, in the long run, equality proves its efficacy. Hitler and Stalin lose. Democracies prove productive. And the more egalitarian a social order, the more healthy it is for everyone concerned.[544]

CONCLUSION

At this juncture it might be best to stand back for a moment and leave definitions of god, religion, science, divinity, and whatnot to the theologians and philosophers. The point at this juncture might simply be to note that we have reached that place where the more religious Left and less religious Left might meet and dialogue; and if they cannot merge, at least they might consider joining efforts. This place is where all parties look at the world and believe that misallocations of power are problematic if not disastrous for themselves their fellow humans; and they worry over doing something about it. Some parties accept these propositions with much faith and fervor, others are more tentative. The faith-full might appreciate that they have something to learn from the skeptical, and skeptical might appreciate that traditions of the faith-full might have something to teach them. The place could be that hill where Jesus and Amos chatted. Presumably Bonhoeffer, Crossan, Heschel and Havel might be welcomed into the conversation. Marx might bring the wine if he promised not to drink too much.

CHAPTER SEVEN
EPILOGUE

The anchor essay of this anthology ("Lawyers, Law and Social Change") was published in 1984. The purpose of this epilogue is to consider the degree to which its assertions have held valid over time.

The article's main thesis was that lawyers could expect to effectuate only a very limited impact in social change work. Truly meaningful social change would be implemented by organizing masses of people. Lawyers might assist those efforts through mundane legal work (relating, e.g., to corporations, taxes, criminal defense, etc.). Beyond that, however, lawyers could expect to have no direct or significant impact on social change.

Additionally, the article critiqued three alternative perspectives on the matter of lawyers and social change:

- One (the a-legal perspective) was associated with Piven and Cloward, who suggested that not only were lawyers not relevant, so was organizing: disruption in the social order moved elites to grant concessions to the oppressed.
- A second (the fusionist perspective) was associated with Harris and Gabel in particular, and the Critical Legal Studies (CLS) movement in general. This perspective argued that lawyers should work to break the hegemonic symbols and practices of law in hopes of overcoming social alienation.
- Last but not least, the public-interest-through-law ("PITL") perspective, which asserted that social change could best be effectuated through recourse to the courts.

From the vantage point afforded by the Year 2001 I will review each of the above in turn.

THE THESIS THAT ORGANIZING IS KEY

In my 1984 essay I pointed to the 1930s labor movement and the 1960s civil rights movement as positive events in the history of social change. I attributed much of the success that they enjoyed to organizing.

I would like to be able to point to a progressive social change movement since 1984 which has enjoyed similar success, but I fear I cannot. What this means is that since 1984 no new historical proofs have arisen to sustain or invalidate my thesis, even though I still believe it remains valid. A few random comments on organizing and its efficacy might nevertheless be ventured:

- One might cite the women's movement or the gay liberation movement as social change events which have transpired since 1984—or 1970. Discussing these movements adequately lies beyond the scope of this essay. Part of the discussion, though, would have to address the degree to which these movements remain unresolved; and indeed, the degree to which they involve the sort of social change that I would applaud. As to the matter of resolution, it is unclear the extent to which various rights of women—and gays—have yet to be secured. As to the matter of the character of these social change movements, my concern is the degree to which they remain an upper class or upper middle-class phenomenon. The labor and civil rights movements brought marked change to the lives of working- and lower-class people. They involved significant transfers of power to broad masses of people. The degree to which working class and lower-class women and gays have benefited from "their" respective movements is a matter which merits further study.[545]

- My client ACORN has continued to organize community groups since the article was written in 1984. In the mid-1990s, the election of John Sweeney to the presidency of the AFL-CIO inaugurated a new and needed attention to organizing on the part of "Big Labor." One can question the degree to which these organizations' focus on organizing has generated success. On the one hand these organizations have so far precipitated no major upheavals that could come close to matching the triumphs of labor in the 1930s or the civil rights movement of the 1960s. On the other hand, these organizations are still alive and winning some victories; moreover, survival over time does constitute some measure of success.

- As to the relevancy of organizing to progressive social change, if my 1984 article suggested that organizing constituted the ONLY key to historical success, then I have qualified that assertion. Organizing on the part of the disenfranchised is one predicate for progressive social change. At least one other is that the established powers themselves have become disorganized, so that they are susceptible to pressure from the lower orders. Such disorganization usually derives from either internal division or external disruption.[546]

- If disorganization can work to the disadvantage of the established powers, so too can disorganization work to the disadvantage of the disenfranchised. In the history of the past 25 years, much of the disorganization in the ranks of the disenfranchised can be placed under the category of "internal division" deriving from the fashionability of "identity politics" and its attendant mores. In an excellent book on the subject, Todd Gitlin has traced the roots of identity politics to the political despair of the middle 1970s.[547] While other causes might be cited to explain the birth and growth of such "multi-culturalism,"[548] Gitlin nevertheless makes many valid points concerning the deleterious impact that identity politics has had on trade unions,[549] Left political practice,[550] and Left political vision.[551]

- Finally, the sad fact is that if any segment of American society has been organizing in any quality and quantity it has been the Right. I would suggest that this explains some of the limits on the success of the Left during the past 15 years; as well as some of the extent of the success of the Right. Since the 1980s, a conservative media network has evolved, linked with conservative think tanks.[552] In their POLITICS BY OTHER MEANS, Benjamin Ginsberg and Martin Shefter describe the Republican grassroots revolution which occurred after Reagan:

> Reaganism was very much a media phenomenon, relying upon a small number of activists and possessing little organizational presence at the grass roots... Gingrich Republicanism, on the other hand, involved a very substantial measure of grassroots organization... The Reagan revolution did not penetrate far from the nation's capital.
>
> By contrast, the forces constituting the Republican coalition of the 1990s are organized at the state, county, and local levels in almost all region of the nation...[553]

Ginsberg and Shefter note the obvious impact on the legal scene which these organizing efforts have wrought:[554]

> ...During the past two decades congressional Democrats and the White House have been locked in a struggle over both the scope of judicial power and who will control the courts... In the 1960s and 1970s the most important beneficiaries of [newly created] judicial powers were liberal forces [e.g., civil rights, environmental and women's groups] that made litigation a major weapon in their arsenal...
>
> The expansion of judicial power during the 1960s and 1970s increased the stakes involved in the judicial appointment process... The Reagan administration attempted to ensure that appointments to all levels of the federal bench—district and circuit courts as well as the Supreme Court—were committed conservatives.[555]

By 1992, Reagan and Bush had appointed almost half of the federal judiciary.[556] More importantly, seven (7) of nine (9) members of the United States Supreme Court had been appointed by Republicans. Five of them—the most conservative five—stopped vote counting in Florida in the 2000 election and ensured that the Presidency of the United States would be awarded to George W. Bush.[557]

THE EFFICACY OF DISRUPTION

Civil disobedience and conscientious disruption may have been common tactics during the 1960s. Since the early 1980s, not many groups have seen fit to employ disruption widely and regularly, as least not to the visible degree of the 1960s. Thus, it is hard to argue one way or another what disruption might achieve historically. Perhaps the disruptionists might argue that its lack of appearance in recent U.S. history directly explains the lack of progressive change in recent U.S. history. Tactics of disruption and civil disobedience have been employed to a limited degree in the following political contexts, but the results are less than conclusive:

- e.g., rightwing pro-life forces have tried harassment and intimidation at abortion clinics and at the homes of abortion providing doctors. In general, their actions have been contained by the courts.

- e.g., leftwing environmentalists have resorted to disruption, most famously in the Seattle world trade talks in late 1999. At this historical juncture it appears their efforts may have contributed more to the development of security precautions than to fair labor practices and environmental safety.

- e.g., ballot counting. In Yugoslavia in 2000, the Yugoslav Supreme Court declared the election of Vojislav Kostunica to be invalid. Social unrest arose which reversed this decision. In Miami in December 2000, a mob organized by Republicans stopped votes from being reviewed in Florida. Five members of the U.S. Supreme Court agreed that no further re-counts should occur in Florida, and there was no social unrest.

THE EFFICACY OF FUSION

In the 1980s, Gabel and Harris suggested that lawyers could break hegenomic symbols of law and overcome social alienation through practices like telling an aggrieved tenant what she might do for herself first; standing by a prisoner in the prisoner's dock; requesting that "standing rules" against children in the courtroom be waived while a client is being sentenced; and so forth.[558] I personally cannot attest to the degree to which such programs have been adopted or implemented anywhere. As already has been observed, certainly not much progressive social change in the United States has occurred since 1980, which means either that the Gabel/Harris program has been ineffectual; or that it has been inadequately implemented.

What might be clearer is the degree to which the CLS movement has declined, due in no small part to its ignoring of organizing considerations. For example, it developed a reputation for being aloof and distant from any grassroots concerns:

> [One law student observed that "while] the liberals were out fighting [the Bork nomination], Duncan Kennedy [a leading CLS theorist] was busy writing dense pieces for publication like the BUFFALO LAW REVIEW, pages few people read and even fewer understood." The fairness or accuracy of such observations is hardly important. What matters is that, certainly in the press, such observations were not uncommon.[559]

On its own home turf–the universities–CLS academics tried some organizing. But they were outmaneuvered and crushed by the Right (which knew how to exercise power when it felt it needed to do so):

> In 1986, Daniel K. Tarullo, a proponent of critical legal studies, became the first assistant professor to be denied tenure by the Harvard Law School in seventeen years. In the following year, Clare Dalton, fell only a few votes short of the two thirds faculty majority necessary for a tenure recommendation. David Trubek–also at Harvard during this year as a visiting professor–won faculty approval by a vote of 30 to 8, but his case for tenure was rejected by the president of the university, Derek Bok. ...

...The plight of the critical legal studies movement was not confined to Harvard. In the 1980s, critical legal scholars protested not infrequently that, owing to their association with the movement, they were being denied appointments, tenure and promotions at other law schools. To proclaim oneself a critical legal scholar, it was felt, was to risk academic rejection or even persecution. There is no doubt that there was some foundation to such fears.[560]

THE EFFICACY OF THE PUBLIC-INTEREST THROUGH-LAW PERSPECTIVE

The moral bankruptcy of the PITL perspective seem to have been well illustrated by the 2000 presidential campaign of Ralph Nader. The PITL perspective which Nader all but founded and embodied made its elitist way through recent history by developing an agenda accountable to no particular group, and relying on smart lawyers to make change through enlightened bureaucrats and wise judges. PITL votaries grounded themselves in populist politics in as limited a fashion as their more extreme CLS counterparts (who also seemed to think that smart arguments unsupported by a mass base could accomplish something). Hence, in early 2000, Nader determined that he would run for President. When various groups with actual constituencies–e.g., labor unions, minority groups, women's groups, gay liberation groups and environmental organizations – suggested that Nader withdraw, he maintained his stance of elitist unaccountability and continued his campaign. The result revealed that rightwing process (Naderite elitism) leads to rightwing substance (Republican reaction): the election was determined by five wise judges who abrogated not only the 500,000-majority vote which Gore secured across the nation; they also stopped a full and accurate re-counting of the contested vote in Florida. Presumably Nader would survive the Bush-the-Younger years with the wealth he refused, in typically unaccountable fashion, to disclose and discuss with the public during the Presidential campaign. The real people in the labor unions, minority groups, women's groups, gay liberation groups and environmental organizations whom Nader disdained would not prove so lucky.

The practical bankruptcy of the PITL approach may finally be revealing itself to practitioners of that perspective. As we have seen, the Right was organizing the grassroots (and thus the courts) while PITL practitioners focused on litigation. In so doing, the organizing Right has all but cut the legs out from under those who might try to reform anything through the courts. The Supreme Court's 5-4 decision appointed George W. Bush as President will affect not only the composition of the federal judiciary (because of the President's appointment power); it may also be expected affect the composition of the U.S. Supreme Court (because of the President's appointment power); which in turn will affect the substance of the federal judiciary (because of the Supreme Court's power to review and overturn lower court decisions). The court decisions which progressives have not enjoyed in the recent past are likely to get worse in the near if not extended future.[561]

If any rejoinder to the preceding might be cited by a PITL advocate, it might allude to the political history of the past 20 years which seem surfeit with lawyers, what with Special Prosecutors, Independent Counsel, legions of lawyers in Florida, etc., etc. Or one might cite a recent observation concerning the degree to which mass torts played out the judiciary have replaced activity in the legislature:

> Hardly a week goes by that we don't read of another gigantic lawsuit with thousands of plaintiffs and billions in damages. Once an esoteric legal device, the class-action lawsuit has become the dominant form of litigation to resolve bitter disputes over collective guilt and innocence that not so long ago played out in Congress. Indeed, our preening national legislature, besotted with special-interest money, seems rivaled by the big budgets and major issues that now thrive in the class-action courtroom.[562]

The problem with the latter view (concerning mass tort litigation) is that it is unclear that the mass tort changes anything: more money gets transferred–if it gets transferred at all–than power. The problem with the former view (concerning the carnival of lawyers) is that it confuses the sound and fury of legal work with actual social change. One of the better commentaries on this aspect of recent U.S. history may be found, again, in Ginsberg and Shefter. The contemporary situation, they argue, has not always obtained in U.S. history. In fact, it is a result of the political preferences and efforts of the American upper classes:

> Full white manhood suffrage was achieved in the United States in the Jacksonian era, and the American electorate was highly mobilized. By the end of the nineteenth century, electoral turnout exceeded 80 percent of eligible voters in presidential elections and approached 70 percent in midterm congressional races. Outside the South, presidential election turnout stood at nearly 90 percent.
>
> ...
>
> During the nineteenth century, voter mobilization (as manifested in electoral turnout) and elite conflict (as manifested in close congressional roll calls) were directly associated. In recent years, however, the relationship between

levels of conflict at the elite and mass levels has collapsed. In sharp contrast with the militarist elections of the nineteenth century, contemporary political forces no longer seem willing to engage in all-out struggles in the electoral arena.

...Why ... has neither party [since the late 1960s] seen fit to engage in nineteenth-century style all-out mobilization in an attempt to overwhelm its opponent at the polls? *One reason is that both political parties are afraid of the implications of a strategy of mobilization.* For the Republicans, expansion of the electorate could threaten an influx of poor voters who wouldn't seem likely to be supporters of the GOP. As for the Democrats, whatever the potential benefits to the party as a whole, an influx of millions of new voters would represent a "leap in the dark" for current officeholders at the local, state and congressional levels. Moreover, *various interests allied with the Democrats—notably upper-middle-class environmentalists, public interest lawyers, antinuclear activists and the like—could not be confident of retaining their influence in a more fully mobilized electoral environment.* Finally, though it is seldom openly admitted, the truth is that many members of both the liberal and the conservative camps are wary of fuller popular participation. Conservatives fear blacks, and liberals often have disdain for working- and lower-middle-class whites.

...

...today's Democratic and Republican parties are dominated by different segments of the American upper middle class. For the most part, contemporary Republicans speak for businessmen and professionals from the private sector, while Democratic politicians and political activists are drawn from and speak for upper-middle-class professionals in the public and not-for-profit sectors. ...neither side has much need for or interest in political tactics that might, in effect, stir up trouble from below.... This trend has created a political process whose class bias is so obvious and egregious that if it continues, it may force Americans to begin adding a qualifier when they describe their politics as being democratic.[563] [emphasis added]

The result is a political quagmire which benefits only the well-to-do beneficiaries of the status quo. If change is going to occur, according to Ginsberg and Shefter, it will have to involve a mobilization of people comparable to those pursued by FDR or Lincoln—or at the very least, Gingrich.[564] But it is not clear that that will happen easily, given the bias of Republicans against the poor, and the comparable biases of Democratic "upper-middle-class environmentalists, public interest lawyers, antinuclear activists, and the like [who] could not be confident of retaining their influence in a more fully mobilized electoral environment."[565]

It does seem clear that if a mobilization of people is going to occur, it will not happen without organizing. And the problem with the years since 1984 is that it seems that outside some exceptions, most of the organizing has been done by the Right.

NYURLSC 40th ANNIVERSARY KEYNOTE (2010)

I appreciate being invited to speak here tonight about the *Review of Law and Social Change*, and this theme of "Page to Practice." Your focus speaks well of your determination to remain in the avant garde of social change writing for lawyers. But to be honest, I have to acknowledge that I am facing a couple of conundrums.

The first is that when it comes to *Lawyers, Law, and Social Change*, the article I wrote in 1984 envisioning a very limited role for lawyers, I am not sure that I have changed my mind a lot.[566] I still don't think much of lawyers. I said in 1984, and I still believe now, that it is organized people (those who have been organized into groups for taking action) that make social change, not lawyers–and if lawyers have anything to contribute to social change, it is by using their skills to help the social changers to organize.

My second problem is that I remain quite ambivalent when it comes to writing pages, even though I like to write a lot as a person and have written a lot as a lawyer. As a lawyer in general, I know that a lot of our job is to invent words to justify the infliction of pain, degradation, and death. Words allow humans to exploit and kill each other with greater ease and less guilt. Words at their worst have been used to justify a lot of obscene violence, including war, torture, executions, incarcerations, elimination of health, destruction of the environment, seizures of property, and more.

As a lawyer worried about social change and organizing, I know that words, in addition to affirming evil, can also assist it by making us into apathetic lumps. If a bad page cannot seduce us into doing evil, it will settle for making us stupid and passive.[567] The Right mobilizes cliché to make us think we live in a best of all possible worlds that should not and cannot be changed. Yet the Left does something similar when it encourages people to believe that polysyllabic logorrhea can serve as a substitute for concrete political action.[568]

So when all is said and done, I must admit that talking about "page to practice" is, for me, almost a contradiction in terms.

However, in the days of my Hegelian/Maoist youth, we used to say that contradictions make the world go 'round–or something like that. So in the limited time I have tonight, I think I can wrestle with some of these contradictions and make some suggestions about what the *Review of Law and Social Change* should consider when it contemplates "page to practice."

FIRST, I would reiterate my theme that we should be careful about our priorities. Our priorities should be organizing first, law second. Good organizing creates good law. Or it creates bad law. Look at what labor unions and African Americans did between 1930 and 1965. But also look at what the New Right has done over the past 40 years.

Beyond being an organizer first, be careful about privileging intellectual work over other forms of work. Even Foucault said "it is not with ideas that history is made to move forward, but with a material force, that of the people reunited in the streets."[569] We should keep in mind that Barack Obama *might* say that his years working as a community organizer on the South Side of Chicago were more valuable than his years on the Harvard Law School Law Review. Of course, had he worked with the *Review of Law and Social Change*, his choice would be clearer…

SECOND, pages from the *Review of Law and Social Change* should put words to *good* work. They should identify bullshit and critique cliché. "Death Tax" should be called "excuse for hereditary aristocracy." "Enhanced interrogation" should be called torture. War criminals should be called war criminals. Pages should expose the myth that humans are nothing but consumption machines and the lie that the market is free and always produces happy endings.

THIRD, the *Review of Law and Social Change* should produce practical pieces that help lawyers working in particular fields. One example that *Social Change* can cite from its own pages includes an upcoming article by K. Babe Howell, who will speak to you tonight as part of the next panel. The title of her article, *Broken Lives From Broken Windows: The Hidden Costs of Aggressive Order-Maintenance Policing* gives you an idea of the type of piece I am referring to.[570]

FOURTH, the *Review of Law and Social Change* should consider publishing occasional war stories. By "war stories" I mean stories of legal work done "in the trenches," so to speak— stories that address details of actual practice that seldom come to the attention of other lawyers unless it's around a nightclub table assisted by a good number of beer bottles. These stories don't have to be long, and they don't have to carry a truckload of footnotes. But I do think a few pages of war stories per issue might give people a sense about how the law works in real life. The stories might provide some hints about how to survive emotionally or financially as a social change lawyer. They might include a hint or two for effective legal practice.

By way of example, in my 1984 article, I wrote one story about law practice in the savannahs of deep Arkansas. The context was an ACORN campaign to give citizens more power over their local utilities. In reflecting on the role of lawyers in social change, I wrote about political theater and my personal experience working with organizers and community members–not speaking for them, but giving them legal research–to help move the campaign forward. In an article I hope to publish in the near future, I will tell a story about a Republican voter suppression effort that ACORN fought in 2004 in Toledo, Ohio. Supposedly it was a grassroots lawsuit objecting to alleged improprieties in ACORN voter mobilization. However, our response to this lawsuit did not restrict itself to the dubious merits of the plaintiffs' allegations. By pursuing corporate research, we demonstrated that the lawsuit was in fact an Astroturf lawsuit bankrolled by the Republican National Committee out of Washington, DC–and, surprise, the supposed grassroots dried up. For the exciting details you should maintain your subscription to *Social Change*.

FIFTH, the *Review of Law and Social Change* should deal with art. When I wrote my article in 1984, I was also working for a Master in Fine Arts degree from the University of New Orleans. I learned a lot about the importance of thinking in a non-linear, non-lawyerly way. If you insist on sticking with words, look at Walter Benjamin's *Arcades Project*, a classic in the technique of presentation through collage with words.[571] But you also have to look beyond words, because today words count even less than they did in 1984. This is so because the power of visual images and other non-literary stimuli have been appreciated and appropriated by corporate advertisers, Rightwing political hacks, fascist dictators, and pseudo-socialist thugs. The visual and the visceral are what is being used more and more to tell people what to buy, how to vote, what to value, how to think, and so forth. The good news is that a good verbal critique may still undercut the efficacy of a non-verbal cue. But the bad news is that it does not always do so. To undercut the efficacy of these images, I conclude that the *Review of Law and Social Change* may want to consider images–or, at the very least, it needs to publish words that evaluate images and investigate other non-literary approaches.

FINALLY, the *Review of Law and Social Change* should remember that it is building community between humans across space and over time. Evolution tells us we are social beings whether we like it or not. When I wrote my article in New Orleans in 1984, it meant something to me that people somewhere–even here in New York–shared an interest in my passions. It means something to me now that so many of us are gathered here to discuss and celebrate our passions.

Beyond the communities we have created in spite of geographical challenges, let us acknowledge the communities we have created in spite of chronological challenges. For my part, I stand amazed at the scope of historical time that is being spanned by the people sitting in this room. Some people here– maybe including me–have written things when other people here were not even born. That to me means that all of us are reaching back to people like seventeenth century Thomas Rainsborough, eighteenth century Mary Wollstonecraft, and nineteenth century Frederick Douglass, all of whom were reaching out to us when we did not exist. And we, through our efforts, will hopefully make our own values and passions available to people who are now toddlers, or who have yet to be born. The English historian E.P. Thompson has called this phenomenon shaking hands across history.[572]

I would like to close with some lines from someone who was trying to shake hands with us when we were not yet alive. In four lines I think he does rather well in summing up these issues of page, practice, and vision:

I will not cease from Mental Fight,
Nor shall my Sword sleep in my hand
Till we have built Jerusalem
In England's green & pleasant Land.

The writer, of course, was William Blake,[573] who wants to shake hands with us and the yet unborn. He and I thank you all for the opportunity to shake your hands and extend our hands to the good dead, the good living, and the yet unborn. Maybe we can still give them a planet that is green, with people living in peace and justice.

NEW YORK UNIVERSITY

REVIEW OF LAW & SOCIAL CHANGE

40TH ANNIVERSARY CELEBRATION

LAWYERS, LAW, CHANGE – UPDATE YEAR 2010

STEVE BACHMANN*

* B.A., Harvard College, 1972; J.D., Harvard Law School, 1976; M.F.A., University of New Orleans, 1984; author of UNBECOMING JANE: AUSTEN, PROUST & DARWIN (& CASANOVA & STENDHAL) (2009); EXTREME PROUST: PHILOSOPHY OF THE "MADELEINE MOMENT" (2007); LAWYERS, LAW, AND SOCIAL CHANGE (2001); NONPROFIT LITIGATION: A PRACTICAL GUIDE WITH FORMS AND CHECKLISTS (1992); CONSTITUTION FOR BEGINNERS (1987). I would like to thank Anjali Bhargava, Katy Mastman, Liz Kukura, and Julia Hiatt for bringing me into this process, and Katherine Greenberg, Alexa Rosenbloom, Alexis Flyer Rodriguez, and Gabriel Jaime for bringing it to fruition. Il miglior fabbro.

TABLE OF CONTENTS

INTRODUCTION

A man with thirty summers on his head
Has seen his best, and is as good as dead[574]

In 1984, the *N.Y.U Review of Law & Social Change* published an article by me entitled "Lawyers, Law and Social Change."[575] The purpose of this article[576] is to investigate what something written some twenty-five years ago might offer to people interested in this topic for the next twenty-five years. At the very least, I view this article as a critique of something written twenty-five years ago, after twenty-five years of reading, thinking, and living the topic.

The main thesis of the 1984 article was that lawyers could expect to have only a limited impact in social change work.[577] Truly meaningful social change would be implemented by organizing masses of people. Lawyers can be most useful in assisting those efforts through legal work when they practice in areas such as corporations, where they can structure organizations in a way to maximize organizing efficacy; taxes, where they can advise progressive organizations as to how to receive the greatest benefits from the tax system without limiting their permissible organizing activities; and criminal defense, where they are instrumental in minimizing the amount of time arrested organizers have to spend in confinement.[578] Beyond such limited roles, I argued that lawyers could expect to have no direct or significant impact on social change. Moreover, to the degree that lawyers directly involve themselves in social change work, to that degree they adversely affect the implementation of social change: sustainable social change requires the mobilization of masses of "ordinary" people who achieve change for themselves, not "experts" or "lawyers" who try to accomplish the change for them.[579]

While I believe this thesis still holds true, this article will explore the degree to which my perspective on the role of lawyers and social change has been modified after twenty-five years. I have been particularly struck by developments in evolutionary brain science,[580] especially new information concerning our conceptions of consciousness, and how this knowledge might affirmatively contribute to progressive theory and practice. These lessons are critical in light of the continuing exploitation of vulnerable groups through systemized inequality,[581] physical violence,[582] and ideological manipulation through physical[583] and metaphysical means.[584] Exploitation, violence, and resistance still depend mainly upon organizing masses of people.[585] While lawyers are not the primary vehicle for social change, they do have a role to play both in organizing groups and establishing legitimacy for various efforts.

In Part I, I explore dialectical materialism as a theoretical basis for discussion of social change. Dialectical materialism has been a useful starting point for dialogues about social change because of its incompatibility with the fundamentalist perspectives that have historically led to the oppression and marginalization of socially weaker groups. Recent developments in evolutionary brain science provide additional support in favor of the dialectical materialist perspective. Additionally, this theoretical framework has led me to adjust some of my notions of what lawyers can contribute to social change work, particularly in constructing public narratives that create consciousness for individuals and delegitimize the status quo.

In Part II, I analyze the lessons on the relationship between organizing and social change that can be drawn from the past twenty-five years. In 1984, I argued that organizing masses of people is the key to social change; events since then have provided further support for this proposition. Modern conservative[586] groups appear to have embraced this premise and as a result have enjoyed substantial success through organizing activities, to a degree equal to, if not surpassing, that of progressives.

In Part III, I discuss how experiences in organizing over the past twenty-five years could lead us to reconsider some of our conventional wisdom about organizing. While dialectical materialism provides a general philosophical orientation for various branches of progressive practice, the more particular questions of organizing remain. I explore the degree to which my original emphasis on socioeconomic factors, such as class, needs to be supplemented with an attention to other material factors relating to culture, organizational behavior science, and evolutionary brain science.

In Part IV, I connect the above threads to social change work by lawyers. While I still believe lawyers play a subordinate role in social change, developments in history and science over the past twenty-five years suggest new areas where lawyers have significant parts to play, particularly in the arenas of voter registration and protection, and in the (de)construction of ideology.

1.

GENERAL THEORY: MIND AND MATTER

[T]he prevailing view is that brain patterns were established during the millenniums when humans were hunters and gatherers, and we live with the consequences.[587]

In my 1984 article, I explored the philosophical tradition of "dialectical materialism,"[588] a worldview that focuses on the interplay between mind and matter: mind derives from matter, while simultaneously, matter derives from the mind, which conceptualizes and constitutes matter. 1 return to this discussion as a starting point for framing a dialogue on "social change," because it both provides a way of understanding reality and encourages individuals to take a proactive role in shaping that reality.[589]

In 1984, I identified five components of dialectical materialism:

1. A thing consists not only of the objective material, but also of the subjective mind that conceives of it.
2. Things are many sided, and perhaps infinitely so.
3. Things change (i.e., to understand something one must know its past and future as well as its present).
4. Consciousness derives from matter…
5. Thought is affected by material conditions, e.g., social, political, economic, and biological.[590]

Since 1984, a number of developments in science, including those involving evolutionary theory and brain science, have reinforced key components of dialectical materialism, in particular the role of matter in creating mind, along with the role that mind plays in creating "reality."[591] Thanks to these developments, phenomena of consciousness have been linked to chemical states and physical networks in the brain.[592] The physiology of the brain has, in turn, been explained in terms of evolutionary development,[593] providing perspective on both the power and the limits of the reactions and networks of the brain.[594]

In addition to structuring a discussion on social change by grounding it in scientific observations, dialectical materialism also provides intellectual grounds for opposition to the various fundamentalisms that attempt to stifle progressive movement.[595] Its postulates about the relationship between mind and matter (and the implied politics) are particularly relevant when thinking about two major theoretical movements I consider progressive-Marxism and feminism.[596] Additionally, these postulates are relevant when thinking about the past, present, and future of legal education.[597]

A. Darwin and the Brain

My conception of dialectal materialism is consistent with the development of evolutionary theory and brain science since 1984. Advances made in evolutionary theory provide support for dialectical materialist theory, which in turn supports progressive movements and social change.[598]

Under Darwinian theory, the motors of evolution include the mutation and mixing of genes through sexual reproduction,[599] and how well or not they interact with external factors like climate and other competing forms of life.[600] These basic principles help drive our understanding of human perceptions, motivations, and inclinations, and suggest the degrees to which they may or may not contribute to survival and reproduction.[601]

The physical construction of the human brain is grounded in an evolutionary history that reveals more about humanity's ability to survive during various phases of human history than it does about our ability to ascertain "truth."[602] That is, rather than solely seeking to discern the factual reality of our physical and social environments, our brains evolved to create, or even fabricate, aspects of reality in order to promote human survival. It is critical to note the degree to which narrative devices such as cause-and-effect and plot are in fact only convenient-and possibly false-human means for surviving reality. The research suggests that patching things into something connected and "coherent" is simply something that human brains are wired to do.[603] Paleontologist R. Dale Guthrie has proffered at least one evolutionary explanation for why this propensity has developed in the human brain: "Tracking is a highly cultivated ability that enables the hunter to imagine the other animal's emotions and behavior....[A] tracker creates a template or story upon which he works to piece together what may have happened and what may be happening."[604] In other words, at least 40,000 years of hunting have pushed the human brain to become a story-making machine-even though these coherent narratives may have little or nothing to do with actual reality."[605]

Brain science and evolutionary theory have provided scientific grounds supporting both the dialectical and materialistic components of dialectical materialism. The material bases of mind are growing clearer with every scientific discovery. The dialectical aspect, which acknowledges the mind's role in creating "reality," is also being increasingly explored,[606] despite its counter-intuitive message that "truth" is in fact "fiction"-or at least, always provisional.

B. Fundamentalism, Plato, and Reaction

Dialectical materialism cuts against the philosophical grounds of retrogressive movements,[607] which today might be subsumed under the category of "fundamentalism." Fundamentalism has been defined as "a movement or point of view characterized by adherence to fundamental or basic principles."[608] Fundamentalism can justify this adherence only if it can establish that the mind can literally apprehend reality (and from it derive basic, fundamental principles). Philosophically, fundamentalism derives from Platonic idealism, which postulates that universal, abstract essences exist and that the human mind can apprehend them.[609] Dialectical materialism cuts at the foundations of this perspective because it holds that reality is too rich for the mind to comprehend. Moreover, dialectical materialism posits that the mind is inherently inadequate to apprehend reality, either because of its physical construction"[610] or because of the tools used to identify and describe reality.[611]

By way of example, the fundamentalism of American conservatism reveals itself in one its founding texts, Richard Weaver's Ideas Have Consequences, written in 1948.[612] Weaver's "central philosophical question" was "whether there is a source of truth higher than, and independent of, man," a question he answered in the affirmative.[613] He asserted that human development regressed starting "in the late fourteenth century...when man had abandoned his belief in transcendental values in favor of William of Occam's nominalism."[614] As a bit of background, William of Occam denied the existence of mind-independent universals or essences, arguing that universals were only names, lacking any non-mental reality.[615] As such he provides an early intimation of anti-fundamentalism by denying any reality inhering in language, an arbitrary invention of fallible human beings. That he was excommunicated for this early version of "dialectical materialism" should surprise no one. That he continued to cause discomfort to people like Weaver centuries later should also surprise no one: he denies them a certain means by which they can order the universe, including other human beings.

The philosophical battle between "essentialism" and "nominalism" continues, as evidenced in the writings of one of the world's most prominent fundamentalists, Pope Benedict XVI. Taking his cue from the Gospel of John (which equates God with Word, or "Logos"), he argues, "The basic reason that man can speak with God is because God himself is speech, word. "[616] Elaborating on John further, he states:

> "In the beginning was the Word [logos], and the Word [logos] was in communication with God."... [T]he Christian mysteries are Logos-mysteries. They reach beyond the limits of human reason, but they do not lead into the formlessness of frenzy or the dissolution of rationality in a cosmos understood as irrational.[617]

If God is postulated as Word, Logos, logical, then the cosmos can be considered essentially rational, and cannot be "understood as irrational."[618] This point is critical to understanding fundamentalism. If God, Being, and Creation are rational, they become accessible to humanity, which is blessed with logos (i.e., language and rational capacity). All fundamentalists subscribe to the notion that Logos (Word) and Ontos (Being) connect in a fundamental fashion.

Another school of fundamentalism that threatens progressive goals is market-oriented fundamentalism, which one leading thinker has defined as "a widely held creed that the markets will take care of all our needs."[619] Adam Smith and his views on economics have been cited to justify asymmetrical power relationships rather than to explain actual phenomena.[620] Smith's faith in the market appears anchored in a belief in a beneficent supernatural Being, or Order, a belief that was explored as a general matter by Nietzsche and Veblen[621] and traced in particular to his embrace of Stoic theology.[622] Smith described the Stoic world as one "governed by the all-ruling providence of a wise, powerful, and good God, [and] every single event ought to be regarded, as making a necessary part of the plan of the universe, and as tending to promote the general order and happiness of the whole."[623] Such observations correlate with his "invisible hand" by which the "selfish rich" are led (almost "by deception") "to help the poor and to serve the interest of society at large;"[624] and as a result, market fundamentalists characterize the exploitation of unequal relations as fair transactions[625] and encourage activity that may have led to the most serious economic turmoil in decades.[626]

Whether you call it Platonism, essentialism, universalism, or fundamentalism, the perspective of dialectical materialism rejects these views. It repudiates the notion that the human brain can precisely ascertain any essences in reality; at best, it can create only provisional approximations of external stimuli. With this understanding at its core, dialectical materialism thus provides an intellectual starting point for opposition to creeds that would order and oppress humanity in the name of something perfect.

C. Marxism

In addition to providing suggestive grounds for opposing reactionary fundamentalism, dialectical materialism also suggests productive avenues for Marxism, a school of thought associated with progressive action. Since the beginning, Marxism has been influenced by dialectical materialism,[627] neo-Marxist thinkers have built on these works and contributed useful progressive theories to the debate.

While this article focuses on writers that postdate my 1984 article, many mid-twentieth century French thinkers did not work their way into the American consciousness until at least the 1980s.[628] Dialectics and materialism can be found in the works of Georges Bataille, whose "base materialism" analyzed the "social body as a kind of sociological metabolism, or as a waste-management system" where abundance and heterogeneous transgression served as constituting concepts as important as scarcity and homogenizing hegemony.[629] Guy Debord, with his experiences during the May days of 1968 in France, raised the question of how human bodies might most effectively organize themselves into action in post-industrial history.[630] Further, Foucault's "biopolitics" focused on collective, disciplinary action on individual bodies, as well as "a second seizure of power...directed not at man-as-body but man-as-species" where the general "population" was the subject for management and regulation.[631]

In 2000, Marxist philosophers Michael Hardt and Antonio Negri "rehabiltiate[d]...'communism'"[632] with the publication of their book, Empire. Hardt and Negri posited that "sovereignty has taken a new form, composed of a series of national and supranational organisms," which they titled Empire"[633] This new global form "is characterized fundamentally by a lack of boundaries,"[634] lacking a "territorial center of power and...fixed boundaries" as a result of "[t]he declining sovereignty of nation-states and their increasing inability to regulate economic and cultural exchanges."[635] Similar to dialectical materialism, Empire opposes fundamentalism by rejecting the notion that global order could arise according to some omniscient, transcendent force or power.[636] Empire is also consistent with the fluidity and interplay between mind and matter that characterize dialectical materialism: its terms are "completely indeterminate, even though they are nonetheless concrete."[637]

D. Feminism

Dialectical materialism also provides theoretical support for feminism- although given the range of authors who might be termed "feminist," composing a singular definition of "feminism" is difficult.[638] For the purposes of this article I will rely on a somewhat simplified definition of feminism as an objection to discrimination against women and the ideologies that have been relied on to justify such discrimination.

Patriarchal ideology contrasts masculine spirit to feminine body and argues that the thought of the former is superior because it is unconnected to and uninfected by earthly clay to the degree of the latter.[639] Dialectical materialism would directly oppose this position by arguing that there exists no thought without matter to create it, and thus, even if such spiritual/material distinction may be validly drawn, neither may be privileged over the other.

Consistent with its contempt for the body, patriarchal thought also denigrates emotion, dismissing it as effeminate, to the point of being worthless as a source for insight.[640] Dialectical materialists would agree with neuroscientist Jill Taylor, who has pointed out how "thought" is inseparable from emotion at the threshold of perception, in that the brain automatically "scan[s] all incoming stimulation" to establish whether to feel emotional responses (anxious or calm, threatened or intimate), before any "thinking" even occurs.[641] The feminist historian Gerda Lerner has pointed out how such patriarchal prejudices have impoverished the range of human consciousness for centuries.[642]

In the face of patriarchal dichotomy between intellect and emotion, between conscious thought and physical reflex, dialectical materialism establishes that there is no such thing as disembodied reason separable from human bodies. There is no pure reason, no pure spirit; rather, human existence is the result of the intrinsic intertwining of reason and spirit. "Reason" comes from imperfect bodies developed over millions of years of evolution. To argue the contrary is to create theoretical justification for intolerance and oppressive violence.[643]

E. Legal Thought and Legal Teaching

Today, the main method for teaching law is the case method.[644] Developed at Harvard Law School in the 1870s, the case method centers on exploring fundamental legal doctrines through discussion of certain critical cases. Rather than lecturing, professors employ rigorous questioning to lead students to induce these doctrines.[645] By the late 1960s and into the 1970s, this use of the Socratic method had developed a reputation for being oppressive, abusive, and reactionary.[646]

From the perspective of dialectical materialism, this should come as no surprise. By divorcing theoretical discussions of casebook law from the work of law as lawyers practice it, the casebook method privileges mind, over matter. As Adorno observed, incompetence-and potentially fascism-lurks in such idealism.[647] The quality of legal teaching and of law school graduates degenerates under the case method in the absence of insight gained through connections with reality and actual practice.[648] The humanity of the people participating in this context suffers for similar reasons. Historically, this began as an unbalanced valorization of thinking and theory (fit for philosophers) over labor and practice (fit for slaves),[649] and it culminates now in the "survival of the fittest" mentality underlying the casebook method.[650]

One stark example lies in the defense of torture. For generations, a broad consensus has existed among civilized nations that torture is beyond the pale;[651] however, under the Bush Administration, some of this country's top legal minds found ways to justify its legal use.[652] Had legal teaching not been so strongly divorced from reality and its method not so saturated with contempt for real-life context and consequences, these arguments might never have gained the level of credence they did. If the autarky of mind in America does not lead to Auschwitz, it does seem to lead to Abu Ghraib.[653] Clinical legal education retains the dialectical nature of the exchange between student and teacher; in addition, it focuses on forcing students to confront the lived human experiences behind litigation and the surrounding social contexts implicated in judicial decisions. Clinical education was already being advocated in 1949 by Jerome Frank, a leader of the legal realist movement,[654] and its array of advocates has only continued to grow.[655]

One should also note the broader political contexts of legal education and the history of formal legal education. Most lawyers in the early American republic learned through a version of clinical legal education: they served as apprentices reading laws with a senior lawyer before they staked out on their own.[656] The need for law schools may have been obvious more to law schools than to lawyers.[657] More significantly, when a law school degree becomes a predicate for certification as an attorney, individuals from lower socioeconomic classes are more easily denied access to the legal profession. This "credentials" revolution thus protects middle- and upper-class privilege.[658] It also promotes ideologies favorable to those class groups by legitimating certain outlooks and practices, and delegitimizing others.[659]

In short, if legal teaching introduced more materialism into its dialectics, two goals could be achieved: lawyers might become more competent,[660] and protections would be established against the prejudice, insensitivity, and violence that can result when idealism is divorced from practice.[661]

11.

PRACTICES OF ORGANIZING: CHANGING SOCIETY

I couldn't survive my own pessimism if I didn't have some kind of sunny little dream.... Human beings will be happier-not when they cure cancer or get to Mars or eliminate racial prejudice or flush Lake Erie but when they find ways to inhabit primitive communities. That's my utopia. That's what I want for me.[662]

In one sense "social change" is a meaningless term, in that any sort of change in social arrangements equals social change. In this article, I maintain the position I have advocated previously,[663] that social change worthy of the name should involve a drive to greater equality[664] and community.[665] More equality makes happier and healthier people, irrespective of economic class.[666] Moreover, it contributes to community, by which I mean a social structure that combines social support with respect for individual autonomy.[667] The template set down by our Paleolithic past suggests that humans remain "wired" to thrive in egalitarian and communitarian societies.[668]

It is important to note the degree to which some social change is impacted by advances in technology. Arguably, the development of birth control has done more to advance the status of women in society than all the rational arguments for women's rights over a number of centuries and all the demonstrations for women's rights over the past few decades.[669] The development of the computer and the internet may lead to further revolutions in human social relations, in terms of how they influence human brains[670] and how they affect political dynamics within a society.[671]

The importance of technology in spreading and supporting social change forces us to confront the question of how to make social change. In confronting this question, we must also ask ourselves whether the work traditionally engaged in the pursuit of social change is effective. In other words, does social change work work? As I did in 1984, I believe that organizing constitutes an effective avenue for actualizing social change. Events since then, including the rise of the new Right and the election of President Obama, have confirmed that belief. Certain structuralist approaches to history might argue for passivity.[672] Such approaches undercut the need to organize, by arguing that social change happens as a result of external factors. However, I believe that individuals cannot rely on external factors to drive social change but must instead take an active role to create it.

In short, I believe that human history requires, at least in part, humans taking steps to act. Historical conditions may help some human actions and thwart or pervert others; however, these historical conditions alone are not responsible for the course of human history. External and social conditions are important, but they only go so far; after that, it is what people do with them that determines the shape of history.[673] Both previous progressive movements[674] and advances in evolutionary science[675] show us that the most important thing to do to create social change is to organize.

A myriad of historical phenomena might be cited as examples of how organizing people might implement social change. Since 1984, the following phenomena have helped confirm this belief: the Republican resurgence, the election of Barack Obama, and the experiences of the community organizing group ACORN.

A. The Republican Resurgence

When I first approached this subject in 1984, it remained unclear whether Reagan represented a resurgence of reactionary politics or a historical aberration. Out of the previous fifty-two years, Republicans had only held the White House for twenty of them.[676] In terms of Congressional control, Democrats controlled the House of Representatives during the forty years from 1955 to 1995[677] and lost the majority in the Senate to Republicans for only six years in that period (from 1981 to 1987).[678]

From the perspective of 2009, it seems clear that Reagan's electoral victories indicated something more than incidental fortuity. Since 1984, Republicans have been very competitive in running for Congress[679] and the White House.[680] When they are unable to win enough popular votes, their conscientious focus on and presence in the judiciary has been important in advancing the Republican agenda.[681]

In short, Reagan's election represented a reassertion of conservative power. The consequences have been significant: economic inequality has dramatically increased,[682] and the federal government's budget has emphasized military spending over funding social welfare programs.[683] The Right accomplished a transformation of society through democratic consent, largely because of its own careful organizing and an absence of counter-organizing (or even affirmative de-organizing) by the Left.[684]

When the Democratic Party represented a majority in Congress, they nonetheless failed to pass legislation benefiting "lower class constituents," including a measure that would help unions organize and expand the Democratic base.[685] At the grassroots level, many liberal activists spent their energies focusing on identity politics, which promoted difference instead of unity[686] and substituted arguments over language in lieu of real political action.[687] By doing little to contribute to organizing, and by doing much that undercut efforts at progressive organizing, the Left proved to be a significant factor contributing to the Right's resurgence.

Additionally, the Right engaged in effective organization and mobilization of their base. While much has been written concerning the conservative ascendancy,[688] a good summary can be accomplished by a simple review of the self-conscious organizing efforts undertaken by the Right during the 1970s.

In August 1971, shortly before his nomination to and confirmation as an associate justice of the Supreme Court, Lewis Powell circulated through the Chamber of Commerce a memo concerning attacks on the "free enterprise" system and how to save it:

> [I]ndependent and uncoordinated activity by individual corporations, as important as this is, will not be sufficient. Strength lies in organization, in careful long-range planning and implementation, in consistency of action over an indefinite period of years, in the scale of financing available only through joint effort, and in the political power available only through united action and national organizations.[689]

The Right did not ignore Powell's advice,[690] it began organizing, with the help of subsidies from wealthy individuals and corporations.[691] Such organizing manifested itself in the founding and financing of a number of organizations and efforts,[692] influencing school curricula,[693] and forming political action committees (PACs).[694] This organizing groundwork of the 1970s led to a conservative resurgence. The battle between Jimmy Carter and Ronald Reagan over the 1980 presidential election illustrated the growing strength of the conservative movement,[695] and popular support for the Right continues to run high, even after the ups and downs of that presidential campaign have been forgotten.[696]

Significantly, after taking the White House in 1981, conservative organizers did not rest on their laurels. When the 1980s Moral Majority foundered, the 1990s Christian Coalition arose to take its place.[697] Talk radio became a new media specialty of the Right, a potent tool for sharing ideas, reinforcing values, and mobilizing voters.[698] When Bill Clinton was elected president in 1992, the Republicans responded with their "Gingrich Republicanism," which relied on "a very substantial measure of grassroots organization...at the state, county, and local levels in almost all regions of the nation."[699] During the 2000 presidential election campaign, the Right's strong focus on organizing could be seen in the candidates' contrasting approaches to the Florida recount: "While Republicans were mobilizing protesters, Gore was imploring journalists."[700] The Bush administration's power was underscored in the 2002 congressional elections, when the GOP strategically recruited candidates, mobilized its base, and targeted thousands of voters from key demographic populations.[701] Even after Barack Obama's election, Karl Rove continued to urge conservative activists to organize.[702] Some of them did so by utilizing online messaging tools such as Twitter and Facebook,[703] others by employing phony "astroturfing" methods.[704] Moreover, during the summer of 2009, a number of commentators observed how opposition to Obama's health care initiative seemed to draw directly from the playbook of progressive organizer Saul Alinksy,[705] while also employing more contemporary modes of organizing involving online media.[706]

Any article discussing the past twenty-five years of organizing and its interaction with the law must address the Federalist Society, an organization of conservative legal activists. Interestingly, the Federalist Society was not officially founded until 1982,[707] just as conservatives were beginning to enjoy political and social victories resulting from a decade of organizing,[708] This timing suggests either that law follows good organizing or that law needs good organizing; either way, the two seem to mutually reinforce each other. Within a few years of the Federalist Society's founding, Harvard Law School-perceived by many on the Right to be an institution that was "out of control" in its promotion of far-Left ideologies-was brought "under control" through an organizing campaign aimed at conservative Harvard Law School alumni and ultimately at the law school itself.[709] Today, the Federalist Society is one of the Right's "most vigorous, durable, and well-ordered organization[s]," endorsing judicial candidates and "building the support structure of the conservative legal network."[710] The Federalist Society's narrative production has expanded my appreciation of what lawyers can do to effect social change.[711]

B. Obama

At least one person on the Left has appreciated the message that organizing can have historical impact: Barack Obama, a former community organizer in Chicago, Illinois. How his experience organizing translated into his successful 2008 presidential campaign was manifested in a number of ways at a number of junctures.

While in some ways Howard Dean's presidential campaign of 2004 served as the prototype for Obama's organizing innovations,[712] a combination of advances in technology,[713] along with a favorable demographic drift,[714] allowed Obama to inaugurate a new era in mobilizing the electorate. In both the primary campaigns and the general election,

> the Obama campaign collected names and contact numbers both from the Internet and at big rallies, including even his acceptance speech in Denver, attended by more than 75,000 people. Most of those digitized names were called, e-mailed, and text-messaged, often more than once, by election day. At some of the rallies the members of the audience were asked to call and e-mail their friends and families and ask them to vote.[715]

These qualitatively new tactics translated into quantitatively impressive numbers. By the end of 2008, Obama's campaign was estimated to have accumulated ten million addresses in its database.[716] The nearly $750 million Obama raised exceeded "what all of the candidates combined collected in private donations in the previous race for the White House."[717] Even after the election he had close to "$30 million in the bank," and his "final tally of individual contributors surpassed 3.95 million."[718] Obama's success could be credited to his appreciation of community organizing: he performed better than Democratic front-runner Senator Hillary Clinton in states where caucuses, rather than general elections, determined the allocation of delegates.[719] Had Clinton taken more seriously her own knowledge of community organizing, she might have put into place the offices, lists, phone lines, doorknockers, car drivers, and phone callers, which could have mobilized sufficient supporters to various caucuses and might have neutralized the numbers delivered by Obama offices.[720]

Shortly after his inauguration, Obama employed some of his organizing tactics to mobilize support for his first proposed budget,[721] and he has continued to build on these organizational tactics.[722] Karl Rove criticized these efforts as ineffective,[723] but Republicans were soon using community-organizing tactics during the health care battle to fight the community organizer they had mocked during their convention.[724]

C. ACORN[725]

In my 1984 essay, I discussed my personal experience as an attorney for the community organization known as the Association of Community Organizations for Reform Now (ACORN).[726] Aspects of ACORN's work are worthy of comment here, as they show how organizing (and lawyers for organizers) can indeed effect change, sometimes in ways one cannot anticipate.

ACORN's approach to community organizing involved the establishment of grassroots neighborhood groups, with the ultimate goal of achieving political power.[727] In 2004, ACORN experienced its first counterattack launched by conservatives, signifying that its activities might have a national impact. In a flurry of legal actions taken against ACORN, a rightwing district attorney in Colorado convened a grand jury, though she ultimately failed to secure an indictment. A private RICO lawsuit filed in Ohio ended when the plaintiffs dropped the charges after ACORN's discovery efforts revealed that the case was being subsidized by parties connected to the Republican National Committee. Two private cases filed against ACORN in Florida were dismissed and abandoned, the first culminating with the court awarding ACORN damages for defamation.[728] While none of these attacks succeeded in stopping ACORN from organizing, they did require the diversion of valuable resources from organizing work to defensive efforts.

Despite these impediments, ACORN continued to organize, and to do so effectively. The significance of ACORN voter mobilization endeavors became clear once again in 2006, when the Republican Party pushed for the Department of Justice to prosecute ACORN voter registration efforts. In Missouri, the Bush Administration replaced U.S. Attorney Todd P. Graves, "who had shown reluctance to bring vote fraud-related cases," with Brad Schlozman.[729] Schlozman showed no such reluctance, filing four indictments against ACORN election workers on November 2, 2006, just before the November 4 election, in apparent violation of DOJ guidelines.[730] The Wall Street Journal duly printed an editorial publicizing the indictments on November 3.[731] Following the election, the Justice Department filed a grand jury referral against Schlozman to investigate whether he had perjured himself in statements to Congress concerning the ACORN indictments.[732]

Because of, or in spite of, November 2006, Republican officials continued their attempts to influence voter registration, and thereby elections, by politicizing the Justice Department. Several U.S. Attorneys were fired on December 7, 2006, including David Iglesias.[733] Iglesias had been "[r]ated a top performer by department officials early in 2005," only to be criticized a year later by Republican lawmakers for "lax voter fraud prosecutions," including failing to prosecute ACORN workers.[734] These attacks on the independence and integrity of the Justice Department led to a public scandal, climaxing in 2007 with the resignation of Attorney General Alberto Gonzales from the Justice Department.[735]

In 2008, the Right did its best to smear Obama with what it perceived to be the tar on an ACORN brush.[736] Conservative media outlets attempted to claim that Obama had been employed as ACORN's counsel, based on his participation as trial counsel for ACORN in a 1990s lawsuit; while this claim was factually unsupported, conservative organizers repeated it in efforts to paint Obama as a radical candidate.[737] ACORN also became the target of allegations that it was pursuing massive voter registration fraud around the country.[738] Most remarkably, during the third presidential debate, Republican front-runner Senator John McCain stated that ACORN was "now on the verge of maybe perpetrating one of the greatest frauds in voter history in this country, maybe destroying the fabric of democracy."[739] Following this, ACORN's offices and workers were subjected to vandalism, hate messages, and physical threats.[740] Reports of an FBI investigation of ACORN surfaced two days later, information that the McCain campaign sought to bring to the foreground of the campaign.[741]

One can debate how much ACORN deserved all this attention-it was hardly the only progressive organization seeking to empower marginalized populations or increase voter registration. At the time of the 2008 presidential campaign, ACORN had merely been continuing its work of organizing and mobilizing low- and moderate-income people.[742] By engaging in organizing efforts with the goal of creating measurable progress, ACORN may have affected the course of history: by increasing voter registration and turn-out among low-income and minority voters, ACORN's voter mobilization (in conjunction with the organizing efforts of similar groups across the country) played a role in tipping the election towards Obama.[743]

111.

THEORIES OF ORGANIZING: CHANGING ORGANIZING

Hedge funds really need a community organizer.[744]

Organizing can be a highly effective endeavor. Like many other ways in which humans engage the world (and history), it holds potential-and, of course, limits. Yet like so many other ways in which humans engage the world, lessons may be learned concerning its forms, practices, and modes of engagement. This section attempts to provide an overview of lessons and questions for the field of organizing that have arisen (for me, at least) over the past twenty-five years. That this list could prove exhaustive is impossible; but even a cursory review of certain issues may help the social changer at least think about these matters and act with a sense of orientation, as opposed to blindly flailing about in the cauldron of history. Specifically, I believe organizing for social change would benefit through refining the role of class, enhancing an appreciation of culture, expanding a knowledge of corporations and corporate behavior, and, finally, exploring further avenues opened by Darwin.

153

A. Class

I continue to find Marx's conception of class, predicated on "self-conscious organization," useful.[745] Marx focused on the proletariat, who not only shared similar material conditions of oppression in the factory, but, by being concentrated in a factory and forced to work cooperatively, was also more amendable to being connected and organized.[746] It also explains his dismal perspectives on the French peasantry: while they experienced similar socioeconomic conditions, they worked in family units isolated from one another, and this hindered their development as an effective class.[747]

That being said, the question becomes how do Marx's nineteenth century observations apply to the twenty-first century? During the twentieth century, Marx's focus on the blue-collar proletariat became outdated because factory workers' centrality to the economies of wealthy countries declined.[748] As the twenty-first century progresses, farmers and factory workers are no longer the center of progressive organizing; instead, the white-collar, post-industrial economy has become dominant because of the information it can gather, analyze, reconfigure, and mobilize.[749]

During the twentieth century, white-collar workers themselves began to become proletarianized.[750] Initially these white-collar workers resembled Marx's French peasantry: similar in condition, but scattered and unable to form common bonds.[751] However, with the invention of broadband, the ability for relatively isolated white-collar people to become less isolated and more socially engaged changed dramatically.[752] The political effects of such technological advancements were evident in the 2006 congressional elections[753] and brought to the fore in the 2008 presidential campaigns, when Obama applied the lessons of community organizing to a generation of people who grew up on this new technology.[754] He took people similarly situated materially and exploited new technology to join them together in a movement that elected him president.

Of course what will happen next remains an open question. Obama's opponents are beginning to explore the potential of newer media for their future organizing efforts.[755] The extent of their success will turn in part on the degree to which class constitutes the premier way by which people experience their lives. In the United States, attempts to organize people from the same socioeconomic class have been impeded by differences across other identities, including materially experienced differences in age, race, gender, and sexual orientation;[756] at the same time, these identities have sufficient commonalities for people to form groupings around, regardless of class differences.[757] The Republican Right has attempted to exploit these means of dividing people with otherwise potentially similar socioeconomic interests.[758] By focusing on identity politics[759] and failing to organize effectively, progressives have missed opportunities to unite people with shared interests that could be advanced by joint progressive action.

Class remains a powerful approach for conceptualizing political action because similar socioeconomic experiences can bring people together, as Obama's electoral success-due in large measure to the mobilization of individuals with shared class interests-has demonstrated. Yet the past twenty-five years have also shown how other material experiences can divide people who could otherwise unite to advance shared interests. Class is an important narrative for comprehending politics, but it can no longer claim to be the only viable narrative.

B. Culture

While class focuses on one set of material forces that group and divide people, culture provides a different set of perspectives and emphases.[760] Cultural narratives remain variegated.[761] One of their most articulated instances is David Hackett Fischer's Albion's Seed, which gives a detailed account of the origins and development of majority American culture, arguing that it derives primarily from four cultures developed in the British Isles: Puritans from eastern English counties, who settled the northeast; Royalist elites from southern England, who settled Virginia; Quakers from the northern midlands, who settled the Delaware Valley; and border country highlanders from Scotland and Ireland, who settled the Appalachians.[762]

It is hard to do justice to Fischer's exhaustive analysis in a paragraph, but by way of summary we might note some observations he emphasizes concerning each culture: Historically, the eastern part of England was a region of religious dissent (e.g., Lollards, Marian Martyrs, Puritans) and political rebellion (e.g., Jack Straw, Wat Tyler, John Ball, Peasants' Rebellion, Oliver Cromwell).[763] In the northern midlands, religious values were expressed by Quakerism, and political values focused largely on opposition to the slave trade.[764] Quakers, like their Viking ancestors, accorded exceptionally high status to and respect for women (whose burial mounds in Scandinavia compared to those for males).[765] As opposed to the egalitarian views espoused by the Quakers, the Royalists who settled Virginia came from regions where slavery and serfdom lasted the longest[766] and where support for entrenched power interests was particularly strong.[767] These characteristics were then transplanted to Virginia, where order was maintained through strict social hierarchies that were often enforced by violent means.[768] Violent tendencies also carried over into recreational activities; "Virginia's favorite amusements were bloodsports."[769] Similarly, the borderlanders who settled the Appalachian region frequently engaged in violence against authorities and against each other.[770] The prevalence of violence throughout their society may have also affected gender roles: "men were warriors, women were workers" and subordinate members of society.[771] Education was low, inequality was high, and "[w]here the warrior ethic [was] strong, the work ethic [grew] weak."[772] Common education was emphasized in Puritan and Quaker cultures, and deemphasized in Royalist and borderlander culture.[773]

Many of Fischer's cultural characterizations suggest an easy melding of Puritans and Quakers into Yankees, and of Anglicans and Highlanders into Cavaliers. The former embraced traditions of egalitarianism and education, while the latter embraced hierarchy and violence.[774] These cultural values translate into contemporary politics: progressive values track those of the Quakers and Puritans, and are predominant in the regions settled by those groups, and the same is true of conservative values and the Royalist and borderland groups.[775] These trends ripened into violent conflict during the Civil War, but the tensions existed before[776] and have continued into the present day.[777] Based on these patterns, Fischer analyzed American elections through the lens of cultural interpretation and regional politics from 1968 to 1988.[778] His analysis remains relevant for elections from 2000 onwards, as regional politics have continued to dominate electoral trends: Republicans continue to win majorities in the regions settled by Royalists and borderlanders, while the Democratic base remains strong in areas first inhabited by Puritans and Quakers.[779]

After recognizing the influence of culture, the task becomes understanding the grounds of culture. Culture manifests itself in patterns of thinking and behavior that are so pronounced that one can identify them as patterns and correlate them to groups;[780] but what causes the patterns? For example, one psychological experiment determined that, when subjected to insult, "Southerners showed much bigger jumps in cortisol [stress] and testosterone [aggression] than insulted Northerners."[781] In other words, cultural conventions about violence and honor correlated with hormone levels. How much of this physiologically measurable reaction derives from genes (nature) and how much from environment (nurture)? These issues are likely to engender debate for quite some time, and there are staunch advocates on each side.[782] On one side stand "environmentalists" who argue that the influence of environmental factors and lived experiences overrides genetic instincts to a strong degree.[783] On the other side are those who believe that much of human history is genetically determined.[784] An intermediate position, one I adopt here, emphasizes the fact that the human mind is predisposed to create certain "wirings" at certain critical junctures in its development.[785]

Narratives that focus on class, race, and gender are important to those who want to organize people into groups. Culture is another narrative, full of suggestive leads for understanding what material influences help bring people together or keep them apart. The study of culture, its existence, its manifestations, and its origins, is in its earliest phases. But it is clear that culture can create inertias for or against political positions that one would like to advance or oppose in particular constituencies. Moreover, it remains to be seen how deeply these cultural inertias are ingrained. They extend over historical time and appear in biochemical manifestations. As evolutionary science advances, the organizer will need to pay attention to the degree to which some of these inertias have a deep genetic basis.[786]

C. Corporations

Much can and should be learned from contemporary studies of the modern corporation, since its profit and nonprofit forms constitute the mode of organization for so many groups. As a matter of general history, corporate forms have instructed human organization since the ancient Roman Empire and the medieval Catholic Church.[787] The history of corporations within the United States begins with chartered corporate enterprise in New England and Virginia.[788] Ironically (or not) it was a for-profit corporation that helped to facilitate the first western revolution, the English Revolution, in that, at the very least, it forced future anti-Royalists to learn how to work together in an organized fashion within an organizational structure.[789] In this section I urge the Left to pay more attention to what business and managerial schools have for some time been thinking and writing about: the rise, decline, and revival or death of organizations.[790] How do movements begin, and how do they coalesce into groups? When do like-minded people join together in an organization, and how? Once an organization has been formed, how is it maintained? It is time for progressives to familiarize themselves with the literature concerning these phases and apply those lessons to their own organizing enterprises. Some of my experiences from the past twenty-five years have raised particularly pointed questions.

For example, my wife and I each started our careers working for organizations in the early stages of their existence. Most young organizations die out;[791] ours did not. Even though my organization was nonprofit and my wife's was for-profit, both enterprises faced similar growth issues over time, many of them relating to the depersonalization that accompanies expansion in terms of numbers, size, and geography.[792] There seem to be plenty of books on how to start a business and how to maintain a business.[793] More literature should be written concerning the transition from a new business, through a transitional company, to a large, established corporation.[794]

There is also the question of leadership. Many insurgent movements begin in an unorganized state, as a result of the comparative lack of power and resources characterizing new movements relative to a well-organized ruling class.[795] Because of this lack of organization, insurgent movements can prove unusually dependent upon charismatic leaders. This dependence, in turn, has made these leaders into particularly attractive targets for members of the established elites, who seek to dismantle a young, unorganized movement by removing the leader that holds it together (e.g., the Gracchi, Spartacus, Caesar, Jesus, Marat, Robert Kennedy, Martin Luther King). When insurgent movements prove successful, their leaders often conclude they are indispensable to the movement and hold on to power at the expense of the egalitarian origins of the movement (e.g., Caesar, Cromwell, Napoleon, Stalin, Mao, Castro, Ralph Nader, Robert Mugabe, Hugo Chavez). At this point the leader becomes "toxic," an issue that has been addressed in corporate studies[796] and to which progressive organizers should pay greater heed. Greater awareness of the dangers posed by toxic leaders may have prevented or mitigated ACORN's major scandal of 2008, when it was discovered that the brother of ACORN founder Wade Rathke had embezzled almost one million dollars from ACORN and affiliated charities in 1999 and 2000, and that founder Wade Rathke had, in defiance of democratic principles, corporate propriety, and legal prudence, failed to disclose that information to board members or law enforcement.[797]

Lessons on the relevance of organizational leadership studies would again have been helpful to ACORN in 2009, when a conservative activist entered ACORN offices dressed as a pimp and asked for help in his prostitution enterprise.[798] Unfortunately, in a number of ACORN offices, employees were videotaped expressing a willingness to help him, and the results were circulated over the internet.[799] The negative fallout from these incidents was enormous,[800] and observers criticized ACORN's failure to adequately "manage its staff" as being responsible for the scandal.[801]

D. Darwin

Materialist theory focuses on the outside material forces that induce humans to form or not form groups.[802] Evolutionary sciences, which have taken radical strides since 1984,[803] are an important source of our knowledge of human group formation (or resistance to it). Understanding the evolutionary drives and philosophical theories behind human group formation and other human behaviors is an important tool for increasing the efficacy of organizing.[804] While scientists continue to debate which traits are genetically inherited and which are socially developed,[805] there does seem to exist some consensus over other physiological issues pertaining to the matter of grouping in general. For the purposes of this article, I will simply highlight illustrative issues that have arisen in four critical areas relating to organizing: the actuality of individuality (group formation); membership recruitment (getting people into the group); organizational maintenance (keeping people in the group); and ideological justification (why one should bother).

1. *Individuality*

The prevalence of human social groups seems remarkable given the incredible diversity that exists among individuals.[806] Given the diversity of humans, and the corresponding diversity of motivations, interests, and reactions, bringing more than one individual into alignment with another constitutes no automatic or easy accomplishment. Group formation occurs along a spectrum of possible structures; at one end of the spectrum, humans organize themselves through love, sympathy, and reasonable persuasion.[807] At the other end, they are organized through terror, violence, and lies.[808] Within this range, organizing can be (1) purely self-conscious, (2) purely unconscious, or (3) a mix between the two. An example of self-conscious organizing is the ideal anarcho-syndicalist commune of free and equal consenting adults pursuing a common project.[809] An example of unconscious organizing is a group of people responding in similar fashion to similar external stimuli, but their knowledge of or coordination with others is limited to nonexistent.[810] An example of organizing characterized by only partial self-conscious awareness is the political party of the Orwellian nightmare, where leaders lead followers, and the followers either do not know why they are being led, or they do not realize that they are being led at all.[811] When one extrapolates beyond two or three persons to larger social groupings, the phenomenon of human organization appears all the more remarkable.

2. *Recruiting*

Disparities between individuals are quite marked, and the more people in a group the more differences among them to account for, thus making the formation of groups a difficult task.[812] Evolutionary science is a valuable source of information about bringing people into new groups. Much of neoclassical economic theory has been built around the notion of the rational, deliberative human actor.[813] Yet developments in neuroscience have demonstrated that human thought is imbued with emotion.[814] Conservatives have made better use of this knowledge than progressives have, utilizing emotional appeals to gain public support for their goals.[815]

Other factors besides emotions affect human responses to various messages.[816] One such factor involves priming or subliminal suggestions.[817] Marketers and branders have become well versed in priming, which is a phenomenon critical for inducing people to buy certain products over others.[818] Similarly, priming could be a powerful tool for organizers to effectively spread their messages.[819]

Organizers should also appreciate how sensitive people are to other subliminal cues, particularly visual ones.[820] Thus, organizers should pay attention to such issues as dress and grooming.[821] Issues of priming aside, organizers can also take steps to ensure that the people to whom they are reaching out feel comfortable, which often means engaging local people to "mute[] the outsider role of the organizer and reduce[] the foreign experience of an organizing drive."[822]

3. Maintenance

Holding a group together requires consideration of the number of members in the group; as Adam Smith has observed, there may be limits to the number of humans that can remain in a viable group.[823] Again, this can be traced back to human diversity: too many members in a group, each with distinct personalities and motivations, can make group cohesion impossible. In identifying where the limits on membership size lie, answers may be derived from prehistoric anthropology. Paleontologist R. Dale Guthrie observed that Paleolithic bands seem to have typically consisted of twenty-five to forty individuals, with approximately five adult hunters. This suggests that the human brain was originally predisposed to work with about five other people and that people find it hard to deal with the complexity of more than forty or so other people.[824] Contemporary literary studies have found that humans can "comfortably keep track of three different mental states at a time," but challenges and difficulties arise when that number is increased.[825] Similarly, "[t]he Navy Seals...typically operate in 13-man units led by two officers and a chief, and frequently break down into subgroups depending on this mission," a principle of group formation successfully employed in 2008 by the U.S. Ryder Cup golf team.[826]

British evolutionist Robin Dunbar has argued that the human brain has evolved to "reckon with about 150 individuals."[827] Consistent with this point is the fact that humanity's closest relatives (the chimpanzees) begin to break into new groups once they reach around 100 members.[828] However, questions remain concerning the quality of relationships. Guthrie argued that the shift from small bands to larger tribes involved a suppression and impoverishment of personality.[829] Kurt Vonnegut seems to have placed himself in Guthrie's camp when he correlates certain quantities of people with certain qualities of life.[830]

In addition to managing the size of the group, effective organizers must consider how to keep group members together. Solidarity tactics might include pep rallies (which wolves do) or sharing food (which chimpanzees do).[831] In the marketplace, efforts at group cohesion find a correlate in the phenomenon of branding, where commercial corporations aspire to establish positive associations through consistent combinations of colors, images, and words.[832] By creating a recognizable visual, corporations are able to utilize human emotion to create a subconscious form of group loyalty, which is demonstrated by maintaining a consumer base.[833] With so many different groups and causes in today's society, not to mention countless other ways to fill time or distract attention, it is crucial that progressive organizers find a way to market their organization effectively, to create the same kind of brand loyalty enjoyed by top consumer products, lest they lose their members to other organizations.

Nor are groups homogenous institutions. Unique organizational structures exist within groups; this intra-group organization is significant to the group's success. After the individuals are organized into a group, the significance of organizing within the group must be acknowledged. Chimpanzees are quite adept at forming alliances to make or break an alpha male.[834] Lower-ranking male baboons will form coalitions with other lower ranking baboons in order to oust higher ranking males,[835] and female gorillas will similarly band together to keep an unruly male gorilla "in line."[836] Though male bonobos are bigger, females maintain solidarity and will gang up on a male if necessary.[837] These examples from the primate world demonstrate how complicated and volatile intra-group dynamics remain, providing important lessons for social change organizers.

4. Ideologies

Many conservative thinkers have cited Darwin and his theories on survival of the fittest as scientific proof that entrenched privilege and resource inequalities are both appropriate and natural.[838] Darwin's work, however, can also be useful to progressive organizers. As Darwinian science develops, progressives can gain insight helpful to advancing progressive goals and also undermine the inaccurate rationalizations conservatives have put forward to advance their positions.

Conservatives start with a Darwinian point concerning the unique nature of every individual[839] and extrapolate it into an assertion that every person is a self-centered, self-serving, isolated monad.[840] Yet evolutionary research suggests that humans have been "hard-wired" towards equity, empathy, cooperation, and solidarity, because of the evolutionary benefits that accrue when those traits are exhibited.[841] For instance, game theory suggests evolutionary grounds for altruism and fair play, contradicting the theory that humans could have evolved solely through short-sighted self-interest.[842] Cooperation in hunting seems to have been a necessary characteristic among land predators hunting large mammals,[843] but the instinct for social interactions goes beyond successful food-obtaining strategies. Empathy can be observed in rats, which have been shown to stop pressing a lever to obtain food once they notice that doing so delivers an electric shock to a neighboring rat,[844] and monkeys have been observed choosing starvation over inflicting pain on other monkeys.[845] In an experiment involving capuchin monkeys, two would receive cucumbers, and then only one would be given more highly prized grapes: "Upon noticing their partner's salary raise, monkeys who had been perfectly willing to work for cucumber suddenly went on strike. Not only did they perform reluctantly but they got agitated, hurling the pebbles and sometimes even the cucumber slices out of the test chamber."[846] Such instances of empathy and solidarity constitute more than an interesting aside: ability to succeed socially has been linked to ability to survive physically. In a study of baboons in Kenya, females with the best social connections proved to have the most surviving offspring.[847]

These traits were not lost when the human species evolved: through his review of art from the Paleolithic period, Guthrie argues that Old Stone Age modes of production pushed humans into cooperative and irenic patterns of behavior.[848] Conservative arguments that support inequalities in resource distribution are based on a flawed ideology that relies on a purely self-involved actor, the existence of which is belied by the evolutionary inclination toward equity and cooperation. Evolutionary science thus provides additional support for progressives seeking to organize a counter to conservative ideology.

IV

WHERE LAWYERS FIT IN

The study of law can be disappointing at times, a matter of applying narrow rules and arcane procedures to an uncooperative reality; a sort of glorified accounting that serves to regulate the affairs of those who have power-and that all too often seeks to explain, to those who do not, the ultimate wisdom and justness of their condition.[849]

The thesis of my 1984 article was that organizing is a far more effective tool for achieving social change than legal strategies, and that if lawyers wanted to affect social change, their best option would be to assist organizing efforts.[850] After twenty-five years, I still hold to that thesis, albeit with some emendations. In my 1984 article I made some suggestions for lawyers who wanted to participate in bringing about social change. I argued, "The lawyer's facilitative role is most obvious and significant in three substantive areas of law: the first amendment, corporations and taxes, and criminal law. Additionally, to be effective, a progressive lawyer should be aware of the rules of civil procedure and ethics."[851] After twenty-five years, those propositions should be supplemented by the following observations.

A. Help Wanted

Whereas in 1984 1 was only beginning to appreciate this point, by 2009 it has become clear to me: while lawyers are not necessary for the traditional organizing work that requires massing people in neighborhoods, lawyers are very necessary for the complicated organizing work that that cuts closer to the heart of the economic system. My experience with ACORN is illustrative of this point. In 1984, ACORN's work involved mainly community organizing, which generally does not raise many issues of

162

governmental regulation.[852] Most of what we had to worry about implicated the five legal areas noted. None of it was overly complicated.

However, as the 1980s proceeded, ACORN helped to start housing organizations and labor unions.[853] Processing real estate involves its own set of complications, but fortunately ACORN Housing Corporation was able to bring in qualified counsel to assist it in this particular field. On the labor front, we learned that establishing a labor union, which faces much more federal red tape,[854] is significantly more complex than forming a community organization.[855]

Perhaps the most dramatic example of the new need for legal expertise was ACORN's experience with electoral politics and voter registration.[856] The many questions surrounding this area of the law have become quite complicated, perhaps by design: incumbents like to remain incumbents and thus prefer a restricted franchise, which they can monitor, as opposed to an open, democratic franchise, which remains unpredictable.[857] While this proposition generally holds true across the political spectrum, some Republican politicians and pundits have been particularly determined in pursuing lawsuits[858] and supporting voter registration rules that would restrict voting.[859] Various conservative thinkers continue to manufacture theories[860] and engage in actions intended to restrict the franchise.[861]

This increase in the use of legal tactics to depress voter turnout may be a matter of history repeating itself,[862] however, the situation is likely to worsen, given that the socioeconomics of twenty-first century global capitalism has less use for democracy than the nineteenth century version: as wealth and power become increasingly consolidated, appealing to the populace becomes a less effective, and less frequent, tool for governance.[863] Because these retrogressive legal tactics can be most effectively countered by progressive legal strategies, the need for progressive lawyers in this specialized area grows.

B. Do You Really Want to Be a Lawyer? (1)

In evaluating the 1960s War on Poverty, former Senator Daniel Moynihan bluntly argued that it was waged less for the sake of the poor than for the professionals; that is, the War on Poverty became a project to engage and divert a growing professional class.[864] Moynihan's assessment may suggest that society will work to ensure that positions for social work lawyers will remain open, in part to maintain social stability.[865] Two years later, his comments were substantiated by a more centrist Democratic leader. In 1969, then-Congresswoman Edith Green, ranking Democrat on the House Education and Labor Committee, observed: "[P]robably our most enduring monument to the problem of poverty has been the creation of a poverty industry. There are more than 100 companies in Washington, D.C., alone which specialize in studying and evaluating the poor and the programs that serve them."[866] Despite the dedication of professionals and resources to solving the problem, poverty still exists, and one could argue that the biggest thing that has changed since we began waging the War on Poverty is the increase it has created in employment opportunities for professionals.

These factors may give a person pause when she contemplates pursuing a legal career for the purpose of effecting social change. ACORN has exemplified a partial response to this issue: it attempts to engage, whenever possible, "ordinary" people in solving their own problems and to resort to lawyers or other professionals only when necessary.[867] Other progressive lawyers have advocated a client-centered approach to lawyering that aims to mitigate the paternalism that can occur between a professional attorney and an unsophisticated client.[868] Whether these approaches solve the issue of professionals working to secure their own profession rather than to advance the goals of their professed clients, however, remains another question. The phenomena of reforms that increase professional opportunities rather than solve social problems simply may be an inherent feature in the dynamics of capitalism.[869]

C. Do You Really Want to Be a Lawyer? (2)

It is one question to ask whether professionals serve themselves or their clients. It is another question to ask whether professionals can in fact remain professionals; that is, whether they can enjoy the "independence of judgment, esoteric knowledge, and immunity to outside criticism that characterize professionals."[870] In 1976, legal work, like many professions, was increasingly focused on material acquisitions and becoming less enjoyable, less prestigious, and increasingly alienating.[871] That trend has continued, and, since legal work is now being outsourced to other countries, it is not likely to stop.[872] While law used to enjoy some cache, practicing it is not what it used to be.[873] Even the inspiration that might attend legal work with a public purpose is not immune to disintegration: fifteen years ago Harvard Law School began including a discussion of "burnout" in a course on providing legal services to indigent clients.[874] The young lawyer must confront all of the issues that attend legal work, regardless of the cause or client. I would urge any person who thinks about becoming an attorney to prepare herself with strategies for coping with disillusionment and emotional fatigue.

D. Get a Day Job!

During the late 1970s and early 1980s, it was possible for progressive attorneys to contemplate a career in private law practice, given a statutory provision that provided for the award of attorneys' fees to prevailing parties in civil rights cases.[875] Conservatives understood that this provision was a critical resource for progressive legal advocacy; thus, subsequent years saw conservatives on the judiciary cutting back the scope of the attorney fee award statute.[876] As legislative revival of this statute is unlikely, beginning attorneys tend to focus on obtaining a salaried position at a public interest institution or at a large law firm with a generous pro bono policy. Since there may be more attorneys seeking these positions than there are positions available, those who would pursue a career in social change lawyering may want to consider other options.

One option is to develop expertise in some area of traditional private practice, providing one with sufficient independence to pursue more controversial work. From the generation of lawyers that preceded mine, two lawyers who followed such a path come to mind: Maurice Sugar and Arthur Kinoy. Sugar, who contributed a significant amount of work to the fledgling labor movement in Detroit during the 1930s,[877] supported himself through private practice work, including criminal defense and constitutional litigation.[878] When his efforts with the labor movement hit a roadblock, he was able to withdraw and retire.[879] By opening a general practice, Arthur Kinoy and his partners were able to participate in cutting-edge civil rights litigation during the 1950s and 1960s.[880]

Another potential source for progressive legal employment is government, whether at the state or federal level. When I graduated from law school in 1976, most of the "real action" supposedly thrived at the federal level, in part because of the critical role the federal government played in promoting civil rights and fighting poverty.[881] Since then, the significance of localized work has risen more to the foreground: state legislatures have played a crucial role in vindicating federal constitutional rights.[882] Justice Brennan has also suggested that state courts may be more protective of fundamental rights.[883] Additionally, state attorneys general are becoming increasingly active in civil actions and criminal prosecutions targeting corporate white-collar crime, securities fraud, internet fraud, and environmental degradation.[884]

E. Civics

Lawyers often enjoy better training and access to resources that enable them to make contributions and exert influence to a greater degree than an "ordinary" citizen is able. Lawyers may play a special role in a variety of ways, affecting local issues, politics, and theories of governance and judging.

Just as an attorney should not restrict her vision to the national stage,[885] neither should she restrict her focus to the landscape set by established political parties. The Working Families Party in New York provides an example of how third parties can impose a progressive vision onto the political dialogue of a state.[886] However, third parties often cannot achieve electoral impact without the proper "fusion" laws in place; so if a lawyer cannot work with a viable third party, she can work to change her state's election laws.[887]

Another arena of politics in which the lawyer may have a special role to play is the selection, evaluation, and retention of judges. With the election of Obama, progressives now may hope to play a role in supporting progressive people for seats on the federal judiciary.

In considering the notion of bringing progressive judges to the bench, progressives should be careful to ensure that their notion of qualification does not fall prey to the ideology of expertise.[888] The more a judicial career seems to qualify one to sit on the Supreme Court, as opposed to a political career where one has had to actually go to voters and find out what they think to secure office, the more an ideology of expertise is advanced. Judging becomes increasingly characterized as the province of elite, specially trained experts who practice a science.[889] The notion that rendering judicial decisions would have any grounding in popular sentiment is dismissed as inappropriate pandering. Progressives who believe the protection of minority rights requires an independent judiciary should see this notion for the false ideology that it is, because the history of the American judiciary reveals an elite protecting mainly elite minorities and white majorities.[890] Rather than seeking to promote judges based solely on years of judging, progressives should support judges who have proven responsive to the people and who have demonstrated a commitment to progressive legal interpretations.

Beyond the question of bringing progressive people to the bench, there remains the question of those already sitting. Since the federal judiciary and, more importantly, the Supreme Court are presently dominated by Republican appointees,[891] progressives today are frequently confronted by a hostile judiciary.[892] In such a context, it is the responsibility of a progressive attorney to recognize that judicial decision making may be improperly influenced by the ideological perspectives held by the individuals who make up the federal bench.[893] She may need to be prepared to engage in aggressive tactics, including impeachment.[894]

F. Narrative and Cliché

This article opened with a discussion of narrative as a way in which humans organize their experiences. Evolution has given us a jerry-built brain that pushes to organize data regardless of truth; in part, perhaps, because Paleolithic humans needed to invent stories to help them track down food.[895] Thus, because of the limits of the brain, narratives are always suspect, but because of the practical necessities involved in living, narratives must be invented and used. By organizing experience in a certain way, narrative can help humans function; however, in doing so, narrative suppresses certain facets of human experience.[896]

There is also a political function to narrative. Narrative allows people to organize into groups. A fundamental organizing tactic involves the review of campaign actions by participants. In the words of community organizer Mike Silver, "The fundamental purpose of reviewing the action is to develop a consensus definition of the experience. This is mainly a process of reality construction."[897] However, such "reality construction" can exact its price in terms of personal individuality: at its worst, it can drown personal individuality in totalitarian terror;[898] more frequently, but just as dangerously, invented narratives can serve as soothing but mind-numbing cliché.[899] By suppressing individuality, cliché enables elites and governments to control their constituents and override the will of the people.[900]

The instances of cliché abuse for population control are legion in the United States. Art high and low constitutes one potential avenue for population control because of its ability to contain and constrain the mind's ability to define things and imagine alternatives. Enzensberger has identified it as the "mind industry."[901] An artist or writer can either participate in this industry by perpetuating cliché or oppose it by attempting to break or transcend cliché.[902]

Attorneys, with their talents for analysis and articulation, can play a unique role in the destruction of cliché at a number of levels. Professor Steven Teles's history of the Federalist Society[903] provides a useful tool in thinking about this because it demonstrates how organized and conscientious lawyers can create a narrative for understanding (or obfuscating) reality. Teles has observed that "a regime is most likely to endure when it can make its ideas seem natural, appropriate, and commonsensical, consigning its opponents to the extreme."[904] The legitimating role played by lawyers and the courts thus influences a regime's ability to "make its ideas seem natural, appropriate, and commonsensical." As for law's role in supporting a particular hegemonic order, Teles writes:

> [F]or legal ideas to be taken seriously by the courts they cannot be seen as wholly novel or outside the realm of legitimate professional opinion. As a consequence, groups with disproportionate control of the institutions that produce and legitimate legal ideas, groups who have legal "authority," will enjoy a significant advantage in persuading judges and other significant legal actors that their demands are legal and appropriate.[905]

The Federalist Society consciously set out to impact which ideas were considered legitimate,

> shaking the self-confidence of liberal lawyers by challenging their perceptions that they had a monopoly on serious legal thought... Conservatives were insufficiently "articulate" and

their ideas poorly developed, and the budding Society claimed that they could build an organization that could help make conservative ideas both convincing and respectable.[906]

The success of the Society is indicated not only by the power that some of its fellows have assumed in the legal and political fields,[907] it is also indicated by the degree to which its ideas, previously largely disregarded by academic and professional establishment, have become mainstream.[908] Inequality is seen as just and natural when, in actuality, the more unequal a society is, the more miserable everyone in it lives, including the rich.[909] Widely-respected members of the legal profession manufacture apologies for torture.[910] These are only a few examples of the ways in which conservative lawyers have legitimated previously unaccepted opinions.

This regime of conservative cliché needs to be challenged by the Left. The American Constitution Society has attempted to assume the role of counterweight to the Federalist Society, but its long-term prospects for success remain to be seen.[911]

As suggestive as the history of the Federalist Society has been concerning lawyers' role in the construction of public narrative (or reinforcement of oppressive cliché), two qualifying points must be reiterated. The first is that the cliché industry functions not only in courtrooms and law schools; it also functions in the public square. While progressive attorneys should engage in consciousness-creating activities promulgated in elite circles, they should remember that they often play a leading role in public discourse.[912] They should respond to the language and ideas promulgated by conservative organizations at the grassroots level.[913] As a general matter, they might want to contrast perceptions of American freedom with evidence of the lack of freedom in the United States[914] and challenge the false assumptions of proponents of capitalist markets.[915] Lawyers would do well to remind themselves and the public that market theory does not always comport with reality[916] and that human beings are more than just automatons seeking to maximize consumption.[917] Human impulses towards empathy,[918] self-actualization, and ecstasy[919] constitute equally, if not more, compelling motivations relative to material desires. Indeed, in seeking to change the shape of public discourse, lawyers may wish to look to the Preamble to the U.S. Constitution, which implicitly sets out goals and criteria by which the government is to be judged.[920]

As Adorno has suggested, the material often trumps the ideological, and often in a very blunt fashion.[921] In his book on the conservative legal movement, Teles focused on elite discourse to the degree that one might conclude that history moves only because smart people weave fascinating narratives.[922] Teles failed to note the laundry list of conservative organizations that preceded the formation of the Federalist Society in 1982.[923] His detail of conservative financing of the Federalist Society is impressive, but he does not seem to acknowledge how that money created salaries and jobs which allowed conservatives elites to manufacture ideas. He discussed a Federalist Society "public effort" to bring Harvard Law School "under control,"[924] but he focused more on the law and economics proponents who were brought into the law school, as opposed to those who were affirmatively excluded.[925] Finally, while Teles minimized the importance of electoral activity,[926] one has to wonder how seriously he or anyone else would be taking the Federalist Society and law and economics if their members had not enjoyed so much success in having their colleagues appointed to judicial benches by elected officials.[927]

In 1984, I alluded to a conception of the law as an argument over values and their implementation. That values are implemented through discourse as well as material struggle is something that the last twenty-five years have underlined. Another quote from Obama provides a closing for this section as well as a segue to the next: "The law is also memory; the law also records a long-running conversation, a nation arguing with its conscience."[928]

CONCLUSION: BACK TO THE FUTURE AND BACK

Fail again. Fail better.[929]

It remains unclear how much longer evolution's experiment with humans will continue. To some degree, I see the last 50,000 to 100,000 years as a sporadic series of candles being lit in darkness. Sometimes there is more light and warmth; a lot of times it is dark to a depressing degree. One idea which has given me comfort comes from the English historian E.P. Thompson, who stated that, while we cannot change the facts of history, there are values expressed in history which we may either repudiate or affirm. In Thompson's words, we have the opportunity to "shake Swift by the hand."[930] Various of my articles (including the 1984 article) have attempted to shake hands with the past and extend handshakes to the future. With this opportunity I have been allowed to shake hands with myself- and extend more offers to the future. The person who wants to engage in work that ratifies and extends the work of Swift and others like him may wish to keep these remarks in mind: on the one hand, we may stand on the brink of some new epoch in human progress; on the other hand, rust never sleeps.[931]

Yet to maintain the spirit of critique, I will add one corrective to Thompson's otherwise wise and moving meditation. To a degree, Thompson gives human actors too little credit for impacting history. Prior to 1960, one would have to work hard to conceive of non-white, non-upper class, non-manly persons appearing on history's stage as actors. It simply made limited sense, given the histories one had read and the histories one had lived. By contrast, by 1975, virtually everyone recognized that nonwhite, non-upper class, non-manly persons could appear on history's stage as actors.[932] In one sense, that was what the 1960s were about: these nonwhite, non-upper class, non-manly persons demanding to be acknowledged. As a result, historians had to look at history anew.[933] The historical facts did not change-non-white, non-upper class, non-manly persons had always been there; rather, it was a matter of posing the question, of deciding what to look for, and of acknowledging what was possible. And thus history changed, because of the efforts of recalcitrant Blacks, uppity women, stubborn Asian peasants, striking Latinos, rioting gays, and so forth.[934]

In short, when one tries to make the history of one's own generation, one not only reaches out to shake hands with those from the past and those in the future. One also enjoys the potential of inducing the review, revision, and rewriting of history.[935] Even lawyers can sometimes do this, but they may wish to pay attention to history (and yes, biology) to ensure that their impact on history has the greatest efficacy. And they should remind themselves and everyone else that if they get it wrong-or do nothing-they also risk having history rewritten in an even more dismal fashion. La lutte continue.

ALSO, BY STEVE BACHMANN

Beyond NOLA: New Orleans Reviews of Art
(with Terrington Calas, Unlimited Publishing LLC, 2002)

EXTREME PROUST
(Unlimited Publishing LLC, 2007)

Non-Profit Litigation
(John Wiley & Sons, 1992)

Preach Liberty
(Four Walls Eight Windows, 1990)

Simulating Sex: Aesthetic Representations of Erotic Activity
(Unlimited Publishing LLC, 2002)

Unbecoming Jane: Austen, Proust & Darwin (& Casanova & Stendhal)
(Harvardwood Publishing and Unlimited Publishing LLC, 2008)

U.S. Constitution for Beginners
(For Beginners LLC, distributed by Random House, expected 2012)

ABOUT THE BOOK

The first edition of *Lawyers, Law and Social Change* (Unlimited Publishing LLC, 2001) consisted of seven essays exploring the relationship that lawyers and law have to social change. Written over the course of the author's 25 years as General Counsel of the Ass'n of Community Organizations for Reform Now (ACORN), it discussed a number of topics, including attacks on the legal profession; living the life of the activist lawyer; the relevance (or lack of it) of law and lawyers to lasting social change; the efficacy of poverty law; the religious perspective; social change concerns; and recent developments in law and social change.

This expanded 2012 second edition adds a 60-page update published by the *NYU Review of Law and Social Change* in 2010, reprinted verbatim in its entirety for the benefit of a new generation of readers. Also added is a transcript of Bachmann's keynote address at the NYURLSC's 40th anniversary.

ABOUT THE AUTHOR

Since graduating from Harvard Law School in 1976, Steve Bachmann has represented a number of organizations working for social change, including neighborhood groups, labor unions, community radio stations, fair housing organizations, and anti-death penalty advocates. His practice has included litigating civil rights actions in federal and state courts nationwide. Bachmann is also the author of *U.S. Constitution for Beginners* (illustrated by Pulitzer prize winner Joel Pett) soon to be updated by For Beginners LLC and distributed by Random House. His other books include *Preach Liberty* (Four Walls Eight Windows) and *Nonprofit Litigation* (John Wiley & Sons) as well as four books of art and literary criticism published by Unlimited Publishing LLC.

ENDNOTES

[1] Karl Marx, CAPITAL, trans. Samuel Moore and Edward Aveling, (N.Y.,1967) ch. IX f.

[2] Ibid., Part VII.

[3] By alienation we mean the worker's loss of control over his/her product, and probably existentially more important, over his/her work situation. Alienation comprises a necessary adjunct to capitalism because in order to ensure that he gets the most of the labor time which he purchases from a worker, the capitalist must ensure that he have as much control over of the labor process as possible. This of course implies less control to the worker. Harry Braverman, LABOR AND MONOPOLY CAPITAL (N.Y.,1975) 57-8.

[4] Alienation in the workplace is cruel because of the degree to which it negates human values of competence, capacity, and self-determination. Alienation is subtle because there is a tendency for "experience in one sphere of life to generalize to all." For examples of degeneration in one's life experience outside the sphere of work (with the sphere of work so poisoned) see Sam Bowles and Herb Gintis, SCHOOLING IN CAPITALIST AMERICA (N.Y., 1976), 69 f.

[5] Braverman, LABOR, 258.

[6] Ibid., 60.

[7] Ibid., 53.

[8] Ibid., 254.

[9] Ibid., 378-81. As Braverman compiles these figures, he defines the working class to consist of individuals who possess nothing but their power to labor, and who sell the power to capital in return for subsistence. Concrete occupations which Braverman fits into this definition include operatives and laborers, craftsmen, clerical workers, service and sales workers, and "occupations not reported." Adding these together, Braverman reaches the percentages cited above.

[10] Ibid., in chapter 18 Braverman puts this figure at 15-20%.

[11] See Richard Parker, THE MYTH OF THE MIDDLE CLASS (N.Y., 1972).

[12] Braverman, LABOR, 241-2. Braverman's remarkable book constitutes one long documentation of this process which came into its own with Taylorism in the latter

part of the nineteenth century, when industrialized monopoly capitalism was just beginning to come into its own.

[13] To see how the historical roots of this view trace back to the seventeenth century (the century of Hobbes, Locke, and the emerging–if not erupting–bourgeoisie) see Macpherson, THE POLITICAL THEORY OF POSSESSIVE INDIVIDUALISM (Oxford, 1962), passim.

[14] Cf. Georg Lukacs, HISTORY AND CLASS CONSCIOUSNESS trans. R. Livingstone (Cambridge, MA. 1971), passim.

[15] E.g., T. Emerson, TOWARDS A GENERAL THEORY OF THE FIRST AMENDMENT (N.Y., 1966), 37, 84-5, 106 f., and T. Emerson, THE SYSTEM OF FREEDOM OF EXPRESSION (N.Y., 1970), 126; Note, "Private Attorneys General," 58 YALE.L.J. (1949).

[16] See NAACP v. Alabama, 357 US 449, 459 f (1958).

[17] A bourgeois is an individual who possesses material resources (i.e., "capital") to the degree that he can live off of them and not be compelled to sell his labor. The joy of his socio-economic life experience relates to the independence, autonomy and opportunities for personal freedom and self-expression which such a happy material state entails.

[18] Jerold Auerbach, UNEQUAL JUSTICE (1976) 41.

[19] A "proletarian" possesses inadequate material possessions to the degree that he must sell his/her labor in order to live. Proletarianization refers to the transformation of American workers from independent producers to dependent producers. The percentage of self-employed in the American population has declined from 4/5 in the early 19th century to 1/3 in 1870 to 1/10 in 1970. Harry Braverman, LABOR AND MONOPOLY CAPITAL (1975) 254.

[20] I was unable to include this observation in 1976, but Thomas Frank has done an excellent job of documenting a parallel historical development: to the degree that American workers become less and less free at work, to that degree American culture defines freedom in terms of consumption outside the factories and offices of the workplace, and inside the stores and malls of the marketplace. Thomas Frank, THE CONQUEST OF COOL (1997); Thomas Frank, ONE MARKET UNDER GOD: EXTREME CAPITALISM, MARKET POPULISM, AND THE END OF ECONOMIC DEMOCRACY (2000).

[21] A petty bourgeois is an individual who is a bourgeois in that he possesses enough material resources so that he can live off them and not be compelled to sell his labor. He is "petty" in that his "capital" is small compared to that, say, of the industrial entrepreneur. The shopkeeper, and arguably the small independent

farmer might be cited as examples of the petty bourgeoisie. This petty bourgeois is to be distinguished from the "new middle class" which has emerged over the course of the last century. (These are "white collar workers" e.g. clerks, technocrats, lower level managers.) The latter are less "bourgeois" than the petty bourgeois in that they work for a wage and have less control over their work situations. By contrast, the petty bourgeois is a petite boss.

[22] This view of the lawyer's circumstance, though, must be qualified. See below.

[23] Karl Llewellyn, "The Bar's Troubles and Poultices–and Cures?" 5 LAW & CONTEMPORARY PROBLEMS, (1938) 104, 106.

[24] Hackin v. Arizona, 389 US 143 at 1590 (1967) (dissent) reh. denied, 389 US 1060.

[25] "The Canons, reflecting values appropriate to a small town, were easily adaptable to an equally homogenous upper-class metropolitan constituency, where they served as a club against lawyers whose clients were excluded from that culture: especially the urban poor, new immigrants, and blue-collar workers." Auerbach, JUSTICE 42.

[26] Ibid., 45-8.

[27] NAACP v. Button, 371 US 415 (1963); United Mineworkers v. Illinois Bar Association, 389 US 217 (1967); Brotherhood of Railway Trainmen ex rel. Virginia State Bar 377 US 1 (1964).

[28] George Bodle, "Group Legal Services–The Case for BRT," 12 UCLAL.REV. 306, 314-5 (1964).

[29] Philip Schuchman, "Ethics and Legal Ethics" 37 GEO.WASH.L.REV. 244, 260 (1968).

[30] Bodle, "Group Legal Services" 315.

[31] Sometimes, as one Chinese philosopher has observed, reactionaries lift a rock only to drop it on their own feet. In order to prove that its Canons were not directed only against the NAACP, the Virginia Bar relied heavily on the Association of American Railroads as it brought suit against the Virginia Brotherhood of Railway Trainworkers. However, the result was Brotherhood of Railway Trainmen ex rel. Virginia State Bar 377 US 1 (1964). Bodle, "Group Legal Services" 320.

[32] Peter Zimroth, "Group Legal Services and the Constitution," 76 YALE.L.J. 966, 968 (1967); see also Auerbach, JUSTICE 270f.

[33] Auerbach, JUSTICE, 50 f. Actually, Auerbach does not work to suggest that these lower-class Jews and Catholics automatically catered to a lower-class clientele. He emphasizes more the point that the American legal profession was a stratified profession; and that the WASPs were on top and used the Canons to stay there. Thus, though Auerbach's point may ultimately attenuate our suggestion that the

Canons were used to stifle potential lower-class lawyers, the point that the Canons still reflect an upper-class bias should be acknowledged.

[34] It is of interest to note that the lawyers attacking Kunstler had more concern for their precious ethics than they did due process. Auerbach, JUSTICE, 294. Due process, it would seem, is less important a value than repressing communists and Blacks. See ibid., 65 f.

[35] Ibid., 193-5.

[36] Hildebrand v. State Bar of California, 36 Cal.2d 504, 225 P.2d 508, 516 (1950) (Carter, dissent).

[37] Hildebrand, 225 P.2d at 521 (Traynor, dissent).

[38] 79 YALE.L.J. 1186n.

[39] Cf. Patrick Oster and Donald Doane, "Changes Coming in Law Practice," U.S. NEWS & WORLD REPORT, 9-22-1975, 30: "George Fee, a Chicago legal consultant, predicts that law firms will become larger in efforts to effect economies through operations on a larger scale. The solo practitioner, unable to keep up with the capital expenditures modernization will entail, is seen as likely to go the way of the blacksmith, surviving mainly in rural and remote areas."

[40] "...the rapid transformation of the U.S. economy is from entrepreneurial capitalism, in which the middle classes maintain the privilege of controlling their work lives, to a corporate capitalism in which white-collar labor is proletarianized and bureaucratized. This transformation leaves children from the relatively well-off families essentially de-classed–part of a new wave of workers integrated into the wage-labor system... The modern period involves another basic economic shift... the proletarianization of the once-independent nonmanual producers. The massive increase in employment in the corporate, state, and non-profit sectors of the economy has eclipsed the self-employed professional and the traditional, small-scale entrepreneurial enterprise–the historical niche of the independent producer. Thus, traditionally elite independent jobs–entrepreneurial, privileged white collar, professional, and technical occupations–are reduced to the condition of wage labor. No longer can professional and small-business people look confidently to a future of controlling their work processes, finding creative outlets in work, or holding decision making power. Some, experiencing a loss in objective power and status, then to become radicalized. They seek to regain the lost ideal of independent and personal control in some sphere of life. Much of the student movement and youth culture has embraced a kind of retrospective radicalism vaunting the ideals of spontaneity and unfettered personal independence. Some young professional, too, have elevated work autonomy and life-style individualism to a commanding position among their personal and social objectives. These ideals may be traced to

the aspirations of the property-owning class in the epoch of petty capitalism. In the corporate era, they constitute an anachronism–granted an inspiring and evocative one–unless altered in ways compatible with the political needs for a radical transformation of the U.S. economic and social structure. Sam Bowles and Herb Gintis, SCHOOLING, 215, 253.

[41] A. KINOY, RIGHTS ON TRIAL: THE ODYSSEY OF A PEOPLE'S LAWYER (1983) [hereinafter cited by page number only].

[42] 380 U.S. 479 (1965).

[43] L. NIZER, MY LIFE IN COURT (1964).

[44] F. BAILEY, THE DEFENSE NEVER RESTS (1971).

[45] The book's jacket suggests that Kinoy provides such insights: "Through all these cases, Kinoy has fashioned revolutionary new approaches to the theory and practice of people's law."

[46] CHAIRMAN MAO TALKS TO THE PEOPLE: TALKS AND LETTERS 1956-1971, at 235 (S. Schram ed. 1974).

[47] P. 233.

[48] 339 F.2d 989 (5th Cir., 1964).

[49] P. 253.

[50] P. 300.

[51] *See, e.g.*, p. 146 (describing the changing public opinion of the HUAC); p. 150 (stating that there is no real hope of change without a massive people's movement); p. 326 (legal battles to enforce freedom and equality have potential for victory only when intertwined with daily efforts of large numbers of people).

[52] 301 U.S. 1 (1937).

[53] In February 1937 C.I.O. organizing had forced settlements from GM, Chrysler, General Electric, and U.S. Steel. The managers of the nation's leading industries had accepted the principle of collective bargaining without waiting for the Supreme Court's ratification. *See* Klare, *Judicial Deradicalization of the Wagner Act and the Origins of Modern Legal Consciousness, 1937-1941,* 62 MINN.L.REV. 265, 266n.7 (1978).

[54] 347 U.S. 483 (1954).

[55] Immediately after *Brown*, hundreds of school districts were integrated. But for many years, the civil rights movement involved primarily students and middle-class Blacks. *See* J. HANDLER, SOCIAL MOVEMENTS AND THE LEGAL SYSTEM 109 (1978). The Eisenhower administration helped to integrate only 49 school districts from 1958 to 1960. *See* R. KLUGER, SIMPLE JUSTICE 754 (1976). Even Montgomery, Alabama lapsed into segregation after the boycott of

1956, and the Blacks returned to sit in the back of the bus. *See* J. HANDLER, *supra,* at 108. The turning point seems to have been the 1962 demonstrations in Albany, Georgia, when civil rights leaders learned to appreciate the effectiveness of mass action. *See* F. PIVEN & R. CLOWARD, POOR PEOPLE'S MOVEMENTS 236 (1977). The results of mass mobilization were dramatic: the proposal of the new Civil Rights Act in 1963; the Freedom Summer in Mississippi; the passage of the new Civil Rights Act; and the twenty-fourth amendment to the Constitution in 1964; and the Selma march and the passage of the Voting Rights Act in 1965; *see also infra* note 53 (discussing other forces that aided mass action).

[56] J. HANDLER, *supra* note 15, at 232-33.

[57] *See id.* At 26-27.

[58] *See id.* At 232-233.

[59] *See* Morehead v. New York 298 U.S. 587 (1936); Coppage v. Kansas, 236 U.S. 1 (1915); Lochner v. New York, 198 U.S. 45 (1905); Plessy v. Ferguson, 163 U.S. 537 (1896); Callan v. Wilson, 327 U.S. 540 (1888); Dred Scott v. Sandford, 60 U.S. (19 How.) 393 (1856). *Brown* reminds us that when courts act to support progressive movements, social reality does not always mirror legal doctrine. *See supra* Note 15.

[60] E. P. THOMPSON, WHIGS AND HUNTERS: THE ORIGINS OF THE BLACK ACT 264-66 (1975).

[61] T. Emerson, quoted on the dust jacket of A. KINOY, *supra* note 1.

[62] Dombrowski v. Pfister, 380 U.S. 479 (1965). *Dombrowski* transformed American federalism by broadening the circumstances under which a federal court might enjoin the proceedings of a state court. *See* 380 U.S. at 489-90; p. 227.

[63] *See* pp. 190-91.

[64] P. 114 (discussing the national campaign against the NLRB by the United Electrical, Radio, and Machine Workers of America); *see also* p. 227 (discussing the importance of victory in light of *Dombrowski*).

[65] *See* p. 252.

[66] *See* p. 70 (recalling distribution to United Electrical Workers of the complaint in the suit against members of the House Education and Labor Committee and several Evanston companies).

[67] *See* pp. 252-54 (preparation for a hearing on the conspiracy of Sheriff Rainey and Deputy Sheriff Price).

[68] *See* p. 56.

[69] P. 71.

[70] P. 225.

[71] P. 228.

[72] P 166.

[73] P 144.

[74] *See, e.g.,* pp. 143, 173, 203, 278.

[75] *See* p. 166 (arguing against the doctrine that failure to object to exclusion of blacks from juries waived the issue); *Dombrowski,* 380 U.S. at 483-87 (broadening federal court ability to enjoin state court).

[76] *See* pp. 99-100.

[77] P. 145.

[78] *See* E. P. Thompson, *supra* note 20, at 264-66.

[79] P.114.

[80] *See* pp. 289-90.

[81] *See* Weiler, *Promises to Keep: Securing Workers' Rights to Self-Organization Under the NLRA,* 96 HARV.L.REV. 1769 (1983).

[82] 60 U.S. (19 How.) 393 (1856).

[83] 163 U.S. 537 (1896).

[84] When appeal to principle does not bear fruit, resort must sometimes be had to intricate legal argument. During the early phases of Kinoy's career, a number of substantive rights were "saved" on "technical" grounds. *See, e.g.,* Christoffel v. United States, 338 U.S. 84 (1948) (reversing jury charge about definition of "competent tribunal" in perjury statute).

[85] P. 146.

[86] P 147.

[87] "I believe no student of labor history is likely to quarrel with the judgment of Philip Taft and Philip Ross: 'The United States has had the bloodiest and most violent labor history of any industrial nation in the world.' Taft and Ross have identified over 160 instances in which state and federal troops have intervened in labor disputes, and have recorded over 700 deaths and several thousands of serious injuries in labor disputes, but one can only underline their warning that this incomplete tally 'grossly understates the casualties.' ... With a minimum of ideologically motivated class conflict, the United States has somehow had a maximum of industrial violence. And no doubt the answer to this must be sought more in the ethos of American capitalists than in that of the workers." Hofstadter, Reflections on Violence in the United States, in AMERICAN VIOLENCE 19-20 (R. Hofstadter & M. Wallace eds. 1970) (quoting Taft & Ross, American Labor Violence: Its Causes, Character, and Outcome, in VIOLENCE IN AMERICA:

HISTORICAL AND COMPARATIVE PERSPECTIVES 270, 380 (H. Graham & T. Gurr eds. 1969).

[88] The rise of mass industry enhanced the American working class' ability to organize and thus increase its power. *See* F. PIVEN & R. CLOWARD, *supra* note 15, at 96-180.

[89] The Depression is the most obvious example of such dislocation.

[90] The importance of aggressive labor militancy is illustrated by the events that immediately followed the Depression:

> [D]etermined unionists in the unorganized industries recognized that they would win bargaining rights not by invoking the law but by showing their own strength. The automobile settlement was to be a major cause of the great wave of strikes that engulfed the nation in the spring and summer of 1934.
>
> ...
>
> In 1934 labor erupted. There were 1856 work stoppages involving 1,470,000 workers, by far the highest count in both categories in many years. A number of these strikes were of unusual importance ... Four were social upheavals–those of auto parts workers at the Electric Auto-Lite Company in Toledo, of truck drivers in Minneapolis, of longshoremen and then virtually the whole labor movement on the shores of San Francisco Bay, and of cotton-textile workers in New England and the South. I. BERNSTEIN, TURBULENT YEARS 185, 217 (1969).

[91] *See supra* note 13 and accompanying text.

[92] Blacks had petitioned the courts for vindication of their rights a hundred years before *Brown v. Board of Education. Dred Scott* was decided in 1856. Eleven years later, Marx published *Capital,* but balked at labeling the United States a capitalist nation. 2 K. MARX, CAPITAL 790-800 (S. Moore & E. Aveling trans. 1967).

[93] President Kennedy knew that Blacks could claim credit for his election. Theodore White writes that when Kennedy called Mrs. Martin Luther King after her husband was arrested in Georgia:

The entire episode received only casual notice from the generality of American citizens in the heat of the last three weeks of the Presidential campaign. But in the Negro community the Kennedy intervention rang like a carillon. The father of Martin Luther King, a Baptist minister himself who had come out for Nixon a few weeks earlier on religious grounds, now switched. "Because this man," said the Reverend Mr. King, Senior, "was willing to wipe the tears from my daughter[-in-law]'s eyes, I've got a suitcase of votes, and I'm going to take them to Mr. Kennedy and dump them in his lap" Across the country scores of Negro leaders, deeply

Protestant but even more deeply impressed by Kennedy's action, followed suit. And where command decision had been made, the Kennedy organization could by now follow through. Under Wofford's direction a million pamphlets were distributed outside Negro churches all across the country. One cannot identify in the narrowness of American voting of 1960 any one particular episode or decision as being more important than any other in the final tallies: yet when one refl ects that Illinois was carried only by 9,000 votes and that 250,000 Negroes are estimated to have voted for Kennedy; that Michigan was carried by 67,000 votes and that an estimated 250,000 Negroes voted for Kennedy; that South Carolina was carried by 10,000 votes and that an estimated 40,000 Negroes there voted for Kennedy, the candidate's instinctive decision must be ranked among the most crucial of the last few weeks.

T. WHITE, THE MAKING OF THE PRESIDENT 1960, at 323 (1961). Arthur Schlesinger, Jr., noted the practical effects of Kennedy's civil rights policies in the international sphere:

President Kennedy's action [concerning James Meredith] had a profound effect around the world, most of all in Africa. As the delegate from Upper Volta put it in the UN General Assembly, segregation unquestionably existed in the United States, but "what is important is that the Government of the United States did not make an institution of this. It does not praise the policy. On the contrary, it energetically fights it. For one small Negro to go to school, it threatens governors and judges with prison ... it sends troops to occupy the University of Mississippi." Three weeks after Oxford, Se'kou Toure and Ben Bella were prepared to deny refueling facilities to Soviet planes bound for Cuba during the missile crisis.

A. SCHLESINGER, JR., A THOUSAND DAYS 948 (1965); see also supra note 15 (discussing mass black mobilization); See generally F. PIVEN & R. CLOWARD supra note 15, at 181-258 (detailing how shifts in socioeconomic tides provide the foundation for black defiance and eventual release from white oppression); Bachmann, Lawyers, Law and Social Change, 13 N.Y.U. REV.L.&.SOC.CHANGE 1 (1984).

[94] B. BRECHT, THE THREE PENNY OPERA, 66-67 (E. Bentley trans.1960)

[95] *See* pp. 74-75 (burden on Kinoy's family); p. 161 (Kinoy's illness and its effects on his family); p. 318 (end of Kinoy's marriage).

[96] P. 264.

[97] P 264.

[98] *See* p. 265.

[99] Some courts have acknowledged the chilling effect of governmental intrusion

into an organization's internal finances. *See, e.g.,* Buckley v. Valeo, 424 U.S. 1, 66 (1975)(invalidating portions of the Federal Election Act of 1974, but upholding financial disclosure provisions because they serve substantial governmental interests); California Bankers Ass'n v. Shultz, 416 U.S. 21, 78-79 (1974)(Powell, J. concurring)(upholding bank recordkeeping and reporting regulations, but stating that some broad language of the Bank Secrecy Act would intrude into individuals' privacy expectations); Ealy v. Littlejohn, 569 F.2d 219, 229 (5th Cir. 1978)(preventing a grand jury from delving into the financing activities, or membership of black citizens' organization); Bursey v. United States, 466 F.2d 1059, 1088 (9th Cir. 1972)(overturning criminal contempt against two immunized witnesses who refused to answer questions concerning the financing of Black Panther overseas travel); Pollard v. Roberts, 238 F. Supp. 248, 256-57 (E.D.Ark.) (quashing a subpoena for the names of individual contributors to the Arkansas Republican Party), *aff'd per curium,* 393 U.S. 14 (1968); NAACP v. Committee on Offenses Against the Administration of Justice, 133 S.E.2d 540, 544 (Va.,1963) (quashing a legislative committee's interrogatories requesting the names of contributors to the NAACP).

[100] G. SINGER, HOW TO GO DIRECTLY INTO SOLO PRACTICE WITHOUT MISSING A MEAL (1976).

[101] J. MOLLOY, DRESS FOR SUCCESS (1975).

[102] M. ALTMAN & R. WEIL, HOW TO MANAGE YOUR LAW OFFICE (1982).

[103] J. FOONBERG, HOW TO START AND BUILD A LAW PRACTICE (1976).

[104] J. FLANAGAN, THE GRASSROOTS FUNDRAISING BOOK. (1977).

[105] E.P. THOMPSON, THE POVERTY OF THEORY AND OTHER ESSAYS 42 (1978) (emphasis in the original).

[106] *See* p. 28.

[107] *See* p. 199.

[108] *See* p. 215-16.

[109] P. 26.

[110] P. 22.

[111] P. 122.

[112] P. 123.

[113] *See* p. 231.

[114] P 238.

[115] *See* p. 245.

[116] P. 193.

[117] P. 299.

[118] Pp. 222-23.

[119] Chapter One contains 38 pages, and Rehnquist's name appears on pages 9, 12, 13, 14, 18, 20, 27, 33, 34, and 38.

[120] *See* pp. 12-13.

[121] 407 U.S. 297 (1972) (rejecting the inherent power theory).

[122] P. 37 (emphasis in original). As Kinoy points out, some "queer" aspects of the Watergate break-in and its official explanation are cleared up by this interpretation:

> …There are puzzling, unresolved questions about the Saturday break-in. For example, why did it occur at all? The bugs and microphones had been installed successfully on May 28. On June 16 the break-in team … had been recalled from Miami … to Washington … Why did they go back into the Democratic National Committee office at the Watergate the next morning? The only explanation ever publicly offered has been that one of the bugs was faulty. But why did five men have to go in to make a repair that could have been done by one? Further, why was this risky adventure carried out at all in light of the known imminence of the Supreme Court decision which would affect so intimately the planned legal cover for the covert operation? Even to the police on the scene the whole affair was strange. One officer in charge of the initial investigation told a reporter that the operation was "bungled too badly" and there seemed to be "three or four more" people there than the operation called for. And finally, why, when the men were arrested on the scene, were they found with all the electronic equipment removed from the ceiling and in their hands, instead of just the one tape that was allegedly not working? P. 36 (emphasis in the original)

[123] P. 38.

[124] *See* p. 37.

[125] P. 12.

[126] *See, e.g.,* J. GOULDEN, THE MILLION DOLLAR LAWYERS 191-240 (1978).

[127] *See* R. KLUGER, *supra* note 15, at 605.

[128] P. 14.

[129] *See* p. 44. For the Communists' perspective on Huey Long, see T. WILLIAMS, HUEY LONG 760 (1969).

[130] Fortunately, some historians have begun to probe the complexity of Long's

personality. *See* A. BRINKLEY, VOICES OF PROTEST (1982); T. WILLIAMS, *supra* note 89.

[131] *See, e.g.,* W. HAIR, BOURBONISM AND AGRARIAN PROTEST (1969); L. GOODWYN, DEMOCRATIC PROMISE (1976); L. GOODWIN, THE POPULIST MOMENT (1978); R. SHUGG, ORIGINS OF CLASS STRUGGLE IN LOUISIANA (1968); T. WILLIAMS, *supra* note 89.

[132] For example, there is no record that Huey Long had black women whipped with barbed wire. *See* W. HAIR, *supra* note 91, at 261.

[133] For discussions concerning the Left and its powerlessness, see P. CLECAK, CROOKED PATHS (1977); P. CLECAK, RADICAL PARADOXES (1973).

[134] *See, e.g.,* R. CONQUEST, THE GREAT TERROR (1968).

[135] *See* T. WILLIAMS, *supra* note 89, at 798.

[136] *See supra* notes 36-37 and accompanying text.

[137] W. SHAKESPEARE, KING LEAR, act 5 scene 3.

[138] K. MARX & F. ENGELS: BASIC WRITINGS ON POLITICS AND PHILOSOPHY 245 (L. Feuer ed. 1959).

[139] W. SHAKESPEARE, *supra* note 97, act 4, scene 1.

[140] T. Adorno, Negative Dialectics 366-67 (E.B. Ashton trans. 1973).

[141] See, e.g., Kennedy, Legal Education and Training for Hierarchy, and Rabinowitz, The Radical Tradition in Law, in The Politics of Law (D. Kairys ed. 1982); and Gabel & Harris, Building Power and Breaking Images, 11 N.Y.U. Rev. L. & Soc. Change 369 (1983).

[142] F. Dallmayr, Twilight of Subjectivity 142 (1981).

[143] Cf. G. Lukacs, History and Class Consciousness (R. Livingstone trans. 1971). Cf. also the method acknowledged, described, and affirmed by Roberto Unger in The Critical Legal Studies Movement, 96 Harv. L. Rev. 561 (1983). For a critique of the latter, see Hutchinson & Monahan, The "Rights" Stuff: Roberto Unger and Beyond, 62 Tex. L. Rev. 1477 (1984).

[144] This is possibly the most underappreciated term of the lot. It is cited in accord with the perception of populism as described by Lawrence Goodwyn, in Democratic Promise (1976), and The Populist Moment (1978).

[145] "Individuality" is also a loaded term, given its potential for abuse by the Right. I understand it to involve a ratification of personhood, to be achieved through social experience. See L. Goodwyn, The Populist Moment, supra note 5, at 295-6: "the Populists believed they could work together to be free individually. In their institutions of self-help, Populists developed and acted upon a crucial democratic

insight: to be encouraged to surmount rigid cultural inheritances and to act with autonomy and self-confidence, individual people need the psychological support of other people. The people need to 'see themselves' experimenting in new democratic forms." See also Unger, supra note 4 at 584; C. Lasch, The Minimal Self 32 (1984).

[146] For various explications of "community" see, e.g., F. Dallmayr, supra note 3, at 140-42, and Unger, supra note 4, at 597.

[147] See, e.g., Unger, supra note 4, at 586.

[148] There are Left theoreticians who emphasize the need to cultivate utopian thought. See, e.g., F. Jameson, The Political Unconscious 285 (1981). Most useful is "a basic premise in Merleau-Ponty's political philosophy–that politics is an order of the real world and therefore that any theory that claims to be political philosophy must also provide for its own realization." J. Bien, in M. Merleau-Ponty, Adventures of the Dialectic xi (Bien trans. 1973). See also P. Clecak, Radical Paradoxes 27 (1973); and Bachmann & Weltchek, Book Review, 30 UCLA L. Rev. 1078, 1081, 1091 (1983).

[149] The perspective of this piece and Dallmayr's point might be better appreciated if it is noted that Dallmayr is counterposing communitarian relations to three other types: that of "communalism" (*"gemeinshaft,"* with its emphasis on organic and quasinatural factors such as kinship, heredity, and ascribed status); that of "association" (reminiscent of the classical liberal view of the world, with its stress on volition and a sphere of pre-social autonomy); and that of "movement" which calls to mind Jean-Paul Sartre's "fused group," which "is defined by its undertaking and by the constant movement of integration which tends to turn into pure praxis while trying to eliminate all forms of inertia from it." See F. Dallmayr, supra note 3, at 140-42. The final quotation is his citation from Sartre. For more on Sartre's notion of the fused group, see his Critique of Dialectical Reason (1976); see also M. Poster, Existential Marxism in Postwar France: From Sartre to Althusser chap. 7 (1975).

[150] The rhetoric derives from Unger, supra note 4, at 588, 666.

[151] See L. Goodwyn, The Populist Moment, supra note 5, at 291. Cf. the debates between Luxemburg and Lenin. N. Lenin, What Is To Be Done (1952); R. Luxemburg, Selected Political Writings (D. Howard ed. 1971).

[152] For some, the existence of lawyers constitutes an expression of alienated social relationships. See, e.g., M. Foucault, Power/Knowledge: Selected Interviews and Other Writings (C. Gordon ed. 1980); Cf. Gabel & Kennedy, Roll Over Beethoven, 36 Stan. L. Rev. 1 (1984). For others, lawyers can be seen as playing a useful role as the society attempts to live up to its sense of justice, See Rabinowitz, supra note 2,

and E.P. Thompson, Whigs and Hunters, The Origin of the Black Act 258-68 (1975). While the existence of law and lawyers might entail its own problematic momentum, my own view is dialectical: systems involving statutes and a legal profession involve their positive and negative aspects. Ultimately their impact—and our evaluation—will depend more on what we see being practiced by living human beings.

[153] Unger, supra note 4, at 667.

[154] This approach can be explained from at least two perspectives: (1) philosophical humility, see T. Adorno, supra note 1, at 5 and M. Merleau-Ponty, Humanism and Terror xxxviii (O'Neill trans. 1969); and (2) historical expediency. When ACORN was founded in 1970, the New Left was dissolving through ideological fragmentation and intolerance. By narrowing the requirements for ideological unity, ACORN formed an operating entity which has lasted almost fifteen years.

[155] Kest & Rathke, ACORN: An Overview of Its History, Structure, Methodology, Campaigns and Philosophy, in Community Organizing Handbook #2, 2 (1978). See also The ACORN People's Platform, e.g.:

> Our riches shall be the blooming of our communities, the bounty of a sure livelihood, the beauty of homes for our families with sickness driven from the door, the benefit of our taxes, not their burden; and the best of our energy, land and natural resources for all people.

> Our freedom shall be based on the equality of the many, not the income of the few. Our freedom is the force of democracy, not the farce of federal fat and personal profit. In our freedom, only the people shall rule.

> Corporations shall have their role: producing jobs, providing products, paying taxes. No more. No less. They shall obey our wishes, respond to our needs, serve our communities. Our country shall be the citizens' wealth and our wealth shall build our country.

> Government shall have its role: public servant to our good, fast follower to our sure steps. No more. No less. Our government shall shout with a public voice, and no longer jump to a private whisper. in our government, the common concerns shall be the collective cause. ACORN MEMBERS HANDBOOK (1983) at 16-17. (The People's Platform was adopted at a national ACORN convention in 1979 by approximately 2000 delegates from across the country.)

[156] The more ambitious may attribute additional labels.

[157] See, e.g., the genesis of Goldberg v. Kelly, 397 U.S. 254 (1970), as discussed in Sparer, Fundamental Human Rights, Legal Entitlements, and the Social Struggle: A

Friendly Critique of the Critical Legal Studies Movement, 36 Stan. L. Rev. 509, 562 (1984).

[158] The tactic of publishing hit lists in newspapers is not new. See W. Hair, Bourbonism and Agrarian Protest 259 (1969).

[159] See note 16 supra.

[160] T. Adorno, supra note 1, at 5.

[161] Like a number of the terms already cited, "dialectical materialism" is one that has suffered much abuse, and has come to mean a number of things to a number of people. For the purposes of this paper it will refer to the approaches embraced by philosophers like Adorno, Marcuse, Horkheimer, Enzensberger, and Merleau-Ponty, who trace their lineages back to Marx and Hegel. See, e.g., M. Merleau-Ponty, supra note 9; Adorno, supra note 1; Marcuse, Reason and Revolution (1941); M. Horkheimer, Eclipse of Reason (1974); H. Enzensberger, Critical Essays (1982).

[162] "Paradigm" alludes to T. Kuhn, The Structure of Scientific Revolutions 10-22 (1970), where it is presented as a mode of approaching, interpreting, and changing reality. A paradigm holds "valid" for as long as it seems to interpret reality productively. The point here is to distinguish dialectical materialism from a dogma which asserts its enduring effectuality.

[163] The role that biology plays in thought is an unresolved issue for dialectical materialists. See, e.g., A. Arato & E. Gebhart, The Essential Frankfurt School Reader 477-96 (1978); H. Marcuse, Eros and Civilization (1955); cf. T. Adorno, supra note 1, at 289 (reason's "prehistory" in "self-preservation").

[164] See F. Dallmayr, supra note 3.

[165] See, e.g., M. Konner, The Tangled Wing (1982); N. Chomsky, For Reasons of State (1973); and K. Marx, Capital 592 (S. Moore and E. Aveling trans. 1967): " . . . a higher form of society, a society in which the full and free development of every individual forms the ruling principle."

[166] See T. Adorno, supra note 1, at 276.

[167] Cf. R. Unger, Knowledge and Politics 123 (1975) (alternate ways of conceiving social action).

[168] "Economic conditions had first transformed the mass of the people of the country into workers. The domination of capital has created for this mass a common situation, common interests. This mass is thus already a class as against capital, but not yet for itself." Class, Status, and Power Social Stratification in Comparative Perspective 9 (R. Bendix and S. Lipset eds. 1966), quoting K. Marx, The Poverty of Philosophy 145-46 (1963).

[169] From the Communist Manifesto: "This organization of the proletarians into class, and consequently into a political party." K. Marx & F. Engels, Basic Writings 16 (D. Feuer ed. 1959).

[170] The following remarks from The Eighteenth Brumaire of Louis Bonaparte afford a sense of Marx's criteria for determining the stage of a class's development:

> The small-holding peasants [of France] form a vast mass, the members of which live in similar conditions but without entering into manifold relations with one another. Their mode of production isolates them from one another instead of bringing them into mutual intercourse. The isolation is increased by France's bad means of communication and by the poverty of the peasants. Their field of production, the small holding, admits of no division of labor in its cultivation, no application of science, and therefore, no diversity of development, no variety of talent, no wealth of social relationships. Each individual peasant family is almost self-sufficient; it itself directly produces the major part of its consumption, and thus acquires its means of life more through exchange with nature than in intercourse with society. A small holding, a peasant and his family; alongside them another small holding, another peasant and another family. A few score of these make up a village, and a few score of villages make up a Department. In this way the great mass of the French nation is formed by simple addition of homologous magnitudes, much as potatoes in a sack form a sack of potatoes. In so far as millions of families live under economic conditions of existence that separate their mode of life, their interests, and their culture from those of the other classes and put them in hostile opposition to the latter, they form a class. In so far as there is merely a local interconnection among these small-holding peasants and the identity of their interests begets no community, no national bond, and no political organizations among them, they do not form a class.

Id. at 338-39.

[171] N. Lenin, supra note 12.

[172] R. Luxemburg, supra note 12.

[173] See generally Chairman Mao Talks to the People (S. Schram ed. 1974).

[174] See note 10 supra.

[175] M. Foucault, supra note 13, at 24-25.

[176] R. Hofstadter & M. Wallace, American Violence 19-20 (1970).

[177] I. Bernstein, The Lean Years ch. 4 (1960).

[178] "When [in 1894]...the newspapers reported that federal troops had killed thirty

Pullman strikers, [Taft] wrote cheerfully, 'Everybody hopes that it is true.'" Id. at 190.

[179] Id. at 191.

[180] In his acclaimed book on Lyndon Johnson's early years, Robert Caro has evoked a sense of the nation in 1932-33:

> That was a winter of despair. When, on December 5, 1932, the lame-duck Congress reconvened, those of its members who had hoped that the tear-gassing of the veterans had frightened the jobless away from Washington received a surprise; crowded around the Capitol steps were more than 2,500 men, women and children chanting, "Feed the hungry! Tax the rich!" Police armed with tear gas and riot guns herded the "hunger marchers" into a "detention camp" on New York Avenue, where, denied food or water, they spent a freezing night sleeping on the pavement, taunted by their guards. Thereafter, Congress met behind a double line of rifle-carrying police, who blocked the Capitol steps...

> As the people saw that their government was going to give them no leadership, there began to be heard throughout America the sound of hungry men on the march. In Columbus, Ohio, 7,000 men in ranks tramped toward the Statehouse to "establish a workers' and farmers' republic." Four thousand men occupied the Lincoln, Nebraska, Statehouse; 5,000 took over the municipal building in Seattle; in Chicago, thousands of unpaid teachers stormed the city's banks. A Communist Party rally in New York's Union Square drew an audience of 35,000.

> ...In Iowa, a mob of farmers, flourishing a rope, threatened to hang a lawyer who was about to foreclose on a farm. In Kansas, the body of a lawyer who had just completed foreclosure proceedings was found lying in a field. In Nebraska, the leaders of 200,000 debt-ridden farmers announced that if they didn't get help from the Legislature, they would march on the Statehouse and raze it brick by brick. A judge who had signed mortgage foreclosures was dragged from his bench by black-shirted vigilantes, blindfolded, driven to a lonely crossroads, stripped and beaten. And in scores of county seats in America's farm belt, the same scene was repeated; when a foreclosed farm was to be auctioned, crowds of armed farmers would appear at the courthouse; prospective bidders would be jostled and shoved until they left...

R. Caro, Lyndon Johnson, The Path to Power 248-49 (1982).

[181] Section 7(a) read as follows:

> Every code of fair competition, agreement, and license approved,

prescribed, or issued under this title shall contain the following conditions: (1) That employees shall have the right to organize and bargain collectively through representatives of their own choosing, and shall be free from the interference, restraint, or coercion of employers of labor, or their agents, in the designation of such representatives or in self-organization or in other concerted activities for the purpose of collective bargaining or other mutual aid or protection; (2) that no employee and no one seeking employment shall be required as a condition of employment to join any company union or to refrain from joining, organizing, or assisting a labor organization of his own choosing; and (3) that all employers shall comply with the maximum hours of labor, minimum rates of pay, and other conditions of employment, approved or prescribed by the President. I. Bernstein, The Turbulent Years 34 (1979).

[182] Id. at 35.

[183] J. Handler, Social Movements and The Legal System 223 (1978), quoting P. Schmitter, Still the Century of Corporatism, Rev. Pol. 85, 112 (1974), the following definition of corporatism: "Corporatism can be defined as a system of interest representation in which the constituent units are organized into a limited number of singular, compulsory, non-competitive, hierarchically ordered and functionally differentiated categories, recognized or licensed (if not created) by the state and granted a deliberate representational monopoly within their respective categories in exchange for observing certain controls on their selection of leaders and articulation of demands and supports." The system that Roosevelt would have established through the NIRA approximated this definition rather closely. Schechter Poultry v. United States, 295 U.S. 495 (1935) prohibited the de jure establishment of corporatism, but it is not unproductive to view the United States as a de facto corporate order. Cf. W. Douglas, Go East Young Man 347 (1974) (characterizing the NIRA as a "structural change" towards "the corporate state").

[184] I. Bernstein, supra note 42, at 34.

[185] G. Kolko, Main Currents in Modern American History 125 (1984).

[186] I. Bernstein, supra note 42, at 39. See also Klare, Judicial Deradicalization of the Wagner Act and the Origins of Modern Legal Consciousness, 1937-1941, 62 Minn. L. Rev. 265, 287n.68 (1978).

[187] I. Bernstein, supra note 42 at 177, 322.

[188] ... Within two months, UMW membership jumped from 60,000 to 300,000, and paid-up memberships reached 528,685 in July 1934; the International Ladies Garment Workers Union quadrupled its membership, reaching 200,000 in 1934; the Amalgamated Clothing Workers, which had reported 7,000 dues-paying

members at its low in 1932, added 125,000 new members. And the Oil Field, Gas Well and Refinery Workers Union, which in 1933 claimed only 300 members in an industry employing 275,000, established 125 new locals by May 1934.

In non-unionized industries "there was a virtual uprising of workers for union membership," the executive council of the AFL reported to its 1934 convention; "workers held mass meetings and sent word they wanted to be organized." The result was that almost two hundred local unions with 100,000 members sprang up in the automobile industry; about 70,000 joined unions in the Akron rubber plants; about 300,000 textile workers joined the United Textile Workers of America; and an estimated 50,000 clamored to join the steel union.

F. Piven & R. Cloward, Poor People's Movements 114 (1977). The extent to which my argument follows those advanced by Piven & Cloward should be acknowledged. I will elaborate on our differences below, which concur with the criticism articulated by J. Handler, supra note 44, at 232 n.71: "They never deal explicitly with the problem of translating gains derived from direct action into long-term gains."

[189] I. Bernstein, supra note 42, at 172-73.

[190] Id. at 184-85.

[191] Id. at 185, 217.

[192] F. Piven & R. Cloward, supra note 49, at 126, citing E. Levinson, Labor on the March (1938).

[193] Schechter Poultry Corp. v. United States, 295 U.S. 495 (1935).

[194] NLRB v. Jones & Laughlin Steel Corp., 301 U.S. 1 (1937).

[195] Klare, supra note 47, at 226 n.7.

[196] I. Bernstein, supra note 42, at 541.

[197] Id. at 640-41.

[198] West Coast Hotel Co. v. Parish, 300 U.S. 379 (1937). This case reversed Adkins v. Children's Hospital, 261 U.S. 525 (1923), which disallowed state establishment of minimum wage laws. Only a year before, the Supreme Court had invalidated another minimum wage law in Morehead v. New York ex rel. Tipaldo, 298 U.S. 587 (1936). Justice Roberts voted to invalidate the minimum wage law in *Morehead,* and "swung" in *West Coast Hotel.* W. Douglas, supra note 44, at 324-26.

[199] W. Douglas, supra note 44, at 324-26.

[200] It should be acknowledged that the Supreme Court decision did appear to affect the rubber industry, 1. Bernstein, supra note 42, at 600.

[201] A. Mason, The Supreme Court, From Taft to Burger 122 (1979).

[202] As to the Memorial Day Massacre, David Milton in The Politics of U.S. Labor 108 (1982) writes:

On May 30 the Steel Workers Organizing Committee (SWOC) called a mass meeting to protest police restrictions on picketing. Some 2,500 strikers and their supporters, including women and children, assembled to listen to speeches by strike leaders in front of the strike headquarters, a few blocks from the Republic mill…At the end of the meeting, the crowd marched behind U.S. flags up to the gates of the plant in an attempt to form a mass picket line. The rest of the story has been recorded in history texts, on newsreel film, at Senate hearings, and in fiction. The Chicago police fired point-blank into the crowd, continued firing at the backs of those who fled, beat the wounded who had fallen, dragged those who were shot to waiting police vans, and refused first aid to the victims. As the LaFollette Committee, after the investigation of the Memorial Day massacre, commented, "Wounded prisoners of war might have expected and received greater solicitude." Despite national outrage, the police were never prosecuted and Republic Steel continued strikebreaking.

[203] NLRB v. Fansteel Metallurgical Corp., 306 U.S. 240 (1939). Of this decision Klare, supra note 47, at 324 writes:

The best that can be said for Hughes' decision is that it blatantly ignored historical and social reality. The Court ignored the fact that the sit-down strikes were essentially a reaction to the widespread and often violent refusal by employers to obey the law between 1935 and 1940. The historical record is clear that the sit-down strikes were an indispensable weapon with which workers stemmed the tide of employer resistance to unions and to the law; inferentially, they thereby helped create the political conditions for the court's leftward shift in West Coast Hotel Co. v. Parrish and NLRB v. Jones & Laughlin Steel Corp. Sit-down strikes contributed rather than detracted from whatever law and order existed in industrial life when Hughes delivered Fansteel. Moreover, in sharp contrast to contemporary but traditionally conducted strikes, the sit-downs in 1936-1938 caused no deaths and little property damage.

[204] See, e.g., D. Guerin, 100 Years of Labor in the U.S.A. 162 (A. Adler trans. 1979).

[205] D. Milton, supra note 63, at 165.

[206] 29 U.S.C. 151.

[207] The point here is that industrialization brought large numbers of workers together, which allowed for mass organizing drives, and ultimately massive

agglomerations of worker power. In addition, the industrialization encouraged some captains of industry to prefer to deal with workers through large industrial unions. I. Bernstein, supra note 42, at 19. For a more dour view of union's stabilizing functions, see G. Kolko, supra note 46, at ch. 5.

[208] Joseph Lowry, quoted in H. Raines, My Soul is Rested 70 (1983).

[209] Brown v. Board of Education, 347 U.S. 483 (1954).

[210] The major exceptions to this initial trend were Little Steel and Ford Motor Company, which finally recognized unionization in 1938, and 1940, respectively. L Bernstein, supra note 42, at 727, 734-35.

[211] Another way to interpret the "victories" of labor and minorities is from the corporatist paradigm, see note 44 supra. That is, before their victories, labor and minorities were not even acknowledged as interest groups by the American system. Afterwards, they were allowed circumscribed participation in the American system, as long as they did not attempt to breach certain "conditions." Labor's conditions are set out in the National Labor Relations Act, 29 U.S.C. 151-68. The minorities' struggles are still being settled around issues of school desegregation, affirmative action, political power, etc. See A. Freeman, Anti-Discrimination Law: A Critical Review, in The Politics of Law (D. Kairys ed. 1982).

[212] During *Brown's* first four years, some 750 school districts underwent at least token desegregation. During the last three years of the Eisenhower administration, a total of 49 more school districts were desegregated. R. Kluger, Simple Justice 754 (1976). See also A. Lewis, Portrait of a Decade 119 (1964).

[213] J. Handler, supra note 44, at 108; Owen v. Browder, 352 U.S. 903 (1956) (per curiam).

[214] R. Bardolph, The Civil Rights Record 373 (1970); see also F. Wilhoit, The Politics of Massive Resistance (1973).

[215] II. Raines, supra note 69, at 109.

[216] F. Piven & R. Cloward, supra note 49, at 256.

[217] J. Handler, supra note 44, at 109.

[218] H. Raines, supra note 69, at 234-36; but see id. at 30.

[219] Id. at 234-37.

[220] As James Farmer aptly said, "It is clear that … the President intended to drop civil rights legislation from the agenda of urgent business in order to safeguard other parts of his legislative program. But he had not reckoned on Birmingham."

By June, however, Kennedy admitted to civil rights leaders privately "that the demonstrations in the streets had brought results, they had made the executive branch act faster and were now forcing Congress to entertain legislation which a few weeks ago would have had no chance." Mass protest had forced federal action. It was a point the attorney general also conceded: "The Administration's Civil Rights Bill…is designed to alleviate some of the principal causes of the serious and unsettling racial unrest now prevailing in many of the states."

F. Piven & R. Cloward, supra note 49, at 244.

[221] R. Bardolph, supra note 75, at 405-06.

[222] See J. Handler, supra note 44, at 121-22; Lewis, supra note 73, at 126; HRaines, supra note 69, at 227.

[223] See J. Handler, supra note 44, at 126.

[224] A number of the Justices were concerned with the politics of implementing a reversal of Plessy v. Ferguson, 163 U.S. 567 (1896):

> As the days passed, Warren's position immensely impressed Frankfurter. The essence of Frankfurter's position seemed to be that if a practical politician like Warren, who had been governor of California for eleven years, thought we should overrule the 1896 opinion, why should a professor object? The fact that a worldly and wise man like Warren would stake his reputation on this issue not only impressed Frankfurter but seemed to have a like influence on Reed and Clark.

> W. Douglas, The Court Years 114-15 (1980). 1 would like to thank Seth Borgos for calling this source to my attention.

[225] One cannot identify in the narrowness of American voting of 1960 any one particular episode or decision as being more important than any other in the final tallies: yet when one reflects that Illinois was carried by only 9,000 votes and that 250,600 Negroes are estimated to have voted for Kennedy; that Michigan was carried by 67,000 votes and that an estimated 250,000 Negroes voted for Kennedy; that South Carolina was carried by 10,000 votes and that an estimated 40,000 Negroes there voted for Kennedy, the candidates' instinctive decision must be ranked among the most crucial of the last few weeks.

T. White, The Making of the President, 1960 322-23 (1961). White here is referring to Kennedy's phone call to Corretta Scott King shortly after her husband had been jailed. The call moved King's father to change his endorsement from Nixon to Kennedy, and the incident was publicized in a million JFK pamphlets circulated in black churches across the country the Sunday before the election. See also F. Piven & R. Cloward, supra note 49, at 225-28.

[226] In Kennedy's message to Congress (February 28, 1963), he noted that race discrimination "hampers our world leadership by contradicting at home the

message we preach abroad." The more practical effects of Kennedy's civil rights position was noted by A. Schlesinger, A Thousand Days 948 (1965):

> ...[P]resident Kennedy's action [concerning James Meredith] had a profound effect around the world, most of all in Africa. As the delegate from Upper Volta put it in the U.N. General Assembly, segregation unquestionably existed in the United States, but "what is important is that the Government of the United States did not make an institution of this. It does not praise the policy. On the contrary, it energetically fights it. For one small Negro to go to school, it threatens governors and judges with prison... it sends troops to occupy the University of Mississippi." Three weeks after Oxford [the location of the University of Mississippi], Sekou Toure and Ben Bella were prepared to deny refueling facilities to Soviet planes bound for Cuba during the missile crisis.

[227] A. Kinoy, Rights on Trial 71 (1983).

[228] Village of Schaumburg v. Citizens for a Better Environment, 444 U.S. 620, 629 (1980).

[229] See, e.g., Lovell v. City of Griffin, 303 U.S. 444, 451-52 (1938).

[230] Hague v. CIO, 307 U.S. 496, 512 (1939).

[231] While the U.S. Supreme Court has stated that access to shopping malls is not a right secured by the first amendment, Lloyd Corp. v. Tanner, 407 U.S. 551, 561-70 (1972), it is a right which may be secured by state constitutions. Pruneyard Shopping Center v. Robins, 447 U.S. 74, 80-88 (1980). At this point one may be surprised that a shopping mail does not qualify as a "public forum" along the lines elucidated in Marsh v. Alabama, 326 U.S. 501, 507-08 (1946), given that "shopping malls ... are now the third most frequented space in our lives, following home and workplace." J. Naisbitt, Megatrends 45 (1982). However, the Court has not been that solicitous to insure access to home and workplace. It is almost as if the court ensured access to spaces only when history made them marginal: access to the streets and other "public places" was vindicated only after mass media had begun to make them obsolete. Contrast Davis v. Massachusetts, 167 U.S. 43 (1897) to Hague v. CIO, 307 U.S. 496 (1939). Alternatively, though, we might note that this expansion of the first amendment was secured in a context of labor militance. See D. Kairys, Freedom of Speech, in The Politics of Law, supra note 2, at 156-59.

[232] U.S. Postal Service v. Council of Greenburgh Civil Associations, 453 U.S. 114, 126-31 (1981). Unfortunately, in rendering this decision the Supreme Court outlawed one means by which Mr. Smith's Boy Rangers attempted to communicate to his constituents when Mr. Smith went to Washington. (Mr. Smith's opponents, alas, controlled most of the media in Mr. Smith's state.)

233 See, e.g., Miami Herald Publishing Co. v. Tomillo, 418 U.S. 2419 254-58 (1974).

234 FCC v. Pacifica Foundation, 438 U.S. 726, 748 (1978); FCC v. Midwest Video Corp., 440 U.S. 689, 708-09 (1979).

235 See, e.g., ACORN v. Golden, 744 F.2d 739 (10th Cir. 1984); ACORN v. City of Frontenac, 714 F.2d 813 (8th Cir. 1983); Dallas ACORN v. Dallas Co. Hosp. Dist., 670 F.2d 628 (5th Cir.), cert. denied, 103 S.Ct. 471 (1982); Urevich v. Woodward, 667 P.2d 760 (Colo. 1983).

236 J. Ely, Democracy and Distrust 84 (1980).

237 Cf. Unger, supra note 4, at 599-600 (new rights required for social transformation).

238 NAACP v. Alabama, 357 U.S. 449, 461 (1958). Cf. notes 29-31 and accompanying text supra (significance of organization for political effect).

239 I.R.C. 501 (c) (3) (1984) (list of organizations which qualify for tax exemption).

240 I.R.C. Reg. Sec. 1.501(c)(3)-1(c)(3).

241 Of course, there are exceptions to this "rule." For example, the publicity generated by Angela Davis's imprisonment might have done more for the Communist cause than any public speeches she would otherwise have been able to give.

242 There are exceptions to this rule, too. Cf. the "fill the jails" strategies of some civil rights activists. H. Raines, supra note 69, at 105, 109, 126, 141, 148.

243 Frequently, the bargaining chip used is a 42 U.S.C. 1983 suit, which requires the lawyer to brush up on her first amendment law.

244 H. Raines, supra note 69, at 441-42.

245 So Mills B. Lane said he would make it possible for me to get outa jail, if I'd call off all the demonstrations, and I never will forget that. That was probably one of the great moments of my life, when I said, "Mr. Lane–" cause God knows nobody knows how bad I wanted to get out that jailhouse–I said, "Mr. Lane, if you get me out today, and those lunch counters and restaurants and things are just as segregated, y'all are going to have to put me back in here tomorrow cause I'm gonna lead another march." [laughs] I don't believe I would have if he' da got me out, but I told him that. He said, "Well, uh, we gonna take care of that, too." He sent his lawyer over. The C&S lawyer came over to my cell and we sat down and we drew this thing up, the desegregation plan, and I got outa jail. The way they did it in Savannah, they formed the Committee of 100, who were the richest and most influential white men and women in that town, this Committee of 100, and they would take blacks and go to the lunch counters to eat. I remember one night they [the Klan] was picketing a theater, and we went to the theater with the head of the

Union Bag, that's the largest plant there ... And the Ku Klux Klan was picketing the filling station, but they worked out at Union Bag, and they saw this man's car and recognized him and ran, took the picket signs and ran. [laughs] Dr. King spoke in Savannah, Georgia, in 1963, and Dr. King said "Savannah Georgia is the most integrated city south of the MasonDixon line." So, I saw some ready results from my works.

Id. at 442-43.

[246] W. Douglas, supra note 44, at 303. A Kinoy, supra note 88, at 102. See also National Lawyers Guild, Representation of Witnesses Before Grand Juries 1 (1974).

[247] See, e.g., United States v. Samango, 450 F. Supp. 1097 (D. Hawaii 1978), aff'd 607 F.2d 877 (9th Cir. 1979); United States v. Basurto, 497 F.2d 781 (9th Cir. 1974); United States v. Gold, 470 F. Supp. 1336 (N.D. 111. 1979); United States v. Phillips Petroleum Co., 435 F. Supp. 610 (N.D. Okla. 1977); United States v. Braniff Air-ways, Inc., 428 F. Supp. 579 (W.D. Tex. 1977); Johnson v. Superior Ct., 15 Cal. 3d. 248, 539 P.2d 792, 124 Cal. Rptr. 32; Arenella, Reforming the Federal Grand Jury and the State Preliminary Hearing to Prevent Conviction Without Adjudication, 78 Mich. L. Rev. 463, 539-75 (1980).

[248] See National Lawyers Guild, supra note 107. See also S. Bachmann, Defenses Against Fishing Expeditions 12-14 (1981).

[249] A. Kinoy, supra note 88, at 70.

[250] Id. at 252. See also Bellow, interviewed in Comment, The New Public Interest Lawyers, 79 Yale L.J. 1069, 1087-88 (1970).

[251] During the early part of this century, contingent fee arrangements were carefully scrutinized because of a fear that they would motivate attacks upon a corporation's profits. Later, the ethical canons were used to attack the NAACP and various unions. The Association of American Railroads spent $325,000 annually to finance offices in New York, Atlanta, St. Louis, Chicago, and Los Angeles to look for possible ethical violations on the part of lawyers retained by union members for workmen compensation claims. As a result, over 1500 investigations were instituted, some of which provided the basis for Bar Association proceedings against union counsel in Iowa, Nebraska, Oklahoma, Montana, Michigan, Ohio, and Virginia. Nascent Office of Equal Opportunity offices were greeted with various lawsuits challenging their legitimacy on "ethical" grounds. J. Auerbach, Unequal Justice 45-48, 270-71 (1976). See Bodle Group Legal Services-the Case for BRT, 12 UCLA L. Rev. 306, 318 (1965); Schuchman: Ethics and Legal Ethics, 37 Geo. Wash. L. Rev. 244 (1968); Zimroth, Group Legal Services and the Constitution, 76 Yale L.J. 966 (1967).

[252] In re Primus, 436 U.S. 412 (1977). See also Brotherhood of R.R. Trainmen v. Virginia Bar, 377 U.S. 1 (1964); NAACP v. Button, 371 U.S. 415 (1963).

[253] Ohralik v. Ohio State Bar Ass'n, 436 U.S. 447 (1978).

[254] See I. Auerbach, supra note 112 at 193-95, 294. See also Hildebrand v. State Bar of California, 36 Cal. 2d 504, 225 P.2d 508, 516, 521 (1950) (Carter, J. and Traynor, J., dissenting).

[255] Model Rules of Professional Conduct Rule 1.7 (1983); Model Code of Professional Responsibility DR 5-105 (1981).

[256] Model Code of Professional Responsibility DR 2-109 (1981). See also Model Rules of Professional Conduct Rule 3.1 (1983).

[257] Model Code of Professional Responsibility DR 7-102 (A) (1981).

[258] Id. at DR 7-106 (C)(5), (6), and (7). See also Model Rules of Professional Conduct Rule 3.4(c) (1983).

[259] Model Code of Professional Responsibility DR 7-106 (1981).

[260] A. Fortas, Concerning Dissent and Civil Disobedience 63 (1968).

[261] See notes 92-95 and accompanying text supra.

[262] H. Raines, supra note 69, at 143-44.

[263] Id. at 143 n*.

[264] Model Code of Professional Responsibility DR 7-107 (1981). See also Model Rules of Professional Conduct Rule 3.6 (1983).

[265] In one sense there is a very important political issue here: Who will choose a movement's leaders, the press or the movement? The press's capacity to misconstrue a movement to the public should not be underestimated. Accordingly, ACORN is very conscientious about ensuring that its members, not its staff, speak to the press. By the same token it prefers that its lawyers also stay in the background when the press appears.

[266] D. Broder, Changing of the Guard: Power and Leadership in America 235 (1980).

[267] [The public-interest movement's] vision of the good society is defined less by what that society decides than by how it decides. Public-interest activists are fundamentally engaged in that most American of occupations, namely, constitution making and revising. ...The attraction the courts hold for the public-interest movement– aside from the obvious fact that its ranks are disproportionately populated by lawyers–is the opportunity they provide for citizens to redress directly their grievances. The judicial system represents the public interest movement's version of direct democracy; it enables individuals and organizations to take the

enforcement of the law into their own hands. The movement's emphasis on the courts is not simply a short-term political tactic; rather, the judicial system is its model of democracy in action. Public interest activists not only want to subject virtually all agency decisions to judicial review; they want agencies themselves to make decisions according to a judicial model. Their goal is to make administrative law a surrogate political process designed to ensure the fair representation of a wide range of affected interests in the process of administrative decisions.

Vogel, The Public Interest Movement and the America Reform Tradition, 95 Pol. Sci. Q. 607, 617 (1980-81) (footnotes omitted).

[268] D. Broder, supra note 127, at 235.

[269] In The Republic, Plato envisioned a state governed by a committee of wise men. Unfortunately, it is questionable whether the public interest advocates would act in such a happily concerted fashion:

> One of them has observed that [m]ost of the people in the public interest law movement tend to be real egomaniacs ... which is why the public-interest-law movement is not a movement. We do not have a bar association, or meetings, or conventions; we do not get together and periodically discuss policy. Everything is done on an ad hoc basis, because there is not one of us who is ready to submerge our thoughts to the group." Broder, supra note 127, at 230.

[270] Vogel has noted the upper-middle-class orientation of public interest advocates and has observed its susceptibility to accusations of elitism. Vogel, supra note 128, at 627. For his part, Broder has noted the reluctance of public interest advocates to engage in the messiness of "nitty-gritty politics." D. Broder, supra note 127, at 238.

[271] D. Broder, supra note 127, at 236.

[272] In Social Movements and the Legal System, Handler studied 35 different cases taken from four major social change areas. He summarized his conclusions as follows:

> [B]y turning to the legal system, social reform groups have appealed to traditional institutions, and their claims for social justice have been based on traditional American constitutional values. It should come as no surprise, then, that law-reform activity by social reform groups will not result in any great transformation of American society. Instead, it is, at its most successful level, incremental, gradualist, and moderate. It will not disturb the basic political and economic organization of modern American society.

J. Handler, supra note 44, at 232-33. See also D. Broder, supra note 127, at

240 (quoting Nader associate Mark Green):

[U]nless you're dealing with a Brown v. Board of Education case, which is rare, the amount of time spent in getting a particular decision in the courts can have a bad cost-benefit ratio in terms of social change. There are a few exceptions, but I find I have more influence as a lobbyist than I did as a litigator.

[273] J. Handler, supra note 44, at 26-27.

[274] E.g., Brown v. Board of Education, 347 U.S. 483 (1954); NLRB v. Jones & Laughlin Steel Corp., 301 U.S. 1 (1937).

[275] E.g., Morehead v. New York ex rel. Tipaldo, 298 U.S. 587 (1936); Coppage v. Kansas, 236 U.S. 1 (1915); Lochner v. New York, 198 U.S. 45 (1905); Plessy v. Ferguson, 163 U.S. 537 (1896); Callan v. Wilson, 127 U.S. 540 (1888); Dred Scott v. Sandford, 60 U.S. 393 (1856).

[276] See note 92 and accompanying text supra.

[277] See, e.g., Conservatives on Supreme Court Dominated Rulings of Latest Term, N.Y. TIMES, July 8, 1984, at 1, col. 1.

[278] [J]ust as bourgeois ideology assumed that everyone was, or could be, a property owner, so does the ideology of the public-interest movement assume that everyone is, or could be, a politically committed citizen. But both views are false and for the same reason: they fail to recognize the extent to which life in a market economy may undermine the ideals of liberal democracy. They mistake the rhetoric of liberal democracy for the reality of capitalism...In sum, the more successful the public-interest movement has been in accomplishing and realizing both its substantive and procedural demands, the more powerful and pervasive has become the role of government. But the greater the intervention of government in American society, the more the exercise of governmental authority is perceived by the citizenry as an illegitimate interference with their lives. Thus, while the public-interest movement promises increased public participation, what it actually delivers to most institutions and individuals is increased regulation. It promises to make public bureaucracies more accountable, but what it has actually done is to increase their number and size. As a result, increased citizen participation has failed to accomplish one of its most important stated objectives, namely, that of increasing the legitimacy of government regulation of business.

Vogel, supra note 128, at 626-27.

[279] Cf. Foucault: "Now my hypothesis is not so much that the court is the natural expression of popular justice, but rather that its historical function is to ensnare it, control it and to strangle it, by re-inscribing it within institutions which are typical

of a state apparatus." M. Foucault, supra note 13, at 1.

[280] [U]sing the legal system itself may exact a high price. The lawyers, with the leaders, often assume a dominant position with regard to tactics and strategy once the group goes the legal route. The membership is confronted with a mysterious procedure and trade language; the specialists take over. There is a danger that the nonlegal activity of the group will languish pending the outcome of the litigation. There will be the inevitable delays that can sap the enthusiasm of the membership. Using the courts might mean framing the issues that, while legally sound, lose political and purposive appeal. And then, there is the risk of losing. J. Handler, supra note 44, at 33.

[281] But see C. Halpern: "The term public-interest law...does not imply a claim that the side represented by the public interest lawyer is always right as a matter of law, policy or morality." D. Broder, supra note 127, at 235. See also Vogel, supra note 128, at 625:

> Public-interest advocates take considerable pains to emphasize that the preferences of the interests they represent are not themselves identical with the public interest. Instead, advocates tend to define the public interest in procedural terms, arguing that public policies are capable only to the extent that all affected parties participate in the policies' formulation. (footnote omitted).

> Vogel himself does not accept this procedural notion of the public interest, but feels that the "emphasis on procedural rights is essentially a tactic designed to advance...substantive goals." Id. at 626; see note 144 infra.

[282] See text accompanying notes 36-87 supra.

[283] Cf. Vogel, supra note 128, at 626:

> Public-interest groups do not want participation for its own sake; they want it for the sake of the concrete victories over business that it promises to bring. They do not really want to participate; what they actually want is to win...In fact, neither business nor the public-interest movement actually favors genuine pluralism: instead both believe that the particular interests they represent are themselves the public interest.

[284] J. Handler, supra note 44, at 209.

[285] Id. at 210.

[286] E. P. Thompson, Whigs and Hunters, supra note 13, at 266 (emphasis in original).

[287] "A-legal," as opposed to "illegal," suggests a sense of the total irrelevance of law, as opposed to a sense that anti-legal activity must be pursued.

[288] Cf. A. Vyshinsky, The Law of the Soviet State 13 (H. Babb trans. 1948) (law as "superstructure," "merely the will of the dominant class elaborated into a statute").

[289] See, e.g., Gabel & Harris, supra note 2, at 369 n.1.

[290] K. Marx & F. Engels, supra note 30, at 397.

[291] See F. Wilhoit, supra note 75, at 34, 47.

[292] Horwitz, The Transformation of American Law, 1780-1860 313 n. 18 *passim* (1977).

[293] The material and moral culture of England presupposes the exploitation of the colonies. The purity of principles not only tolerates but even requires violence... In refusing to judge liberalism in terms of the ideas it espouses and inscribes in constitutions and in demanding that these ideas be compared with the prevailing relations between men in a liberal state, Marx is ... providing a formula for the concrete study of society which cannot be refuted by idealist arguments... it is not just a question of knowing what the liberals have in mind but what in reality is done by the liberal state within and beyond its frontiers ... An aggressive liberalism exists which is a dogma and already an ideology of war. It can be recognized by its love of the empyrean of principles, its failure ever to mention the geographical and historical circumstances to which it owes its birth, and its abstract judgments of political systems without regard for the specific conditions under which they develop. Its nature is violent, nor does it hesitate to impose itself through violence.

M. Merleau-Ponty, supra note 15, at xiii, xiv, xxiv.

[294] R. Hofstadter & M. Wallace, supra note 37, at 11. Readers are referred to Hofstadter and Wallace for a convenient compilation of establishmentarian terror.

[295] F. Piven & R. Cloward, supra note 49, at 36-37.

[296] It should be noted here that Piven and Cloward do not focus on issues of law, nor do they employ the Marxist perspective that focuses on masses becoming classes-in-themselves. I am merely extrapolating positions suggested by their work. They might or might not agree with similar extrapolations. However, the two do express doubts about the efficacy of organization in social movements; see, e.g., id. at xv-xvi.

[297] See P. Clecak, supra note 9.

[298] For an even humbler perspective, see Gabel & Kennedy supra note 13 at 53-54.

[299] See E.P. Thompson, Whigs and Hunters, supra note 13, at 264-66.

[300] It should also be noted that conscientious practices also play a role in conscientious disruption. The labor upheavals owed much to communist and C.I.O. agitators. D. Milton, supra note 63, at 108. The civil rights movement began

moving when NAACP reforming was replaced by aggressive organizing on the part of SCLC and SNCC. See text accompanying notes 79 and 80 supra.

[301] Cf. E.P. Thompson, The Poverty of Theory and Other Essays 42 (1978) (History as a process of affirming and transmitting past values),

[302] H. Enzensberger, supra note 22, at 60.

[303] To an extent this position might be identified with the Critical Legal Studies Conference and the National Lawyers Guild Theoretical Studies Committee. While it would be a mistake to cite fusionism as a "party line" for either body, nevertheless, leading figures in both organizations provide the source for this partially articulated point of view. See, e.g., D. Kairys, Freedom of Speech and Gordon, New Developments in Legal Theory, in The Politics of Law note 2 supra; Gabel & Harris, supra note 2. This discussion will focus particularly on the latter article, because it is one piece which explicitly claims that it:

> [I]s a first attempt to link the theoretical advances made by the Conference with the accumulated practice of creative Guild attorneys, and in so doing to outline a new theory of practice that can be of value to lawyers who often lack the time or opportunity to situate their work within a broad political context.

Gabel & Harris, supra note 2, at 370-71.

[304] Gabel & Harris, supra note 2, at 369-70.

[305] Id. at 376. The positions the fusionists espouse might be garnered from the following remarks:

> Hierarchical social relations are fashioned and reproduced principally through cultural conditioning rather than through the direct use of force. One element of this conditioning process is the creation of legal concepts and doctrines to establish the political legitimacy of the existing order…The function of law is thus not so much to "enforce" existing social relations as to legitimize them . . . the legal system is an important public area through which the State attempts-through manipulations of symbols, images, and ideas-to legitimize a social order that most people find alienating and inhumane…The principal role of the legal system…is to create a political culture that can persuade people to accept both the legitimacy and the apparent inevitability of the existing hierarchical arrangement…"Democratic consent" to an inhumane social order can be fashioned only by finding ways to keep people in a state of passive compliance with the status quo, and this requires both the pacification of conflict and the provision of fantasy images of community that can compensate for the lack of real community that people experience in their everyday lives.

Id. at 369-70 n. 1, 370, 372.

[306] Id. at 408.

[307] Id. at 399-400.

[308] Id. at 400.

[309] Id. at 379-84, 389-94.

[310] E.g., id. at 394 n.40, 408.

[311] Id. at 371, 372 n.6.

[312] Id. at 376 n.13.

[313] Id. at 376-77 n. 13. Gabel elsewhere emphasized the disparity between people's "real lives" and the "imaginary political community" which people project. See Gabel & Kennedy, supra note 13, at 28-29. In response to these points I would observe that in the real world unreal abstract groups do have their impact. The Swedish Catholics and American Baptists have lived at least two different experiences which will not only obstruct their capacities to relate to one another. They will also make it easier for them to relate to fellows from their own groups. At some levels, then, human beings do relate abstractly, and that is a function of their lived conditions, not of alienation. Indeed, it might be observed that for the abstraction of legal personage (i.e., one is treated with a certain regard) Gabel is substituting another abstraction (the human being).

[314] For a more critical evaluation of love, see J. Tweedie, In the Name of Love 71-81 (1979).

[315] Gabel & Harris, supra note 2, at 370 n.l.

[316] See note 10 and accompanying text supra.

[317] J. Sartre uses the bus line to illustrate this phenomenon. Sartre, supra note 10, at 256-570.

[318] 179. Cf. J. Sartre, supra note 10, at 306-07 n.89 (speculations as to the possibility of "elimination of *all* forms of alienation").

[319] "In short, the democratic group in fusion, not the elite Leninist party, was the proper revolutionary organization." M. Poster, supra note 10, at 220. Sartre cited situations from the French Revolution in 1789 to establish his point, although many people saw a re-confirmation of his views in the May days in France in 1968. The point, however, is that "*social transformation in advanced society must concentrate on the immediate creation of new relations of reciprocity rather than concentrate on overthrowing the enemy.*" Id. at 395.

[320] See note 179 and accompanying text supra.

[321] Gabel and Harris cite Sartre as an informing mentor, along with Marcuse. Gabel

& Harris, supra note 2, at 371 n.5.

[322] Value and human nature involve two sides of the same coin, for one's values develop from a sense of what is possible and desirable in human experience. Discussions of "human nature" are frequently identified with Rightist discourse because of its potential for justifying the status quo. Nevertheless, the Left must confront these issues because, as Noam Chomsky has observed, a vision of a future social order is ... based on a concept of human nature. If in fact man is an indefinitely malleable, completely plastic being, with no innate structures of mind and no intrinsic needs of a cultural or social character, then he is a fit subject for the "shaping of behavior" by the state authority, the corporate manager, the technocrat, or the central committee. Those with some confidence in the human species will hope that this is not so and will try to determine the intrinsic characteristics that provide the framework for intellectual development, the growth of moral consciousness, cultural achievement, and participation in a free community.

N. Chomsky, supra note 26, at 404. See also M. Konner, supra note 26; P. Clecak, supra note 9, at 124; and Hutchinson & Monahan, Law, Politics, and the Critical Legal Scholars: The Unfolding Drama of American Legal Thought, 36 Stan. L. Rev. 199, 240 (1984). Contrast Gabel & Kennedy, supra note 13, at 14-15.

[323] It might be acknowledged that Gabel "claims separateness." Gabel & Kennedy, supra note 13, at 3. However, it is not clear that his values allow for anything beyond "unalienated relatedness." Id. Separateness is claimed, but only because it constitutes a component of ideal intersubjectivity.

[324] Biologically, every creature is unique, to the extent that some geographic extremes of the same species finally prove unable to reproduce together. (The grass frog, *Rana pipiens,* affords an example of this. W. Johnson, L. Delanney, E. Williams & T. Cole, Principles of Zoology 324 (1969)). At this point it is appropriate to note that my difference with fusionism may be philosophical. I am clearly relying on the fundamental postulate of dialectical materialism which looks to material as the grounds for consciousness. A major reservation I have concerning the phenomenological/existentialist inspired wing of Marxism is the extent to which it ignores the social, economic, and biological groundings of thought. N. Chomsky, supra note 26, at 404, for example, explains the biological postulates which support his social vision. But what, if any such postulates are entertained by fusionists? Cf. J. Sartre, supra note 10, at 524.

[325] See note 10 and accompanying text supra.

[326] Thus, unlike Sartre, I do not look for a thorough abolition of alienation. Gabel might call this a "paranoid" abstraction from contemporary conditions, Gabel &

Kennedy, supra note 13 at 15. My responses are: (1) his is an unrealistic psychoanalytic denial, see C. Lasch, supra note 6, at 20; (2) his is an unjustified abstraction derived from the abstractions of existential phenomenology (again the quarrel with dialectical materialism. Cf. T. Adorno, The Jargon of Authenticity (1973)); and (3) just because you are paranoid does not mean they are not out to get you. I do not know why we should sacrifice a qualified, but hopeful vision for an even more optimistic (utopian?) vision that entails enormous historical risks of repression (for the sake of some ideal "group"). See Sparer, supra note 18, at 514, 530-31; P. Clecak, supra note 9, at 27; E.P. Thompson, Whigs and Hunters, supra note 13, at 258-269; M. Horkheimer, Critique of Instrumental Reason 66-68 (1974).

[327] The rhetoric and the rules of society are something a great deal more than sham. In the same moment they may modify, in profound ways, the behavior of the powerful, and mystify the powerless. They may disguise the true realities of power, they may curb that power and check its intrusions. And it is often from within that very rhetoric that a radical critique of the practice of the society is developed ...

E.P. Thompson, supra note 13, at 265.

[328] At this point, the fusionists are being insufficiently dialectical. Nothing is simply good or bad, there are many sides to one phenomenon. Law, as a practice, implements values that a society of contending groups have temporarily agreed upon. If the values that are being implemented are not all good, that is more the problem of history and those of us who participate in making it, less of law.

[329] With its roots in French thought, fusionism may have an overweening appreciation for French structuralism, and its proclivity for passive historical agents. Cf. E.P. Thompson, The Poverty of Theory, supra note 162, at 147.

[330] E.g., Professor Trubek has cited empirical studies which cast doubt on the extent to which working people passively accept dominating images of society. Trubek, Where the Action Is: Critical Legal Studies and Empiricism, 36 Stan. L. Rev. 575, 613-15 (1984).

[331] The undialectical approach resembles ostensibly socialist condemnations of the popular television program, The A-Team. While its militarism and violence are apparent, this program nevertheless also intimates relationships of community where individual characteristics are respected in a context of loyalty and common endeavor. Popularity, like hegemony, is a complicated, dialectical matter. See H. Enzensberger, supra note 22, at 60.

[332] Dialectically, one might note that the little pranks lawyers get away with only serve to emphasize all the more poignantly one's powerlessness. In the courtroom one works on the turf of the rulers. As ACORN and Foucault maintain, the sooner one returns to one's own turf—the communities and streets—the more effective one

is.

[333] See text accompanying notes 37-40 supra.

[334] The army and rightist goon squads crushed Sartre's fusing groups of the French Revolutions of 1789 and 1968. P. Gay & R. Webb, Modem Europe 497 (1973); Reflections on the Revolution in France: 1968 95-107 (C. Posner ed. 1970).

[335] While Marx believed that socialism might be established by election, he had no illusions that classes will accept elections: "as soon as [the English middle class] finds itself outvoted on what it considers vital questions we shall see here a new slave-owners' war [referring to the United States in 1861]." K. Marx, The First International and After 400 (1974).

[336] See Sparer, supra note 18, at 569.

[337] See L. Goodwyn, The Populist Moment, supra note 5, at 300.

[338] M. Merleau-Ponty, supra note 15, at xviii.

[339] See M. Poster, supra note 10, at 394.

[340] M. Merleau-Ponty, supra note 15, at xviii, xxxii, xxxiii, xxxviii.

[341] Gabel & Harris, supra note 2, at 370 n. 1. For one perspective on the role of force in social control, see G. Kolko, supra note 46, at 174-76. See also R. Hofstadter & M. Wallace, supra note 37, at 11, 19-20.

[342] Gabel & Harris, supra note 2, at 376-77. See Sparer, supra note 18, at 529. See also Lynd, Communal Rights, 62 Tex. L. Rev. 1417 (1984).

[343] See notes 105-06 and accompanying text supra.

[344] This indeed is one of the espoused purposes of the Gabel and Harris article. See Gabel & Harris, supra note 2, at 369-70. Of course, it is also fair to observe that this article grows out of the praxis of lawyers who work with organizers.

[345] The author received a M.F.A. degree from the University of New Orleans in 1984.

[346] H. Marcuse, Soviet Marxism 117 (1961).

[347] See A. Arato & E. Gebhardt, supra note 24, at 188, 220, and T. Adorno, Aesthetic Theory 321, 329 (C. Lenhardt trans. 1984).

[348] T. Adorno, supra note 1, and T. Adorno, supra note 208, at 321, 329, 331.

[349] See Sparer supra note 18, at 569; L. Goodwyn, supra note 5, at 300.

[350] For instance, where art played such a role see generally J. Willett, Art & Politics in the Weimar Period (1978).

[351] John Milton sacrificed poetry and his eyesight for the English revolutionary government. After the Restoration, barely escaping execution, he concentrated on

his major poems, although he did take advantage of occasional relaxation of the censorship laws. C. Hill, Milton and The English Revolution passim (1977). W. Haller, The Rise of Puritanism passim (1938).

[352] E.P. Thompson, The Poverty of Theory and Other Essays, supra note 162, at 42.

[353] Id. at 96.

[354] Here we might postulate a portion of "human nature" which has an innate sense of fairness and survives and observes despite all "hegenomic" practices. See, e.g., H. Raines, supra note 69, at 172.

[355] Id.

[356] See, e.g., Virginia State Bd. of Pharmacy v. Virginia Citizens Consumer Council, Inc., 425 U.S. 748 (1976) (first amendment protects pharmacists' rights to advertise drug prices); Bates v, State Bar of Arizona, 433 U.S. 350 (1977) (first amendment protects lawyers' rights to advertise services at reasonable fees).

[357] See Kennedy in The Politics of Law, supra note 2, at 57-58.

[358] Cf. Simon, Visions of Practice in Legal Thought, 36 Stan. L. Rev. 469 (1984) (The relation of extra-legal considerations to "pure" lawyerly activity).

[359] K. Marx & F. Engels, supra note 30, at 397-98. 22 1. See id.

[360] See id.

[361] At this point one can debate over where Marxism falls. One can cite a barrage of quotations to prove that Marx looked to technology or political will as the chief historical determinator. See, e.g., Vyshinsky, supra note 149, at 13-14; K. Marx & F. Engels, supra note 30, K. Marx & F. Engels, The German Ideology 42, 50, 60, 116 (1972).

[362] K. Marx & F. Engels, supra note 30, at 245.

[363] 273 Ark. 498, 621 S.W.2d 470 (1981).

[364] The primary source for the narrative are my own recollections and that of my partner Andrew Weltchek, who assumed primary responsibility for the case when I began concentrating on New Orleans cases.

[365] Charles Fried, *The Trouble With Lawyers,* N.Y. TIMES, Feb. 12, 1984, (Magazine), at 61. I would like to thank Charles Fried, my former torts professor, for helping me extract his quote from the archives of the NEW YORK TIMES. I assume that, as one of President Reagan's former U.S. Solicitor Generals, Professor Fried would appreciate a statement that certain political opinions expressed in this review are the author's and not his. In any case, as Nietzsche might say, a student repays his teacher poorly if he always remains a pupil.

[366] For elaborations on the ACORN perspective, see Steve Bachmann, *Lawyers, Law, and Social Change*, 13 N.Y.U. REV. L. & SOC. CHANGE 1, 5-7 [hereinafter Bachmann, *Lawyers*]; *see also* STEVE BACHMANN, NONPROFIT LITIGATION: A PRACTICAL GUIDE WITH FORMS AND CHECKLISTS 93-95 (1992) [hereinafter BACHMANN, NONPROFIT LITIGATION].

[367] For elaborations of this perspective, *see* Bachmann, *Lawyers*, *supra* note 2, at 29-33.

[368] The term "public interest" is itself misleading. Who is the "public?" Who defines its "interests?" Many would argue, myself among them, that there can be no such thing as "public interest"–there are only various class interests. "Public interest" is a public relations coinage, crafted by a caucus of clever or naive individuals who would try to win other people to their cause by presenting a posture of content neutrality and scientific disinterest. Attempts to secure legitimacy through claims of universal validity for a particular political perspective is nothing new: during the French Revolution, the French bourgeoisie did it with their declarations of universal human rights (even though some of these "universally valid rights" had deleterious effects on humans who worked for wages). The free marketeers do it in contemporary America when they claim that an untrammeled market will benefit "everyone"–even though an untrammeled market clearly benefits the wealthy and disenfranchises those with less economic power.

[369] Bachmann, *Lawyers*, *supra* note 2.

[370] Bachmann, *Lawyers*, *supra* note 2, at 11-21.

[371] *See, e.g.,* MADELEINE ADAMSON & SETH BORGOS, THIS MIGHTY DREAM (1984); GARY DELGADO, ORGANIZING THE MOVEMENT (1986).

[372] GERALD N. ROSENBERG, THE HOLLOW HOPE: CAN COURTS BRING ABOUT SOCIAL CHANGE? 4 (1991).

[373] *Id.* at 5.

[374] *Id.* at 4.

[375] *Id.* at xi.

[376] *Id.* at 9.

[377] *Id.* at 7.

[378] *Id.*

[379] *Id.* at 3.

[380] *Id.* at 4.

[381] *Id.* at 2-3.

[382] *Id.* at 10-13.

[383] *Id.* at 13-15.

[384] *Id.* at 15-21.

[385] *Id.* at 24.

[386] *Id.* at 30.

[387] *Id.* at 35.

[388] *Id.*

[389] DIETRICH BONHOEFFER, ETHICS 233-234 (E. Bethge ed. & N. H. Smith trans., 1965).

[390] 347 U.S. 483 (1954).

[391] Rosenberg, supra note 8, at 70-71.

[392] Id. at 52.

[393] *Id.* at 60-61. Rosenberg provides numerous and easily decipherable tables and graphs depicting his factual findings. The clarity of his presentation of the wealth of factual evidence is a remarkable strength of the book. One table shows a Black voter registration rate at 20% in 1952, reaching to 28% in 1960 and 29.4% in 1962. In 1964 the rate jumps to 40%, and by 1970 the figure is 66.9%, a percentage which begins to approximate the white registration rate.

[394] *Id.* at 65.

[395] Id. at 69.

[396] Id. at 71.

[397] *Id.* at 179.

[398] 410 U.S. 113 (1973).

[399] Rosenberg, *supra* note 8, at 183.

[400] *Id.* at 205.

[401] *Id.* at 203-04.

[402] *Id.* at 205-212.

[403] *Id.* at 185-201.

[404] *Id.* at 214-219.

[405] *Id.* at 227.

[406] at 200.

[407] at 203-05 & nn. 3 & 9.

[408] *Id.* at 25-26.

[409] *Id.* at 112-116.

[410] *Id.* at 123.

[411] Id. at 126.

[412] *Id.* at 130.

[413] *Id.* at 132.

[414] *Id.* at 134.

[415] *Id.* at 140-41.

[416] *Id.* at 145.

[417] *Id*

[418] *Id.* at 139-40.

[419] *Id.* at 229-30.

[420] *Id.* at 235.

[421] at 237.

[422] at 239.

[423] *Id.* at 242.

[424] *Id.* at 257.

[425] *Id.* at 269-335.

[426] John Patrick Diggins, *Power, Freedom and the Failure of Theory,* HARPER'S, Jan. 1992, at 15.

[427] Rosenberg, *supra* note 8, at 3.

[428] THEODOR ADORNO, NEGATIVE DIALECTICS 366-67 (E.B. Ashton trans., 1973).

[429] Compare King's point that those who do not resist evil participate in it: "We must come to see that human progress never rolls in on wheels of inevitability. It comes through the tireless efforts and persistent work of [people] willing to be coworkers with God, and without this hard work time itself becomes an ally *of* the forces *of* social stagnation." Martin Luther King, Jr., *Letter from Birmingham City Jail,* in THE WORLD TREASURY OF MODERN RELIGIOUS THOUGHT 614 (Jaroslav Pelikan ed., 1990).

[430] Cf. GLENN E. TINDER, THE POLITICAL MEANING OF CHRISTIANITY (1991)

[431] *See* BONHOEFFER, *supra* note *25,* at 30-31 (exploring the significance of Matthew's exhortation to "Judge not, that ye shall not be judged").

[432] Rosenberg, *supra* note 8, at 8.

[433] *Id.* at 155-56.

[434] *Id.* at 159.

[435] *Id.* at 160.

[436] *Id.* at 162.

[437] *Id.* at *247-49*. Rosenberg acknowledges that many women voluntarily or involuntarily left the workplace after the war. However, he points out that the percentage of women in the workplace did not decrease to its pre-war level.

[438] *Id.* at 250.

[439] *Id.* at 251.

[440] *Id.* at 252.

[441] This is a question which engages "liberals," "conservatives," and "disinterested" political theorists. The liberals premise their PITL perspective upon a certain conception of historical change. The conservatives adopt the same conception when they fulminate over the pernicious abuses perpetrated by an "activist" judiciary–unless, of course, they are only trying to manufacture political discontent among an irritated electorate. The "disinterested" political theorists might claim they stand beyond the din of contemporary politics and wish only to learn how to design a reasonable polity. Yet questions concerning the practical and theoretical power that one gives to the judicial branch are premised on certain conceptions of societal change. One would not pose the question if one did not have some concern with its impact on history.

[442] Id. at 339.

[443] The lot of humanity is epistemological uncertainty. *See, e.g.,* Bachmann, *Lawyers,* supra note 2, at 7-8, n.21.

[444] "We must use time creatively, and forever realize that the time is always ripe to do right." Martin Luther King, Jr., *supra* note 65, at 614.

[445] Bonhoeffer inspired my use of these Biblical examples. *See* BONHOEFFER, *supra* note 25.

[446] Rosenberg, *supra* note 8, at 242, 252-53.

[447] *Id.* at 235.

[448] *Id.* at 208.

[449] Gayle v. Browder, 352 U.S. 903 (1956).

[450] DAVID J. GARROW, BEARING THE CROSS 80-82 (1986).

[451] *Id.* at 83.

[452] JOEL F. HANDLER, SOCIAL MOVEMENTS AND THE LEGAL SYSTEM: A THEORY OF LAW REFORM AND SOCIAL CHANGE 108 (1978).

[453] For example, lawyers had to help defend Martin Luther King, Jr. from perjury charges relating to a tax case. King, not to mention his supporters, was also cited as a defendant in the landmark case of New York Times v. Sullivan, 376 U.S. 254 (1964), TAYLOR BRANCH, PARTING THE WATERS 308, 312 (1988). It should be acknowledged though, that on occasion, some civil rights leaders abjured the use of the law altogether when it came to dealing with prison ban. Hosea Williams relied on mass, militant, and nightly demonstrations. HOWELL RAINES, MY SOUL IS RESTED 439-43 (1977). *See also* BACHMANN, NONPROFIT LITIGATION, *supra* note 2, at 25.

[454] GARROW, *supra* note 86, at 451.

[455] RAINES, *supra* note 89, at 143-44.

[456] A. Strindberg, THE RED ROOM (trans. E. Sprigge, 1967) 161-163.

[457] STATISTICAL ABSTRACT OF THE UNITED STATES (1993) Table 735.

[458] Sargent Shriver, "The War on Poverty Is a Movement of Conscience," in THE GREAT SOCIETY READER (ed. Gettleman & Mermelstein)(1967) 205.

[459] Excerpts from attorney General Robert F. Kennedy's Address on Law Day, May 1, 1964, at the University of Chicago Law School.

[460] THE AMERICAN HERITAGE DICTIONARY OF THE ENGLISH LANGUAGE (ed. W. Morris,1973) 1027.

[461] Ibid., 1535.

[462] R. Funk & R. Hoover, THE FIVE GOSPELS (1993) 115, 258-9, 440.

[463] At least for the years 1959 through 1991 the U.S. Department of Commerce never marked the poverty rate at lower than 11%. STATISTICAL ABSTRACT OF THE UNITED STATES (1993) Table 735.

[464] Ibid.

[465] K. Phillips, THE POLITICS OF RICH AND POOR (1990) 203-205 STATISTICAL ABSTRACT OF THE UNITED STATES (1993) Table 735, 739.

[466] STATISTICAL ABSTRACT OF THE UNITED STATES (1993) Table 736.

[467] K. Phillips, THE POLITICS OF RICH AND POOR (1990) 203-205.

[468] Andrew Hacker, "Unjust Desserts?" NYRB March 3, 1994 23-24.

[469] D. T. Ellwood and L. H. Summers, "Poverty in America: Is Welfare the Answer or the Problem?," in FIGHTING POVERTY, WHAT WORKS AND WHAT

DOESN'T (ed. S. Danzier & D. Weinberg, 1986) 84, 85, 88.

[470] G. Burtless, "Public Spending for the Poor: Trends, Prospects, and Economic Limits," in FIGHTING POVERTY, WHAT WORKS AND WHAT DOESN'T (ed. S. Danzier & D. Weinberg, 1986) 46-47.

[471] D. Black, SOCIOLOGICAL JUSTICE (1989).

[472] Obviously Black is not the only person to have made such observations. Organization's role in the development of power is an elementary point for various schools of political theorists, including, most obviously perhaps, that of Karl Marx. See the discussion in S. Bachmann, "Law, Lawyers and Social Change," 13 NYU REVIEW OF LAW & SOCIAL CHANGE (1984-85) 8-11. In another context it might be observed that Prof. Charney at Harvard in a course on employment law appropriately raises the question of "whether there can be satisfactory protection of worker rights without collective institutions (unions) to engage in negotiation and enforcement." HARVARD LAW SCHOOL PRELIMINARY REGISTRATION BULLETIN 1994/95 p. 17. That this essay would answer the preceding question with a resounding NO should be clear. The point of this footnote, though, is to observe that this essay will focus less on political theory than on empirical studies (like Black's) to substantiate its assertion that individual capacity needs organized support in order to become something more concrete than a dream.

[473] Ibid., 90.

[474] Ibid., 41-43.

[475] Ibid., 45.

[476] Ibid., 41.

[477] Ibid., 49.

[478] Ibid., 85.

[479] Ibid., 46, 47.

[480] G.M. Luebbert, LIBERALISM, FASCISM, OR SOCIAL DEMOCRACY: SOCIAL CLASSES AND THE POLITICAL ORIGINS OF REGIMES IN INTERWAR EUROPE (1991) 184-185.

[481] Ibid., 18-19.

[482] See, e.g., S. Bachmann, "Law, Lawyers and Social Change," 13 NYU REVIEW OF LAW & SOCIAL CHANGE (1984-85) 21-29.

[483] Michigan Bar Journal, January 1994 p. 9.

[484] Louisiana Bar Journal, Vol. 41, No. 5, p. 476.

[485] The Washington Lawyer, January/February 1994 p. 13.

[486] A. LaFrance, M. Schroeder, R. Bennett, W. Boyd, LAW OF THE POOR (1973) xxi, B. Burdno, POVERTY, INEQUALITY AND THE LAW (1976) xvii.

[487] HARVARD LAW SCHOOL PRELIMINARY REGISTRATION BULLETIN /95 p. 34, 37.

[488] For a description of one law school clinical program which focuses on transactional (not litigation) law for organizational (as opposed to individual) clients, see J. Lehman & R. Lento, "Law School Support for Community-Based Economic Development in Low-Income Urban Neighborhoods," 42 JOURNAL OF URBAN AND CONTEMPORARY LAW 65 (1992).

[489] For an empirical study concerning the inefficacy of litigation (particularly as opposed to politics) see G. Rosenberg THE HOLLOW HOPE: CAN COURTS BRING ABOUT SOCIAL CHANGE? (1991). F. Piven & R. Cloward, POOR PEOPLE'S MOVEMENTS (1977) argues that poor people's movements should ignore courts and traditional politics and pursue disruptive actions in hopes of effectuating change. For a discussion of various of these options see S. Bachmann, "Lawyers, Law & Social Change," 13 NYU REV. OF LAW & SOCIAL CHANGE 1 (1984-1985).

[490] For some history concerning the attacks on labor union organizing see, e.g., I. Bernstein THE LEAN YEARS (1960); I. Bernstein THE TURBULENT YEARS (1979). At 29 USC 151 Congress declared "it ... to be the policy of the United States ... to encourage[e] the practice and procedure of collective bargaining."

[491] For some discussions concerning the non-professional matters attending the professionalization of the medical and legal professions, see B.Ehrenreich & D. English

FOR HER OWN GOOD (1978) (doctors) and J. Auerbach UNEQUAL JUSTICE (1976) (lawyers).

[492] C. Lasch, THE CULTURE OF NARCISSISM (1979) 385.

[493] By the [1986 Joint Economic Committee's] measurement, American's top 420,000 households alone accounted for 26.9 percent of U.S. family net worth–in essence, 26.9 percent of the nation's wealth. K. Phillips, THE POLITICS OF RICH AND POOR (1990) 11, 241.

[494] The top 10 percent of households, meanwhile, controlled approximately 68 percent [of the nation's wealth]." K. Phillips, THE POLITICS OF RICH AND POOR (1990) 11. In evaluating income distribution from 1977-1988, Phillips noted that the top 20% of American families saw an increase in average income, while the bottom 80% experienced decline. 17, 23-4. By 1991 the top 20% of Americans were taking over 43% of all after tax income, compared to 24% for the second

highest quintile and 4.5% for the bottom quintile. See statistics cited in C. Sunnstein, "Well Being and the State," 107 HARV.L.REV 1303, 1317 (1994).

[495] Barbara Ehrenreich FEAR OF FALLING (1989) 134, 153.

[496] Albert Boime, ART IN AN AGE OF REVOLUTION, 1750-1800 (1987) ch 1. Boime is not the only source of inspiration for this point. The points elaborated in this and the following two sections were inspired in part by discussions provided by Elinor Graham: "…separation of the poor from the rest of the society by means of need requirements increases the visibility of the low-income earners. This is a "war" on poverty–the very nature of such a proposal requires an exposure of "the enemy" in its human form. In addition, separation of the poor creates a donor-donee relationship whether it exists between the income-tax-paying middle and upper classes and the low-income earner, or the social worker and his client. In the context of American social philosophy, such a situation enhances the self-image of the well-to-do and places a stigma of failure and dependency upon aid recipient Above all, it is "the American way" to approach social-welfare issues, for it places the burden of responsibility upon the individual and not upon the socio-economic system. Elinor Graham, "The Politics of Poverty," in THE GREAT SOCIETY READER (ed. Gettleman & Mermelstein)(1967) 216.

[497] This insight is applicable not only to paintings from the 18th century, it also applies to images from most if not all of other historical periods. For example, art from Communist China entails its own propaganda, as does art from Norman Rockwell, a Coca Cola ad or Miller High Life ad.

[498] The demise of the National Welfare Rights Organization (NWRO) suggests the problems attending a poor people's movement which does not make cross class alliances. The successful (so far) history of Association of Community Organizations for Reform Now (ACORN) suggests the promise of cross class alliances for low- and moderate income people. M. Adamson & S. Borgos, THIS MIGHTY DREAM (1984) 113-136.

[499] Michael R. Sosin, "Legal Rights and welfare Change, 1960-1980," in FIGHTING POVERTY, WHAT WORKS AND WHAT DOESN'T (ed. S. Danzier & D. Weinberg, 1986) 260 f.

[500] Elinor Graham, "The Politics of Poverty," in THE GREAT SOCIETY READER (ed. Gettleman & Mermelstein)(1967) 217.

[501] K. Phillips, THE POLITICS OF RICH AND POOR (1990) 41.

[502] Daniel Patrick Moynihan, "The Professionalization of Reform," in THE GREAT SOCIETY READER (ed. Gettleman & Mermelstein)(1967) 464.

[503] Ibid., 463.

[504] Ibid., 470.

[505] These privileges include not only better wages than the proletarians command. It also includes the "independence of judgment, esoteric knowledge, and immunity to outside criticism that characterize professionals" observed by Moynihan. This privileged work situation clearly does not occur in most blue collar and many white-collar jobs.

[506] Elinor Graham, "The Politics of Poverty," in THE GREAT SOCIETY READER (ed. Gettleman & Mermelstein) (1967) 224-230; Tom Haydn, "Welfare Liberalism and Social Change," in THE GREAT SOCIETY READER (ed. Gettleman & Mermelstein) (1967) 481.

[507] HARVARD LAW SCHOOL PRELIMINARY REGISTRATION BULLETIN 1994/95 p. 42.

[508] ROBERT RODES, PILGRIM LAW (1998) xi.

[509] S. Bachmann, "The Politics of the First Amendment," 6 CARDOZO ARTS & ENTERTAINMENT LAW JOURNAL 327, 329n.15 (1988).

[510] Steven Weinberg, "A Designer Universe?," THE NEW YORK REVIEW OF BOOKS, 10-21-99, p. 48.

[511] See CHRISTOPHER HILL, THE CENTURY OF REVOLUTION (1961) (citing David Ogg) 224. My own prejudice might go beyond that characterization in that I think that much of what is good in our modern world was conceived by Martin Luther and incarnate with the execution of Charles I.

[512] This is my answer to Weinberg, who argues that slavery was more sustained by religion than undercut by it. My general position differs from Weinberg in that I think religion and science are dialectical phenomena. Religion can help people do good and it can help people do evil. A rationalist perspective can inspire a tolerant democrat or an oppressive Social Darwinist. On the matter of slavery, it might be noted that one of the earliest justifications for slavery—that of Aristotle—derived from a naturalist, non-religious perspective.

[513] In one sense this argument can be made on behalf of slaves, serfs and farmers who also do the direct labor. The factor that makes the proletariat special in the Marxian vision is that factory workers are concentrated together in large groups. Thus, it is easier for them to organize themselves and take power.

[514] Rodes, PILGRIM, 57.

[515] Rodes, PILGRIM, 58.

[516] Rodes, PILGRIM, 61.

[517] Rodes, PILGRIM, 62.

[518] Rodes, PILGRIM, 85, 122.

[519] Rodes, PILGRIM, 96.

[520] E.g., "Peasants could be subjected to the lash and the stocks, but the higher orders could not. Even the church went along with this tenderness for the moral authority of the ruling class." Rodes, PILGRIM, 57.

[521] E.g., "if you pollute whole counties and poison long stretches of ocean, or–what is more likely–if you and several others in the same business do so in combination, the market cannot be structured so that it will automatically make your bear your share of the cost …other social costs are less easy to assign. When a factory cuts its work force in half, it is all very well to make the owners pay unemployment compensation to the laid off workers, but what of the grocer who loses half his customers, or the automobile dealer who will sell fewer cars? What of the high school graduate who will no longer be able to look to the factory for entry-level jobs?" Rodes, PILGRIM, 61.

[522] "Your right to a job may be so well protected that you cannot be fired for habitual drunkenness at work, but you can do nothing if your employer decides to move its whole operation to Hong Kong. Or your right to the privacy of your home may be so well protected that you can get away with murder if the police do not have a search warrant when they find the murder weapon under your bed, but you can do nothing if the city decides to take your property by eminent domain and put a parking garage on the site. Only if individual rights are founded on a human destiny outside the limits of the whole managerial enterprise can they provide a basis for scrutinizing managerial agendas and calling their authors to account." Rodes, PILGRIM, 129.

[523] Rodes, PILGRIM, 105.

[524] Rodes, PILGRIM, 107.

[525] Rodes, PILGRIM, 106.

[526] Rodes, PILGRIM, 98. 99.

[527] Rodes, PILGRIM, 105.

[528] I.e., Administrative Procedure Acts, Sunshine laws and Freedom of Information Acts, conflict of interest laws, and Whistleblower Protection laws. Rodes, PILGRIM, 126.

[529] See, e.g., Rodes, PILGRIM, 22-23.

[530] D. Crossan, WHO IS JESUS? (1996), 108-09,110, 116,172.

[531] D. Crossan, in M. Borg JESUS AT 2000 (1998) 53.

[532] D. Bonhoeffer, A TESTMENT TO FREEDOM, THE ESSENTIAL

WRITINGS OF DIETRICH BONHOEFFER (Kelly, Nelson) (1990) 533.

[533] Luke 4:18-19, Isaiah 61: 1-2.

[534] For more elaboration on this point see A. Heschel, THE PROPHETS (1962).

[535] V. Havel, DISTURBING THE PEACE (trans. P. Wilson) (1990) 9,11.

[536] S. Carter, THE CULTURE OF DISBELIEF (1993) 25.

[537] Bonhoeffer quoted in Larry Rasmussen, DIETRICH BONHOEFFER, HIS SIGNIFICANCE FOR NORTH AMERICANS (1990) 123; Bonhoeffer, TESTAMENT, 536.

[538] Bonhoeffer, e.g., is unrelenting in his critique of the doctrine of the resurrection:

"Between humiliation and exaltation lies oppressively the stark historical fact of the empty tomb. What is the meaning of the news of the empty tomb, before the news of the resurrection? ... Was it really empty? ... Empty or not, it remains a stumbling block. We cannot be sure of its historicity. The Bible itself shows the stumbling block, when it makes clear how hard it was to prove that the disciples had not stolen the body. Even here we cannot escape the realm of ambiguity. Even in the testimony of Scripture, Jesus enters in a form which is a stumbling block. Even as the risen one he does not lift his incognito..." For a comparable perspective see T. Sheehan, THE FIRST COMING (1986).

[539] "It is not the religious act that makes the Christian, but participation in the sufferings of God in the secular life." Bonhoeffer, A TESTAMENT TO FREEDOM, 533.

[540] The argument here would be that Jesus must be understood from his inaugural address, which alluded directly to the messages of justice and mercy advocated by the Hebrew prophets. In other words, through loving encounters with fellow humans, through an attempt to implement justice, mercy and liberation, through an attempt to empathize with and mitigate suffering, does one gain a sense of what is sacred in human life. See Bonhoeffer, TESTAMENT, 536.

[541] T. Kuhn, THE STRUCTURE OF SCIENTIFIC REVOLUTIONS (1970).

[542] Heterodox Catholic theologian Hans Kueng gives an interesting discussion of Kuhnian paradigms and their relevance for theology in THEOLOGY FOR THE THIRD MILLENNIUM (trans. P. Heinegg, 1988) passim.

[543] The openness of this position should be noted, along with its open approach to the Bible as a guide for action. This perspective alludes to Michael Bakhtin's interpretation of Dostoevsky (see Mikhail Bakhtin, PROBLEMS OF DOSTOEVSKY POETICS) (trans. C. Emerson, 1984)). According to Bakhtin, Dostoevsky's works forced the reader into freedom by confronting the reader with

multiple, contradictory perspectives. The Bible, with its multitude of contradictory perspectives seems constructed with this approach in mind, which should not be surprising, given the extent to which Dostoevsky himself was influenced by the Bible. See Bachmann, "Cubism and the Bible," NEW ORLEANS ART REVIEW (Sept.Oct.1992).

[544] New York Times economic columnist Louis Uchitell reports "social scientists are beginning to assess the damage that [inequality] inflicts on Americans–the rich as well as the much less rich–in their daily lives. ….in any attempt to understand American social problems, enduring income inequality must now be considered as well, said Christopher Jencks, a professor of sociology at the Kennedy School of Government at Harvard University. "If you had asked me a year ago if there was evidence that income inequality had some social consequence, I would have said, 'Gee, I don't know,'" said Mr. Jencks, who recently began a study of the subject with two other academics. "But the data seem to say that if you are of average income, living among people of average income, you are less likely to have a heart attack than if you live more stressfully in a community where there is you in the middle, and a bunch of rich people and a bunch of poor people. That seems hard to believe, but it is the direction in which the evidence seems to point."

[545] Some of these issues are discussed in G. Rosenberg, THE HOLLOW HOPE (1991), 185-201, 214-219; as well as T. Skocpol, PROTECTING SOLDIERS AND MOTHERS (1995) 537-539.

[546] "A classic instance of [internal division] involves differences between the northern and southern ranches of the American power elite during the black civil rights movement. ... Another example is provided by the successes of the American labor movement in the 1930s when certain leaders of industry looked to unionization as a means of stabilizing the workplace ... Instances of [the contribution of war, an external disruption,] to revolution, such as the Paris Commune and the Russian Revolution S. Bachmann, "The Politics of the First Amendment," 6 CARDOZO ARTS & ENTERTAINTMENT LAW JOURNAL 327 (1988) 328n.8.

[547] T. Gitlin, THE TWILIGHT OF COMMON DREAMS (1995) 146.

[548] One of my favorites is that which notes how identity politics is convenient for and consistent with the new international capitalist order. During the 19th century white males enjoyed all but exclusive power of the world's resources, guns, and money. The 20th century broke this monopoly (e.g., African liberation, Arabian oil, Asian revolution). Accordingly, the 21st century has been preceded by a new found "respect" for whatever groups can suggest that they have some sort of buying power. (The groups are not only ethnically defined; women, teen-agers and gays

have also been discovered by the market, and have, accordingly, been accorded "respect.")

549 Gitlin observes that the trade union holds significant potential for "cross-racial, cross-ethnic, cross-gender, cross-regional solidarity." Yet unions "are also undermined by *other* special interests. 'Strong organizations and group affinities based on sex, sexual preference, racial and ethnic ties, religion, physical handicap and the like ... have severely compromised the status or trade unions,' the economist Michael J. Piore writes. 'Federal labor policy ... has substituted legislative remedies to the particular grievances of .... groups (the handicapped, the aged, the racial minorities) for collective bargaining, and in the process has encouraged people to define their grievances and organize in this way.' No idle bystanders to social trends, many companies encourage the growth of particularist organizations in the workplace—one example is the antiunion Digital Equipment Corporation, which cultivates groups of women, blacks, and gays, to the point of buying a corporate page in the program of the Boston Gay Rights parade." Gitlin, TWILIGHT, 226.

550 "Cut off from ecumenical political hopes, the partisans of identity politics became preoccupied with what they might control in their immediate surroundings—language and imagery. Thus, the singular influence of literary and cultural studies and the virtually self-satirizing obsession with rectifying the language of opponents. Like the rest of American society, the practitioners of identity politics resorted to legalistic regulation to address social problems... Affirmative action substituted for economic reconstruction. The new academic Left tended to mistake strong language for steady, consequential political engagement. They spoke confidently, belligerently, or 'disruptions,' 'subversions,' 'ruptures,' 'contestations.' The more their political life was confined to the library, the more their language bristled with aggression." Ibid., 146-147.

551 "A necessary if not sufficient condition for the reversal of these tendencies [inequality, punishment of the poor, civic breakdown] is the emergence of a vital Left, but this is precisely what is thwarted by the obsession with group difference. ... A Left that was serious about winning political power and reducing the inequality of wealth and income would stop lambasting all white men, and would take it as elementary to reduce frictions among white men, blacks, white women, and Hispanics.... To recognize diversity, more than diversity is needed. The commons is needed. To affirm the rights of minorities, majorities must be formed. Democracy is more than a license to celebrate (and exaggerate) differences.... It is a system of mutual reliance and common moral obligations. Mutuality needs tending.... Enough of the perfection of differences!

We ought to be building bridges." Ibid., 230, 234, 236, 237.

[552] B. Ginsberg, M. Shefter, POLITICS BY OTHER MEANS (1999) 37, 68.

[553] B. Ginsberg, M. Shefter, POLITICS BY OTHER MEANS, 66. Examples cited include the Christian Coalition, the National Taxpayers Union, the National Federation of Independent Business, associations dedicated to defending property rights, right-to-life groups, and the Home School Legal Defense Association.

[554] One example of rightwing organizing in the legal sphere which Ginsberg and Shefter do not discuss is that of the Federalist Society. See, e.g., C. Cotts, "Lawyer Steps Up as Voice of the Left," THE NATIONAL LAW JOURNAL, 12-14-1998, p. A9.; Neil A, Lewis, "A Conservative Legal Group Thrives in Bush's Washington," THE NEW YORK TIMES, 4-18-2001 p. A1; Thomas Edsall, "The Force Is With Them," THE WASHINGTON POST NATIONAL WEEKLY EDITION, April 23-29, 2001 p. 14.

[555] B. Ginsberg, M. Shefter, POLITICS BY OTHER MEANS, 148, 150, 152.

[556] B. Ginsberg, M. Shefter, POLITICS BY OTHER MEANS, 156.

[557] The Republicans who appointed G. W. Bush include Rehnquist (Nixon), Scalia (Reagan), O'Connor (Reagan), Kennedy (Reagan) and Thomas (Bush). The Republican dissenters were Stevens (Ford) and Souter (Bush). The Democrat appointees were Breyer and Ginsburg, both appointed by Clinton.

[558] See S. Bachmann, "Lawyers, Law and Social Change" 13 NEW YORK UNIVERSITY REVIEW OF LAW & SOCIAL CHANGE (1984-1985) 1, 37.

[559] N. Duxbury, PATTERNS OF AMERICAN JURISPRUDENCE (1995) 494.

[560] N. Duxbury, PATTERNS OF AMERICAN JURISPRUDENCE (1995) 496, 498.

[561] Indeed, as this book was going to press, the United States Supreme Court issued another 5 to 4 decision in *Buckhannon Board & Care Home v. W.Va. Department of Health & Human Resources*, No. 99-1848 (May 29, 2001). In this case, the five justices who appointed George W. Bush President abrogated the "catalyst theory" which the federal courts had been using for awarding attorneys fees for the past thirty years. "The ruling will have a 'profound adverse effect on the economics of public interest litigation,' says veteran environmental litigator John Eccheverria of Georgetown University School of Law." THE NATIONAL LAW JOUNAL, June 11, 2001, page 1. With this decision the Right needs to worry less about the sort of judges that Bush will be able to appoint, because fewer public interest lawyers—and groups—will be able to handle the newer and more risky economics of public interest litigation. *Buckhannon* provides yet another proof of the proposition that good long term organizing always trumps short term litigation. The sad fact is that

it is the Right which is providing the proofs.

562 HARPER'S MAGAZINE (Nov. 2000) 37.

563 B. Ginsberg, M. Shefter, POLITICS BY OTHER MEANS, 18, 21, 22, 46.

564 B. Ginsberg, M. Shefter, POLITICS BY OTHER MEANS, 186, 66.

565 B. Ginsberg, M. Shefter, POLITICS BY OTHER MEANS, 191.

566 Steve Bachmann, *Lawyers, Law, and Social Change*, 13 N.Y.U. REV. L. & SOC. CHANGE 1 (1984–85).

567 *See* THEODOR ADORNO, THE CULTURE INDUSTRY (J.M. Bernstein ed., 1991) (comparing popular culture to a factory producing standardized cultural goods); HANS MAGNUS ENZENSBERGER, CRITICAL ESSAYS 3–14 (1982) (criticizing what the author calls the "mind industry"); MARCEL PROUST, TIME REGAINED 296–99 (Andreas Mayor & Terence Kilmartin trans., 1993).

568 *See, e.g.*, TODD GITLIN, THE TWILIGHT OF COMMON DREAMS 147 (1995) ("The new academic left tended to mistake strong language for steady, consequential political engagement.").

569 MICHEL FOUCAULT, POWER/KNOWLEDGE 24–25(Colin Gordon ed., Colin Gordon, Leo Marshall, John Mepham & Kate Soper, trans., 1980).

570 33 N.Y.U.REV. L. & SOC. CHANGE 271 (2009). In her article, Powell argues that policing minor offenses aggressively creates significant hidden costs that undermine the legitimacy of the criminal justice system and create substantial burdens for poor people.

571 WALTER BENJAMIN, THE ARCADES PROJECT (Howard Eiland & Kevin McLaughlin trans., 1999). Other notable instances of juxtaposing disparate segments of narrative to create a higher, meta-narrative would include JOHN REED, TEN DAYS THAT SHOOK THE WORLD (1919); JOHN DOS PASSOS, U.S.A. (Houghton Mifflin Co. 3d ed. 1960); DORIS LESSING, THE GOLDEN NOTEBOOK (1962); Kurt Vonnegut, BREAKFAST OF CHAMPIONS (1973). Under the rubric of "postmodernism" this method of representation has become common, bordering on the orthodox. *See, e.g.*, Catherine Constable, *Postmodernism and Film, in* THE CAMBRIDGE COMPANION TO POSTMODERNISM 43, 47. (Steven Connor ed., 2004) (explaining how Jean Baudrillard's nihilist presentation of the postmodern has been widely disseminated). Lawyers may wish to familiarize themselves with this cultural form, if not employ it; to a degree, the law school case book might be viewed as a crude approximation of the genre.

572 E.P. THOMPSON, THE POVERTY OF THEORY AND OTHER ESSAYS 42 (1978).

[573] William Blake, *Milton, in* A SELECTION OF POEMS AND LETTERS 161, 162 (J. Bronowski ed., 1958).

[574] JOHANN WOLFGANG VON GOETHE, FAUST: PART TWO 97-98 (Philip Wayne Trans., Penguin Books 1959) (1832).

[575] Steve Bachmann, *Lawyers, Law and Social Change*, 13 N.Y.U. REV. L. & SOC. CHANGE 1 (1984). This Essay Was Supplemented and Reprinted in STEVE BACHMANN, LAWYERS, LAW, AND SOCIAL CHANGE 35-107 (2001). to Avoid Confusion, All Subsequent Citations to the 1984 Article Will Refer to the Book's Pagination.

[576] I Began Working on This Article in the Fall of 2008 and Completed the Majority of It in December 2009. the Dates Are Relevant Because My Discussion of Certain Recent Historical Events Will Be Limited by What I Knew When I Finally Surrendered This Article to the Printers.

[577] BACHMANN, *Supra* Note 2, at 39.

[578] *Id.* at 66-70.

[579] *Id.* at 39, 64.

[580] *Cf.* Patricia Cohen, *NEXT BIG THING IN ENGLISH: KNOWING THEY KNOW THAT YOU KNOW*, N.Y. TIMES, Apr. 1, 2010, at C1 (discussing the growing application of evolutionary psychology to English literature).

[581] *See, e.g.*, Tony Judt, Ill Fares the Land, N.Y. REV. BOOKS, Apr. 29, 2010, at 17, 17 (observing that the current socio-political climate is one marked by "growing inequalities of wealth and opportunity; injustices of class and caste; economic exploitation at home and abroad; corruption and money and privilege occluding the arteries of democracy"). Such inequality continues to occur in part because of efforts to alternatively valorize or disguise its existence. See Stefan Collini, *Blahspeak*, LONDON REV. BOOKS, Apr. 8, 2010, at 29, 29 (criticizing the use of rhetoric "intended to deflect attention from the basic fact that the most important determinations of [socioeconomic status] are...the pre-existing distribution of wealth and power in society"); Judt, *supra*, at 18 (describing ubiquitous "symptoms of collective impoverishment" that "are so endemic that we no longer know how to talk about what is wrong"); Nicholas Spice, *Don't Look Down*, LONDON REV. BOOKS, Apr. 8, 2010, at 11, 12 (discussing the "refusal of all parties" to discuss gross inequalities in British education).

[582] *See generally* NAOMI KLEIN, THE SHOCK DOCTRINE: THE RISE OF DISASTER CAPITALISM (2007) (describing the ruling orders' tendency to use torture, assassination, martial law, coups, and war to maintain control).

[583] *See, e.g.*, Duff Wilson, *Poor Children Likelier to Get Antipsychotics*, N.Y. TIMES,

Dec. 12, 2009, at A1 (finding that low-income children on Medicaid are prescribed antipsychotic medication at higher rates and for less severe conditions than privately insured children).

[584] JEAN BAUDRILLARD, THE VITAL ILLUSION 25 (2000) (concluding that the structures of popular culture suppress individuality).

[585] The most advanced forms of organization in contemporary society remain the state and the multinational corporation, which enhances their abilities to exploit and destroy. See NOAM CHOMSKY, FAILED STATES: THE ABUSE OF POWER AND THE ASSAULT ON DEMOCRACY 110 (2006) (noting the United States' adoption of characteristics of failed and outlaw states); KLEIN, *Supra* note 9, at 23 (describing the mobilization of corporate and governmental resources for brutal forms of coercion). For examples of organizing as a tool of resistance against societal oppression, see KIM BOBO, JACKIE KENDALL & STEVE MAX, ORGANIZING FOR SOCIAL CHANGE: MIDWEST ACADEMY MANUAL FOR ACTIVISTS (3d ed. 2001).

[586] Throughout this article, I use the terms "conservative," which I equate with "the Right," and "progressive," which I use interchangeably with "the Left." About twenty years ago I argued, "The Right tends to support and intensify unequal concentrations of power between human beings. The Left tends to support and accelerate trends towards more equal distributions of power between human beings." Steve Bachmann, *The Politics of the First Amendment*, 6 Cardozo Arts & Ent. L.J. 327, 329-30 n.15 (1988). Historically, the Right has identified with privilege, while the Left has opposed established elites. See Norman Davies, Europe: A History 696-97 (1996). More recently, the Right supports interests relating to the exclusivity of property rights, while the Left focuses on interests relating to the distribution of social benefits. Compare Barton H. Thompson, Jr., The Public Trust Doctrine: A Conservative Reconstruction & Defense, 15 SOUTHEASTERN ENVTL. L.J. 47, 56 (2006) (identifying conservative concerns over protecting private property rights as a source of opposition to the public trust doctrine), with Sagit Leviner, *From Deontology to Practical Application: The Vision of a Good Society and the Tax System*, 26 VA. Tax Rev. 405 (2006) (arguing in favor of redistributive tax systems from a community-oriented view of society).

Of course, this Left/Right dichotomy fails to capture the nuances that exist on both sides. Modern American conservative groups disagree over the ideal involvement of government, ranging from none at all (radical libertarian), to only enough government to protect property (conservative), to only enough government to protect property and morality (moral majority). See, e.g., DONALD T. CRITCHLOW, THE CONSERVATIVE ASCENDANCY: HOW THE GOP

RIGHT MADE POLITICAL HISTORY 22-23 (2007) (characterizing some of the ideological differences among conservatives in the context of the founding of the publication *National Review*). Liberal groups differ on conceptions and definitions of equality, either equality of respect (neoliberal), equality of opportunity (liberal), or equality of condition (socialist). *See, e.g.*, Walter Benn Michaels, *What Matters*, LONDON REV. BOOKS, Aug. 27, 2009, at 11 (arguing that the neoliberal focus on anti-racism and anti-sexism obscures continuing class disparities).

[587] David Brooks, Op-Ed., *Is Chemistry Destiny?*, N.Y. TIMES, Sept. 17, 2006, § 4, at 14.

[588] The term was first used by the Russian Marxist G.V. Plekhanov in 1891 to describe a philosophical approach to logic, ontology, and epistemology that began with Hegel, Feuerbach, and Marx. Since then, it has been associated with persons as diverse as Mao Zedong and Theodor Adorno. See H.H. Acton, *Dialectical Materialism*, in 2 ENCYCLOPEDIA OF PHILOSOPHY 389 (Paul Edwards ed., reprint ed. 1972). My vision of dialectical materialism aligns itself with the work of neo-Marxists working outside the orthodoxies developed by successful Communist parties in Russia and China, particularly with Adorno. *See, e.g.*, ERNEST BLOCH, THE PRINCIPLE OF HOPE (Neville Plaice, Stephen Plaice & Paul Knight trans., The MIT Press 1986) (1938-1947); GUY DEBORD, THE SOCIETY OF THE SPECTACLE (Ken Knabb trans., Rebel Press 2004) (1967); HERBERT MARCUSE, REASON AND REVOLUTION: HEGEL AND THE RISE OF SOCIAL THEORY (1954). Thus, I have not engaged the thesis/antithesis/synthesis language that attends some discussions of dialectical materialism.

[589] From the perspective of 2010, I would note that much of the "theory" (legal, political, aesthetic, or otherwise) that occurred between 1980 and 2000 served more as a substitute for political action than a guide to real political action, given a political environment that was both frustrating and hostile. See PIERRE BOURDIEU, FIRING BACK: AGAINST THE TYRANNY OF THE MARKET 2, at 19 (Loic Wacquant trans., The New Press 2003) (2001) (calling on scholars to avoid "'paper revolutionism' devoid of genuine target or effect"); TODD GITLIN, THE TWILIGHT OF COMMON DREAMS: WHY AMERICA IS WRACKED BY CULTURE WARS 147 (1995) ("The new academic Left tended to mistake strong language for steady, consequential political engagement."). Dialectical materialism provides an alternative to this nihilistic despair; one that, hopefully, provides more truth and more hope. As Marx has argued, "The philosophers have only interpreted the world, in various ways; the point, however, is to change it." Karl Marx, *Theses on Feuerbach*, in BASIC WRITINGS ON POLITICS AND PHILOSOPHY: KARL MARX AND

FRIEDRICH ENGELS 243, 245 (Lewis S. Feuer ed., 1959).

[590] BACHMANN, *Supra* note 2, at 44. One sentence that I cited in 1984 as a particularly compelling summary of dialectical materialism was from the philosopher Theodor Adorno: "The name of dialectics says no more, to begin with, than that objects do not go into their concepts without leaving a remainder, that they come to contradict the traditional norm of adequacy." THEODOR ADORNO, NEGATIVE DIALECTICS 5 (E.B. Ashton trans., The Continuum Publ'g Co. 1973). See BACHMANN, *Supra* note 2, at 44. Another way of putting this is to say that a thought or concept inside a human head is never adequate to describe or understand an external subject, and that external subjects exist only insofar as they may be comprehended by human intellect. The first part of this formulation makes it "materialist" (because of the focus on external material reality); the second part makes it "dialectical" (because a second agent-the human subject-must still comprehend the external input).

[591] *See, e.g.,* NICHOLAS HUMPHREY, SEEING RED: A STUDY IN CONSCIOUSNESS 13-19 (2006) (explaining how when a person sees something, she both acquires ideas and creates visual sensations about what she sees).

[592] *See* DAVID J. LINDEN, THE ACCIDENTAL MIND: HOW BRAIN EVOLUTION HAS GIVEN US LOVE, MEMORY, DREAMS, AND GOD 144 (2007) (arguing that consciousness is largely a product of brain functions that are themselves products of human evolution). *See generally* HELEN FISHER, WHY WE LOVE: THE NATURE AND CHEMISTRY OF ROMANTIC LOVE (2004) (using data from brain scans, psychological literature, animal studies, and questionnaires to explore the phenomenon of romantic love and its biological aspects).

[593] *See, e.g.,* R. DALE GUTHRIE, THE NATURE OF PALEOLITHIC ART 227 (2005) ("Many of our behaviors and emotions are from older parts of the brain dating back to the early roots of mammals and evolved before we and they diverged from a common stock.").

[594] The capacity to create narrative is a potent example of how evolutionary processes resulted in a function that was important for survival, but in a way that may have been flawed; while the ability to create narrative is an important tool for us to organize and understand our surroundings, it prevents us from perfectly perceiving the world around us. *See* LINDEN, *Supra* note 19, at 83 (observing that, as the result of evolutionary needs, our sensory perceptions emphasize important information and ignore other stimuli); Nassim NICHOLAS TALEB, THE BLACK SWAN: THE IMPACT OF THE HIGHLY IMPROBABLE 62-84 (2007) (exploring the concept of narrative fallacy, including the flush of dopamine

that seems to occurs when a brain forms patterns).

595 *See infra* Part I.B.

596 *See infra* Parts I.C-D.

597 *See infra* Part I.E.

598 *See infra* Parts I.C-E.

599 *See, e.g.,* WILLIAM R. CLARK, SEX & THE ORIGINS OF DEATH 63-66 (1996) (describing the evolutionary advantages of reproduction through sex because of the creation of offspring that are genetically different from their parents); LINDEN, *Supra* note 19, at 243 ("[V]ariation in gene structure underlies brain structure."); CARL ZIMMER, EVOLUTION: THE TRIUMPH OF AN IDEA 230-33 (2001) (observing that sex may provide an evolutionary advantage because it allows the mixing and selection of genes between two organisms, as opposed to one organism reproducing itself through cloning).

600 *See* Joe G. Kingsolver, *Physiological Sensitivity and Evolutionary Responses to Climate Change,* in CARBON DIOXIDE, POPULATIONS, AND COMMUNITIES 3 (Christian Korner & Fakhri A. Bazzaz eds., 1996) (discussing evolutionary adaptations to environmental factors). *See also* Nicholas Wade, *Human Culture, an Evolutionary Force,* N.Y. TIMES, Mar. 2, 2010, at DI (examining genetic adaptations to "sustained cultural changes, like new diets").

601 *See* DAVID F. BJORKLUND & ANTHONY D. PELLEGRINI, THE ORIGINS OF HUMAN NATURE: EVOLUTIONARY DEVELOPMENTAL PSYCHOLOGY 27 (2002) ("Our current genetic makeup...most likely reflects adaptations to our hunter-gatherer past, which may or may not be adaptive for us today."); Jonah Lehrer, *Depression's Upside,* N.Y. TIMES, Feb. 28, 2010, Magazine Section, at 38 ("We are not a blank slate but a byproduct of imperfect adaptations, stuck with a mind that was designed to meet the needs of Pleistocene hunter-gatherers on the African savanna."). See also GARY MARCUS, KLUGE: THE HAPHAZARD EVOLUTION OF THE HUMAN MIND (2008) (arguing that the human brain is a "kluge," a haphazard design-effective but not ideal-that continues to be replicated as a process of evolution).

602 *See* BJORKLUND & PELLEGRINI, *Supra* note 28, at 215 (observing that humans evolved "several specific cognitive abilities" in order to exist in a social community, and that as a result, "formal logic is something that humans are not particularly good at, unless the logic is in the context of social exchange").

603 LINDEN, *Supra* note 19, at 225 ("[O]ur brains have become particularly adapted to creating coherent, gap-free stories.... The creation of [these] coherent narratives in the brain is not limited to manipulation of low-level perception but

extends to higher perceptual and cognitive levels.").

[604] GUTHRIE, *Supra* note 20, at 227.

[605] LINDEN, *Supra* note 19, at 225-26. See also DAVID BERREBY, US AND THEM: THE SCIENCE OF IDENTITY 109 (2005) (describing experiment wherein participants "were unaware that some of their 'memories' were actually alterations or additions"); TALEB, *Supra* note 21, at 62-84 (describing various tendencies of the human brain to exaggerate facts or invent patterns for narrative consistency, despite the accompanying lack of accuracy); William Easterly, *The Anarchy of Success*, N.Y. REV. BOOKS, Oct. 8, 2009, at 28, 28 ("Humans are suckers for finding patterns where none really exist...")

[606] *see, e.g.,* HUMPHREY, *Supra* note 18.

[607] See *infra* notes 90-95 and accompanying text for definitions of progressive and regressive social change. Generally, I put it in terms of more or less equality.

[608] THE AMERICAN HERITAGE DICTIONARY OF THE ENGLISH LANGUAGE 735 (3d ed. 1992).

[609] A.D. Woozley, *Universals*, in 8 ENCYCLOPEDIA OF PHILOSOPHY, *Supra* note 15, at 194, 194-98.

[610] See *Supra* Part I.A.

[611] Friedrich Nietzsche has been credited with making "the first argument...that a single true view of reality was rendered impossible by the structure of language." WILLIAM R. EVERDELL, THE FIRST MODERNS: PROFILES IN THE ORIGINS OF TWENTIETH-CENTURY THOUGHT 349 (1997). More recently, this argument has been divided into five core principles of modernist thought: self-reference and recursion, radical subjectivity, multiple perspective, inductiveness, and discontinuity. *Id.* at 347. It is no accident that fundamentalism has been considered by many to constitute a panic attack in the face of modernity's certain uncertainties. *See, e.g.,* KAREN ARMSTRONG, THE BATTLE FOR GOD, at xiii (2001) (describing various forms of religious fundamentalism as "motivated by common fears, anxieties, and desires...[in] response to some of the peculiar difficulties of life in the modern secular world").

[612] See JEROME L. HIMMEISTEIN, TO THE RIGHT: THE TRANSFORMATION OF AMERICAN CONSERVATISM 50 (1990) (identifying *Ideas Have Consequences* as perhaps "the most revered and influential [of the traditionalist texts] among conservatives"). See also JOHN MICKLETHWAIT & ADRIAN WOOLDRIDGE, THE RIGHT NATION: CONSERVATIVE POWER IN AMERICA 46-47 (2004) (recognizing Weaver and his work as emblematic of the nostalgia that imbued post-war conservatism).

[613] HIMMELSTEIN, *Supra* note 39, at 50 (internal quotation marks omitted).

[614] MICKLETHWAIT & WOOLDRIDGE, *Supra* note 39, at 47.

[615] Woozley, *Supra* note 36, at 203.

[616] Benedict XVI, *On the Theological Basis of Prayer and Liturgy, in* THE ESSENTIAL POPE BENEDICT XVI: HIS CENTRAL WRITINGS & SPEECHES 155, 162 (John F. Thornton & Susan B. Varenee eds., 2007).

[617] Benedict XVI, *The Regensburg Tradition and the Reform of the Liturgy*, in THE ESSENTIAL POPE BENEDICT XVI, *Supra* note 43, at 167, 174 (first and second alterations in original).

[618] *Id.*

[619] GEORGE SOROS, OPEN SOCIETY: REFORMING GLOBAL CAPITALISM, at xii (2000). Soros observed that market fundamentalism is only the latest incarnation of the nineteenth century predilection towards laissez-faire governance, which supports private interests but fails to protect the common interest. *Id. See also* Jackson Lears, *Naderland*, LONDON REV. BOOKS, Apr. 8, 2010, at 7 (criticizing the view that wealth might be utilized to bring about economic social change).

[620] *See* EMMANUEL TODD, AFTER THE EMPIRE: THE BREAKDOWN OF THE AMERICAN ORDER 63 (C. Jon Delogu trans., Columbia Univ. Press 2003) (2002) (observing that traditional economics "perceives...an ideal, perfectly symmetrical world in which the status of all nations is equivalent and all work for the common good," a perception that does not align with "the troubling fact that globalization is not organized around a principle of symmetry but of asymmetry").

Smith is more than his "Hollywood" version, For example, he anticipates Veblen with his comments on the noxious rich: "With the greater part of rich people, the chief enjoyment of riches consists in the parade of riches, which in their eyes is never so complete as when they appear to possess those decisive marks of opulence which nobody can possess but themselves." ADAM SMITH, THE WEALTH OF NATIONS BOOKS I-III 277 (Penguin Classics 1986) (1776). He anticipates discussions of the degradation of labor under the factory system: "[The ploughman's] understanding, …being accustomed to consider a greater variety of objects, is generally much superior to that of the [mechanic], whose whole attention from morning till night is commonly occupied in performing one or two very simple operations." *Id.* at 231. He anticipates Marx when he observes that "masters, being fewer in number, can combine much more easily." *Id.* at 169. He also observed, before Marx, that rural people "dispersed in distant places, cannot easily combine together." *Id.* at 230.

621 See FRIEDRICH NIETZSCHE, HUMAN, ALL TOO HUMAN: A BOOK FOR FREE SPIRITS 25 (R.J. Hollingdale trans., Cambridge Univ. Press 1986) (1878) ("[A] theory like that of free trade, presupposes that universal harmony must result of itself in accordance with innate laws...."); Gary G. Hamilton & Misha Petrovic, *Thorstein Veblen and the Organization of the Capitalist Economy*, in THE OXFORD HANDBOOK OF SOCIOLOGY AND ORGANIZATION STUDIES: CLASSICAL FOUNDATIONS 351, 356 (Paul S. Adler ed., 2009) ("'With Adam Smith...the ultimate ground of economic reality is the design of God...'") (quoting Veblen).

622 A.L. Macfie & D.D. Raphael, *Introduction* to ADAM SMITH, THE THEORY OF MORAL SENTIMENTS 5-8 (A.L. Macfie & D.D. Raphael eds., Oxford Univ. Press Liberty Classics ed. 1982) (1792). A rigorous theologian might note that Stoicism has its roots in Greek philosophy, where both Plato and Aristotle, consistent with fundamentalists like Pope Benedict, embrace the notion that mind can identify reality.

623 SMITH, *Supra* note 49, at 36.

624 Macfie & Raphael, *Supra* note 49, at 8.

625 *See, e.g.*, FERNAND BRAUDEL, AFTERTHOUGHTS ON MATERIAL CIVILIZATION AND CAPITALISM 62-63 (Patricia M. Ranum trans., paperback ed. 1979) ("The basic inequality of partners that underlies the capitalistic process is visible on every level of social life.").

626 *See, e.g., The Financial Crisis and the Role of Federal Regulators: Hearing Before the H. Comm. on Oversight and Government Reform*, 110th Cong. 2 (2008) (statement of Alan Greenspan, former Chairman, Federal Reserve) (admitting that reliance on "the self-interest of lending institutions to protect shareholder's equity" has been "a central pillar of our financial markets' state of balance"); Robert H. Frank, *Flaw in Free Markets: Humans*, N.Y. TIMES, Sept. 13, 2009, Business Section, at 4 (arguing that free market competition can protect "society from excessive financial risk" only when certain conditions exist); Paul Krugman, How Did Economists Get It So Wrong?, N.Y. TIMES, Sept. 6, 2009, Magazine Section, at 36 (describing two major contemporary schools of economics and arguing that recessions and depressions can only be avoided when economists accept that markets do not function perfectly); George Soros & Judy Woodruff, *The Financial Crisis: An Interview with George Soros*, N.Y. REV. BOOKS, May 15, 2008, at 8, 8 (asserting that the financial crisis was the result of "market fundamentalism," or the belief "that markets are self-correcting," and that "generally the intervention of the authorities... saves the markets when they get into trouble").

627 *See, e.g.*, Danny Goldstick, *Applying Dialectical Materialism*, 16 NATURE, SOC'Y

& THOUGHT 277, 277 (2003) ("For textbook purposes, Marxist philosophy is commonly divided into dialectical materialism and historical materialism, and historical materialism is often said to be the application of dialectical materialism to history."); Robert L. Heilbroner, *Through the Marxian Maze*, N.Y. REV. BOOKS, Mar. 9, 1972, at 9 (explaining the dialectics of Marxist thought); Robert Skidelsky, *What's Left of Marx*, N.Y. REV. BOOKS, Nov. 16, 2000, at 24 (identifying the strains of thought that influenced Marx's development of dialectical materialism).

[628] *See, e.g.*, MARK POSTER, FOUCAULT, MARXISM & HISTORY (1984).

[629] EUGENE THACKER, THE GLOBAL GENOME: BIOTECHNOLOGY, POLITICS, AND CULTURE 122-23 (2005). *See also* GEORGES BATAILLE, EROTISM: DEATH & SENSUALITY (First City Lights 1986) (1957).

[630] See DEBORD, *Supra* note 15.

[631] THACKER, *Supra* note 56, at 22-23. See also MICHEL FOUCAULT, THE BIRTH OF BIOPOLITICS: LECTURES AT THE COLLEGE DE FRANCE, 1978-1979 (Michel Senellart ed., Graham Burchell trans., Palgrave MacMillan 2008) (2004).

[632] Ed Vulliamy, *The Observer Profile Michael Hardt: Empire Hits Back*, OBSERVER (London), July 15, 2001, at 23.

[633] MICHAEL HARDT & ANTONIO NEGRI, EMPIRE, at xii (2000).

[634] *Id.* at xiv.

[635] *Id.* at xii.

[636] *Id.* at 3.

[637] *Id.* at 20.

[638] A wide variety of perspectives and priorities falls under the heading of "feminist," including liberal feminism, which advocates the equality of men and women through political and legal reform, *see, e.g.*, BELL HOOKS, FEMINIST THEORY: FROM MARGIN TO CENTER (2d ed. 2000); radical feminism, which focuses on a patriarchal, capitalist hierarchy as the source of gender-based oppression, *see, e.g.*, ALICE ECHOLS, DARING TO BE BAD: RADICAL FEMINISM IN AMERICA, 1967-1975 (1989); multiracial feminism, which explores the experiences of women of color and the intersection of oppression based on gender, race, and class, *see, e.g.*, Maxine Baca Zinn & Bonnie Thornton Dill, *Theorizing Difference from Multiracial Feminism*, in FEMINIST THEORY READER: LOCAL AND GLOBAL PERSPECTIVES 353 (Carole R. McCann & Seung-Kyung Kim eds., 2003); and other theoretical offshoots. Within each feminist movement, various definitions for "feminism" exist, predicated on different notions of the source of oppression, the goals of feminist activity, and the

recommended means for pursuing these goals.

Dialectical materialism is consistent with this multitude of definitions, because it naturally questions the notion of essences or the idea that there could be any single definition for terms like "female." This makes the matter of trying to contain something like feminism within the confines of a definition of "female" all the more problematic. *Cf.* John Lancaster, *Short Cuts*, LONDON REV. BOOKS, Oct. 8, 2009, at 28 (noting the difficulty in defining sex as many female athletes have male Y chromosomes and variations in hormone levels); Jeré Longman, *South African Runner's Sex- Verification Result Won't Be Public*, N.Y. TIMES, Nov. 20, 2009, at BIO (describing controversy over sex-determination testing for female athlete given "athletes who may have both male and female characteristics").

[639] *See, e.g.,* BRAM DIJKSTRA, IDOLS OF PERVERSITY: FANTASIES OF FEMININE EVIL IN FIN-DE-SIÉCLE CULTURE 210-34 (1986) (summarizing the works of patriarchal writers who described men and women as two complementary, and completely different, types of beings, characterizing intelligence and morality as male, and weakness and physicality as female).

[640] *E.g.* GERDA LERNER, THE CREATION OF FEMINIST CONSCIOUSNESS: FROM THE MIDDLE AGES TO EIGHTEEN-SEVENTY 46-47 (1993) (discussing the consequences of "[t]he concept that women are born inferior...[and] are more subject to emotions...than men"). See also Robin L. West, *The Difference in Women's Hedonic Lives: A Phenomenological Critique of Feminist Legal Theory*, 3 Wisc. Women's L.J. 81 (1987) (arguing that, because women's joys and sufferings differ from men's, feminism must go beyond the liberal focus on equality and autonomy and focus also on happiness and pleasure, including the erotic).

[641] JILL BOLTE TAYLOR, MY STROKE OF INSIGHT: A BRAIN SCIENTIST'S PERSONAL JOURNEY 17 (Plume 2009) (2006). *See generally* JONAH LEHRER, HOW WE DECIDE (2009).

[642] *See* LERNER, *Supra* note 67, at 10, 46-52 (noting that misogynist beliefs that women were inferior and incapable of abstract thought prevented women from forming an authentic self and made them uncertain of their right to think).

[643] See DIJKSTRA, *Supra* note 66, at 209, 401 (arguing that the forces underlying cultural hatred of women led not only to fantasies of gynecide, but also to actual genocide by the Nazis). Once the mind presumes to separate itself from and privilege itself over material existence and manual labor, it produces barbarism. *See* ADORNO, *Supra* note 17, at 366-67 (arguing that the sanitization of intellect and culture and the separation of mind from manual labor made possible the atrocities committed during the Holocaust).

[644] NEIL DUXBURY, PATTERNS OF AMERICAN JURISPRUDENCE 18 (1995). While the practice of Socratic questioning in a law school class first took root at Columbia Law School, Harvard Law School developed and popularized the practice. *Id.* at 13, 18.

[645] *Id.* at 14-16.

[646] *See* SCOTT TUROW, ONE L 296 (1977) (observing that the Socratic method "can become an instrument of terror"); Duncan Kennedy, *Legal Education as Training for Hierarchy*, in THE POLITICS OF LAW 54, 60-61 (David Kairys ed., 3d ed. 1998) (characterizing the case method of teaching as "bullying" and criticizing it for misleading students by setting up a false dichotomy between legal reasoning and ethical or political discourse). *See also* JEROME FRANK, COURTS ON TRIAL 225 (1950) (criticizing the case method for creating a "core of somewhat neurotic attitudes" and for perpetuating mythical beliefs in the American legal system); JOHN JAY OSBORN, JR., THE PAPER CHASE (1971) (offering a negative portrayal of the Socratic method in popular culture).

[647] See ADORNO, *Supra* note 17, at 366-67.

[648] The case method fails to adequately educate law students on the impact human competence, interest, and personality have on legal outcomes-on "the human side of the administration of justice." FRANK, *Supra* note 73, at 235. Additionally, clinical legal education may be more engaging, and therefore more effective, for many students than the case method is. See *Id.* ("It is like the difference between kissing a girl and reading a treatise on osculation.").

[649] See MARCUSE, *Supra* note 15, at 41-42, 166-67.

[650] DUXBURY, *Supra* note 71, at 16-17.

[651] For example, Article 3 of the Geneva Conventions of 1949 prohibits torture against civilians and prisoners of war. Geneva Convention Relative to the Treatment of Prisoners of War art. 3, Aug. 12, 1949, 6 U.S.T. 3316, 75 U.N.T.S. 135.

[652] Frank Rich, Op-Ed., *The Banality of Bush White House Evil*, N.Y. TIMES, Apr. 26, 2009, Week in Review Section, at 14 (observing that Justice Department memoranda authorizing the United States to use torture in the War on Terror were written by graduates of top law schools who had worked at prestigious firms).

[653] *Cf.* ADORNO, *Supra* note 17, at 366-67.

[654] FRANK, *Supra* note 73, at 234-36.

[655] *See, e.g.,* Becky L. Jacobs, *A Lexical Examination and (Unscientific) Survey of Clinical Experiences in U.S. Law Schools*, 75 TENN. L. REV. 343, 362 (2008) (advocating for law school clinics, which "not only teach students knowledge and skill, they also

integrate valuable ethical and social concerns").

[656] *See* FRANK, *Supra* note 73, at 230. Frank argues against dedicating three years to teaching case law dialectics. *Id.* at 236-37. See also Christopher T. Cunniffe, *The Case for the Alternative Third-Year Program*, 61 ALB. L. REV. 85, 85 (1997) ("There has never been a persuasive justification for uniformly requiring all law students...to spend their third year of legal training within a law school."). However, case law teaching can process more students at less cost than clinical teaching, through larger class sizes and fewer input requirements. DUXBURY, *Supra* note 71, at 19.

[657] *Cf.* DUXBURY, *Supra* note 71, at 19 ("[T]he primary merit of the case method is its low cost.").

[658] BARBARA EHRENREICH, FEAR OF FALLING: THE INNER LIFE OF THE MIDDLE CLASS 78-81 (1989).

[659] *See* STEVEN M. TELES, THE RISE OF THE CONSERVATIVE LEGAL MOVEMENT: THE BATTLE FOR CONTROL OF THE LAW 14 (2008) ("[D]isciplines tend to reproduce themselves....As a result, we would expect law faculties to reproduce themselves ideologically, even in the absence of an explicit individual desire to discriminate, by defining alternative ideological research projects as marginal or unimportant.").

[660] *See* FRANK, *Supra* note 73, at 237-38.

[661] *See* ADORNO, *Supra* note 17, at 366-67.

[662] David Standish, *Interview with Kurt Vonnegut*, PLAYBOY, July 1973, at 20, reprinted in CONVERSATIONS WITH KURT VONNEGUT 76, 80 (William Rodney Allen ed., 1988).

[663] To a degree my stance is defined by embracing historical movements associated with leftwing, rather than rightwing, ideologies. *See Supra* note 13.

[664] *See* BACHMANN, *Supra* note 2, at 172 ("Because power distributions have been and remain so unequal and so detrimental to the dignity of human beings, I postulate that in the foreseeable past and foreseeable future, most impulses towards the Left should be considered progressive, humane, and/or good.").

[665] *See Id.* at 37 (advocating communitarianism and "an appreciation of community" as laudable social goals).

[666] *See* RICHARD WILKINSON, MIND THE GAP: HIERARCHIES, HEALTH AND HUMAN EVOLUTION 11 (2001) (arguing that greater equality in society is positively correlated with longer life expectancy rates and overall better health); RICHARD WILKINSON & KATE PICKET, THE SPIRIT LEVEL: WHY MORE EQUAL SOCIETIES ALMOST ALWAYS DO BETTER 181, 213 (2009) (noting that greater inequality in a society increases the prevalence of mental illness,

death rates, discrimination, and other harmful effects, not just within disadvantaged groups, but across the population); Judt, *Supra* note 8, at 19 ("Inequality, then, is not just unattractive in itself; it clearly corresponds to pathological social problems that we cannot hope to address unless we attend to their underlying cause."). *See generally* RICHARD WILKINSON, UNHEALTHY SOCIETIES: THE AFFLICTIONS OF INEQUALITY (2001) (connecting health inequalities with social and economic inequalities).

[667] *See* BACHMANN, *Supra* note 2, at 37-38 (citing FRED R. DALLMAYR, TWILIGHT OF SUBJECTIVITY: CONTRIBUTIONS TO A POST-INDIVIDUALIST THEORY OF POLITICS 140-42 (1981)).

[668] *See* GUTHRIE, *Supra* note 20, at 256 (noting that Paleolithic humans not only had to cooperate both to hunt and kill large prey, but that the size of the prey encouraged egalitarian sharing and distribution).

[669] *See* MICHELLE GOLDBERG, THE MEANS OF REPRODUCTION: SEX, POWER, AND THE FUTURE OF THE WORLD 11-12 (2009) (arguing that reproductive rights are directly related to women's economic freedom, educational possibilities, health, and social status).

[670] DON TAPSCOTT, GROWN UP DIGITAL: HOW THE NET GENERATION IS CHANGING YOUR WORLD 97-98, 100-09 (2009) (describing scientific evidence that digital immersion - spending significant time on activities such as playing video games and using the internet - can change the brain, including how information is processed).

[671] MORLEY WINOGRAD & MICHAEL D. HAIS, MILLENNIAL MAKEOVER: MYSPACE, YOUTUBE, AND THE FUTURE OF AMERICAN POLITICS 111 (2008). *See* also Noah Shachtman, *Social Networks as Foreign Policy*, N.Y. TIMES, Dec. 13, 2009, Magazine Section, at 62 (describing how the United States is using social networks to further its foreign policy goals, including facilitating access to Twitter during pro-democracy protests in Iran).

[672] For example, consider the remarkable similarities between the Peloponnesian War and a nineteenth century Polynesian War. *See* MARSHALL SAHLINS, APOLOGIES TO THUCYDIDES: UNDERSTANDING HISTORY AS CULTURE AND VICE VERSA (2004). The number and significance of comparisons between the two wars could support a determinist approach to social change, suggesting that the only way two wars, in different times and eras, could be so similar is if events are somehow preordained. If that were the case, then fighting to bring about social change and to overcome the pre-existing order is futile.

[673] Karl Marx, *Excerpts from The Eighteenth Brumaire of Louis Bonaparte*, in BASIC WRITINGS ON POLITICS AND PHILOSOPHY, *Supra* note 16, at 318, 320

("Men make their own history, but they do not make it just as they please; they do not make it under circumstances chosen by themselves, but under circumstances directly encountered, given, and transmitted from the past.").

[674] In 1984, I cited the 1930s labor movement and the 1960s civil rights movement as instances when significant social change was achieved directly as a result of organizing efforts. BACHMANN, *Supra* note 2, at 49.

[675] The findings of evolutionary science concerning the benefits of organization remain tentative yet intriguing. *See, e.g.*, BERREBY, *Supra* note 32 (identifying evolutionary and neural bases for group formation around shared traits); ERIC CHAISSON, EPIC OF EVOLUTION: SEVEN AGES OF THE COSMOS 392 (2006) (describing the social organization of insects, which is "almost entirely programmed by genes"); RICHARD MCELREATH & ROBERT BOYD, MATHEMATICAL MODELS OF SOCIAL EVOLUTION: A GUIDE FOR THE PERPLEXED (2007) (illustrating mathematical models based on scientific theories of reciprocity, altruism, and other forms of social interaction).

[676] AmericanHeritage.com, People, The Presidents, http://www.americanheritage.com/people/presidents/ (last visited Mar. 16, 2010) (click on links of names of individual presidents to see party affiliation).

[677] Office of the Clerk, U.S. House of Representatives, House History, Party Divisions of the House of Representatives (1789 to Present), http://clerk.house.gov/art_history/house_history/partyDiv.html (last visited Sept. 9, 2010).

[678] U.S. Senate, Art & History Home, Origins & Development, Party Division in the Senate, 1789-Present, http://www.senate.gov/pagelayout/history/one_item_and_teasers/ partydiv.htm (last visited Sept. 9, 2010).

[679] *Supra* notes 104-01.

[680] *See* AmericanHeritage.com, *Supra* note 103.

[681] One potent example of conservative presence on the judiciary influencing politics was "the Court's shameful decision in *Bush v. Gore*, when five conservative justices declared George W. Bush president on grounds that they had themselves rejected in past cases and that they conceded would have no application in future ones." Ronald Dworkin, *Justice Sotomayor: The Unjust Hearings*, N.Y. REV. BOOKS, Sept. 24, 2009, at 37, 37. The broader and more subversive effects of a conservative presence in the judiciary are discussed in RONALD DWORKIN, THE SUPREME COURT PHALANX: THE COURT'S NEW RIGHTWING BLOC (2009) (focusing on the Supreme Court appointments of the openly conservative John Roberts and Samuel Alito as examples of rightwing political influence over judges with serious implications for constitutional jurisprudence). *See also* JAMES

MACGREGOR BURNS, PACKING THE COURT: THE RISE OF JUDICIAL POWER AND THE COMING CRISIS OF THE SUPREME COURT (2009) (observing that politicians have sought to "pack" the Court with justices that share their political beliefs, enabling such ideologies to retain influence long after they have passed out of popularity among the American public).

[682] *See* Robert B. Reich, *How to End the Great Recession*, N.Y. TIMES, Sept. 3, 2010, at A21 ("In the late 1970s, the richest 1 percent of American families took in about 9 percent of the nation's total income; by 2007, the top 1 percent took in 23.5 percent of total income.").

[683] *See* HOWARD ZINN, THE TWENTIETH CENTURY: A PEOPLE'S HISTORY 319 (1984) (observing that, among a group of industrialized countries, the United States dedicates the largest percentage of its gross national product to military expenditures). *See* also FRANCES FOX PIVEN & RICHARD A. CLOWARD, THE NEW CLASS WAR (1982) (examining the efforts of conservative, corporation-oriented parties to dismantle social welfare programs).

[684] *See infra* notes 116-29 and accompanying text.

[685] BACHMANN, *Supra* note 13, at 351-52.

[686] *See* BACHMANN, *Supra* note 2, at 197-98 (citing GITLIN, *Supra* note 16, at 146-47, 226, 230, 234, 236-37).

[687] *See* GITLIN, *Supra* note 16, at 146-47.

[688] *See generally* SIDNEY BLUMENTHAL, THE RISE OF THE COUNTER ESTABLISHMENT: THE CONSERVATIVE ASCENT TO POLITICAL POWER (Sterling Publ'g Co. 2008) (1986) (describing the rise, beginning in the 1980s, of a new conservatism, characterized by a specific mode of ideological politics and the realignment of elites); CRITCHLOW, *Supra* note 13 (exploring the ideological inconsistencies marking the new conservative coalition and how conservative ideologies achieved political power in the second half of the twentieth century); HIMMELSTEIN, *Supra* note 39 (examining the social conditions and political strategies that contributed to the sustained growth of American conservatism); MICKLETHWAIT & WOOLDRIDGE, *Supra* note 39 (describing American conservatism and arguing that this conservatism is what sets the United States apart from other wealthy nations); RIGHTWARD BOUND: MAKING AMERICA CONSERVATIVE IN THE 1970s (Bruce J. Schulman & Julian E. Zelizer eds., 2008) (presenting a number of scholarly articles on the conservative ascendancy in the 1970s); Teles, *Supra* note 86 (tracing the increasing influence of the conservative legal movement that resulted from popular organizing beginning in the 1970s).

[689] Memorandum from Lewis F. Powell, Jr., to Eugene B. Sydnor, Jr., Chairman,

Educ. Comm., U.S. Chamber of Commerce (Aug. 23, 1971) (emphasis added), available at http://old.mediatransparency.org/story.php?storyID=22. Some of Justice Powell's suggestions for organizing efforts included evaluation of social science textbooks, balancing faculties, monitoring television, direct political action, and "exploiting judicial action" with "a highly competent staff of lawyers," as exemplified by the ACLU. *Id.*

[690] *See* LEARS, *Supra* note 46, at 9 ("Powell urged the defenders of capitalism to retake the field...by establishing think tanks, media outlets and university professorships ...").

[691] *See* LEWIS H. LAPHAM, TENTACLES OF RAGE, HARPER'S MAG., sept. 2004, at 31, 3435 (detailing the extent and scope of the conservative organizing that began in the 1970s, funded in part by donations from "senior officers of the Fortune 500 companies").

[692] Some of the more significant organizations include the Business Roundtable, founded in 1972, *see* Micklethwait & Wooldridge, *Supra* note 39, at 79; STOP ERA, in 1972, *see* Marjorie J. Sprull, Gender and America's Rights Turn, in RIGHTWARD BOUND, *Supra* note 115, at 71, 78-79; the American Association of Christian Schools, in 1972, *see* Joseph Crespino, Civil Rights and the Religious Right, in *Rightward Bound, Supra* note 115, at 90, 101; the Heritage Foundation, in 1973, *see* MICKLETHWAIT & WOOLDRIDGE, *Supra* note 39, at 77; the Committee for the Survival of a Free Congress, in 1974, *see Id.* at 82; the Conservative Caucus, in 1974, *see Id.* at 82; the Eagle Forum, in 1975, *see* Sprull, *supra*, at 78-79; Students in Free Enterprise, in 1975, *see* Bethany E. Moreton, *Make Payroll, Not War: Business Culture as Youth Culture*, in *RIGHTWARD BOUND, Supra* note 115, at 52, 58; the Cato Institute, in 1977, *see* MICKLETHWAIT & WOOLDRIDGE, *Supra* note 39, at 77; the National Conservative Political Action Committee, in 1978, *see Id.* at 82; and the Moral Majority, in 1979, *see Id.* at 83. *See also* CRITCHLOW, *Supra* note 13, at 120-22 (identifying conservative organizations and corporate donors that were active in funding conservative policy and research).

[693] Conservative influence over public school curricula can be seen by the increased focus on economics: the U.S. Chamber of Commerce has distributed its "Economics for Young Americans" kits into some 12,000 schools, Moreton, *Supra* note 119, at 57, and the "undergraduate business major became America's default core curriculum," *Id.* at 62.

[694] The number of corporate PACs increased exponentially. "In 1974, labor 'political action committees' (PACs) outnumbered corporate PACs by 201 to 89. Two years later the ratio was reversed, with 433 corporate PACs and 224 labor

ones, and by 1984 companies had a 4 to 1 advantage..." MICKLETHWAIT & WOOLDRIDGE, *Supra* note 39, at 79. *See* also CRITCHLOW, *Supra* note 13, at 128 ("By 1978 the National Conservative Political Action Committee...became the largest conservative political action committee in the country, distributing more than $1.2 million in cash and in-kind contributions to political campaigns in its first five years.").

[695] *See* Donald T. Critchlow, *When Republicans Became Revolutionaries: Conservatives in Congress*, in THE AMERICAN CONGRESS: THE BUILDING OF DEMOCRACY 703, 712 (Julian E. Zelizer ed., 2004) ("[A] revitalized conservative movement in the Republican party set the stage for the 1980 election between Carter and the hero of many conservatives, Ronald Reagan.").

[696] *See* MICHAEL SCHALLER & GEORGE RISING, THE REPUBLICAN ASCENDANCY: AMERICAN POLITICS, 1968-2001 (2002) (tracing the increasing popularity of the Republican Party). *See* also ALAN M. DERSHOWITZ, SUPREME INJUSTICE: HOW THE HIGH COURT HIJACKED ELECTION 2000, at 189 (2001) ("[F]or the first time in modern American history, virtually all the branches of government are effectively controlled by Republicans and conservatives.").

[697] Paul Weyrich and Reverend Jerry Falwell founded the Moral Majority in 1979, mobilizing millions of devout Christian voters and connecting them with social conservatives. MICKLETHWAIT & WOOLDRIDGE, *Supra* note 39, at 83-85. The Christian Coalition was formed in 1989 from the remnants of Reverend Pat Robertson's presidential campaign. *Id.* at 111. The meticulous organizing skills of Ralph Reed contributed to the organization's expansion, as evidenced by the growth of its members so that at "the end of 1990, the Christian Coalition had amassed 125 chapters with 57,000 members. By 1997 it had 2000 chapters and 1.9 million members." *Id.*

[698] *See Id.* at 112-13 (chronicling the rise in popularity and influence of Rush Limbaugh and his talk radio show).

[699] BENJAMIN GINSBERG & MARTIN SHEFTER, POLITICS BY OTHER MEANS: POLITICIANS, PROSECUTORS, AND THE PRESS FROM WATERGATE TO WHITEWATER 66 (rev. and updated ed. 1999).

[700] JEFFREY TOOBIN, TOO CLOSE TO CALL: THE THIRTY-SIX DAY BATTLE TO DECIDE THE 2000 ELECTION 178 (2001). During the controversy over the election, a scuffle by Republican protesters to delay and obstruct ballot recounts, which later became known as the "Brooks Brothers riot," was yet another example of Republican street organizing success. *Id.* at 156, 178-79.

[701] CRITCHLOW, *Supra* note 13, at 267-69.

702 *See* Karl Rove, *How the GOP Should Prepare for a Comeback*, WALL ST. J., Dec. 11, 2008, at A 17 (recommending several organizing initiatives to mobilize Republican supporters, including training party leaders, registering likely Republican voters, and utilizing new media).

703 *See* Christopher Rhoads, *Playing Catch-Up, the GOP Is All Atwitter About the Internet*, WALL ST. J., Jan. 30, 2009, at Al (describing efforts by Republicans to make greater use of new social networking technologies in order to increase their electoral competitiveness).

704 "Astroturfing" is "a tactic used by professional lobbyists to make their efforts appear to be part of grass-roots movements." Stephanie Strom, *Firm Wants U.S. Inquiry in Lobby Case*, N.Y. TIMES, Aug. 29, 2009, at A 14. *See* also Editorial, *Another Astroturf Campaign*, N.Y. TIMES, Sept. 4, 2009, at A20 (detailing a campaign by the oil lobby to block climate change legislation through "a grass-roots citizen movement" funded by the oil industry and inaccurately representing aspects of the opposed legislation).

705 *See* Noam Cohen, *Know Thine Enemy*, N.Y. TIMES, Aug. 23, 2009, Week in Review Section, at 5 ("It is an irony of the current skirmishing about health care that those who could be considered Mr. Alinsky's sworn enemies-the groups, many industry sponsored, who are trying to shout down Congressional town hall meetings-have taken a page (chapters, really) from his handbook on community organizing."). Saul Alinsky is widely considered to have been one of the founding fathers of American community organizing. *See Id.* (describing Alinsky as an "activist whose street-smart tactics influenced generations of community organizers, most famously [President Obama]").

706 For example, as part of the opposition to health care reform in 2009, "[t]he Family Research Council, a conservative Christian organization, issued an electronic 'Town Hall Kit' to help its followers, including pastors, set up their own meetings 'to inform and activate the people in your pews and communities' against the health care overhaul proposals moving through Congress." Katherine Q. Seelye, *Actual Town Hall Not Included*, N.Y. TIMES, Aug. 26, 2009, at A 14. *See* also James P. Othmer, Op-Ed., *Don't Tweet About Health Care*, N.Y. TIMES, Sept. 14, 2009, at A21 (observing the successful use of web sites and messaging services like YouTube and Twitter to undermine health care reform efforts). But *see* Kate Zernike, NYTimes.com, The Caucus Blog, Notes from the Tea Party Convention (Feb. 6, 2010), http://thecaucus.blogs.nytimes.com/2010/02/06/notesfrom-the-tea-party-convention (observing that a session on using new technology "got hung up on basics" due to the lack of tech-savvy among Tea Party convention attendees).

707 *See* TELES, *Supra* note 86, at 138 ("The first Federalist Society activity was a symposium on federalism at Yale Law School held in April 1982.").

708 *See Supra* notes 116-19 and accompanying text.

709 *See* TELES, *Supra* note 86, at 196-98. *See* also George Hicks, *The Conservative Influence of the Federalist Society on the Harvard Law School Student Body*, 29 HARV. J.L. & Pub. Pol'y 625 (2006) (arguing that the conservative shift of Harvard Law School's student body is due in large measure to the organizing efforts of the school's Federalist Society).

710 TELES, *Supra* note 86, at 179.

711 *See infra* Part IV.F.

712 *See* WINOGRAD & HAIS, *Supra* note 98, at 155, 157, 184 (describing Dean's innovative campaign tactics, many of which were utilized to greater effect during Obama's campaign). While Dean lost his presidential bid, he was elected chairman of the Democratic National Committee. He thus played a large role in orchestrating the Democratic party's recapture of Congress in 2006, which included some of tactics developed during his presidential bid. *See* id at 118-19,121.

713 *See Id.* at 1-2 ("The presidential campaign of 2008 is the first real test of the willingness of candidates to embrace social networking technologies. ...").

714 *See Id.* ("Recent survey research on the political attitudes of [youth] show a high tolerance for lifestyle and ethnic differences and support for an activist government to societal and economic issues...").

715 Elizabeth Drew, *The Truth About the Election*, N.Y. REV. BOOKS, Dec. 18, 2008, at 92, 92.

716 *Id*

717 Michael Luo, *Obama Hauls In Record $750 Million for Campaign, with Plenty Left to Spend*, N.Y. TIMES, Dec. 5, 2008, at A29.

718 *Id*

719 Susan Davis, WSJ.com, Washington Wire Blog, Obama's Caucus-State Magic (Feb. 6, 2008), http://blogs.wsj.com/washwire/2008/02/06/obamas-caucus-state-magic/.

720 *See* ROGER MORRIS, PARTNERS IN POWER: THE CLINTONS AND THEIR AMERICA 119, 133-34 (1996) (detailing Clinton's background with and apparent dismissal of community organizer Saul Alinsky).

721 *See* Helene Cooper & Carl Hulse, *Obama's Effort on Budget Echoes Fall Campaign*, N.Y. TIMES, Mar. 18, 2009, at A16.

722 *See* Jim Rutenberg & Adam Nagourney, *Melding Obama's Web to a YouTube*

Presidency, N.Y. TIMES, Jan. 26, 2009, at Al (citing administration's goal of harnessing the presidential campaign's innovative organization to support administration policies); Sheryl Gay Stolberg, *Obama Steers Health Debate Out of Capital*, N.Y. TIMES, June 30, 2009, at Al (documenting the President's mobilization of grassroots supporters and use of new social networking technologies in his campaign to pass health care reform legislation).

[723] Karl Rove, *The President Is "Keeping Score,"* WALL ST. J., Apr. 2, 2009, at A17.

[724] *See* Cohen, *Supra* note 132 (detailing Republican use of tactics similar to those of Alinsky and other progressives). *See* also Mark Leibovich & David D. Kirkpatrick, *On Center Stage, Palin Electrifies Convention*, N.Y. TIMES, Sept. 4, 2008, at Al.

[725] Much of the information in this section and Part IV comes from my experience working as ACORN's General Counsel and is not always covered by sources amenable to citation.

[726] BACHMANN, *Supra* note 2, at 40-43.

[727] *Id.* at 41.

[728] *See* Brief of ACORN as Amicus Curiae in Support of Petitioners at 15-16 & nn.39-47, Crawford v. Marion County Elections Bd., 553 U.S. 181 (2008) (No. 07-21) (citing Final Order of Dismissal with Prejudice and Judgment in Favor of ACORN, Stuart v. ACORN, No. 04-22764 (S.D. Fla. Dec. 6, 2005); Final Order of Dismissal with Prejudice as to Specified Pleadings, Rousseau v. ACORN, No. 04-61636 (S.D. Fla. Nov. 23, 2005)).

[729] Evan Perez, *Investgation into US. Attorneys Scandal Advances*, WALL ST. J., June 16, 2008, at A3.

[730] *Id. See* also Editorial, *The Acorn Indictments*, WALL ST. J., Nov. 3, 2006, at A10 (reporting approvingly on the Missouri indictments); Editorial, *It's Subpoena Time*, N.Y. TIMES, June 8, 2007, at A28 (citing "Justice Department[] guidelines [that told] prosecutors not to bring vote fraud investigations right before an election'").

[731] *See* Editorial, *The Acorn Indictments*, *Supra* note 157.

[732] PEREZ, *Supra* note 156.

[733] Christopher Drew & Eric Lipton, *Anger of Swing State Republicans Eased US. Attorney Toward Exit*, N.Y. TIMES, Mar. 18,2007, § 1, at 1.

[734] *Id.*

[735] Philip Shenon & David Johnston, *A Defender of Bush's Power, Gonzales Resigns*, N.Y. TIMES, Aug. 28, 2007, at A1.

[736] Indeed, as much as this section should be read from the perspective of ACORN and its attempts to organize, it also provides some insight as to rightwing

organizing strategies and tactics.

[737] *E.g.*, Editorial, *Obama and Acorn*, WALL ST. J., Oct. 14, 2008, at A20 ("Acorn is now getting more attention as John McCain's campaign makes an issue of the fraud reports and Acorn's ties to Mr. Obama."). The case in which Obama's participation served as the basis for these inaccurate allegations was ACORN v. Edgar, 56 F.3d 791 (7th Cir. 1996). At the time, I held the position of General Counsel for ACORN, a post I did not share with the future President.

[738] These allegations were made in traditional news media outlets as well as newer, more subjective forms of media. *E.g., Editorial, Justice and Voter Fraud*, WALL ST. J., Oct. 27, 2008, at A18 ("If voter fraud would ever be ripe for investigation, this would seem to be the year with the Association of Community Organizations for Reform Now (ACORN) having been caught filing thousands of bogus voter registrations in at least 14 states."); Michael Massing, *Obama: In the Divided Heartland*, N.Y. Rev. Books, Dec. 18, 2008, at 26 ("[C]olumnists like Jonah Goldberg, Charles Krauthammer, Mark Steyn, Michael Barone...and Ann Coulter...all join[ed] together to produce firestorms of manufactured rage about Obama's purported ties to Bill Ayers, Tony Rezko, Jeremiah Wright, ACORN, Castro, Chavez, Ahmadinejad, and Karl Marx.").

[739] Katharine Q. Seelye, *McCain's Warning About Voter Fraud Stokes a Fiery Campaign Even Further*, N.Y. TIMES, Oct. 26, 2008, at A19. *See* also Bob Herbert, Op-Ed., *The Real Scandal*, N.Y. TIMES, Oct. 21, 2008, at A29 (noting McCain's statement and describing the allegations on which it was based).

[740] Greg Gordon, *Death Threat, Vandalism Hit ACORN After McCain Comments*, McClatchy, Oct. 17, 2008, http://www.mcclatchydc.com/251/story/54360.html.

[741] *See* Michael Falcone, *F.B.I. Offices Examining Activities of ACORN*, N.Y. TIMES, Oct. 17, 2008, at A19; Seelye, *Supra* note 166.

[742] *See* BACHMANN, *Supra* note 2, at 104-05. While ACORN's goals are laudable, like any other organization, its record has not been without error. *See, e.g.*, Steve Friess, *ACORN Charged in Voter Registration Fraud Case in Nevada*, N.Y. TIMES, May 5, 2009, at A18 (detailing allegations of voter registration fraud against the Las Vegas ACORN branch); Sara Jean Green, *Local ACORN Cleans Up Act After Scandal*, SEATTLE TIMES, October 29, 2008, at Al (describing fraudulent voter registrations by the Washington ACORN branch and its efforts to prevent such issues).

[743] See Conor Dougherty, *Minority Turnout Was Critical to Obama's Election, Data Show*, WALL ST. J., July 21, 2009, at A3 (noting Obama's success in swing states could be attributed in part to an increase of nearly five million voters in the 2008 presidential election, the vast majority of them people of color, an increase "reflect[ing] a long-

term demographic shift. .. [and] attest[ing] to the success of the Democrats' extensive campaign to register their supporters and get them to the polls"); Greg Gordon, *More Minorities Voted This Year, but White Turnout Dropped*, MCCLATCHY, Nov. 18, 2008, http://www.mcclatchydc.com/homepage/story/56113.html ("Barack Obama's 8.5 million-vote margin over John McCain was fueled by a more than 20 percent surge in minority voting...appear[ing] to reflect the success of...liberal voter registration groups...").

[744] Open Letter from Clifford S. Asness, Managing and Founding Principal, AQR Capital Mgmt., LLC (May 4, 2009), available at http://zerohedge.blogspot.com/20 09/05/cliffasness-i-am-ready-for-my.html.

[745] *See* Bachmann, *Supra* note 2, at 46.

[746] *Cf. Id.* at 57 n.68 (describing the labor movement in the 1930s in the United States, wherein "industrialization brought large numbers of workers together, which allowed for mass organizing drives, and ultimately massive agglomerations of worker power").

[747] *See Id.* at 46 n.31 (citing Marx, *Supra* note 100, at 338-39).

[748] *See* DANIEL BELL, THE COMING OF POSTINDUSTRIAL SOCIETY: A VENTURE IN SOCIAL FORECASTING 14 (1973) (describing post-industrial society as characterized in part by increased focus on "the professional and technical class"). *See* also Ursula K. Heise, *Science, Technology, and Postmodernism*, in THE CAMBRIDGE COMPANION TO POSTMODERNISM 136, 141 (Steven Connor ed., 2004); Julian Murphet, POSTMODERNISM AND SPACE, IN THE CAMBRIDGE COMPANION TO POSTMODERNISM, *supra*, at 116, 123, 133.

[749] *See* Ruy Teixeira, *Postindustrial Hopes Deferred: Why the Democratic Majority Is Still Likely to Emerge*, BROOKINGS REV., Summer 2003, at 40, 41 (describing the impact of postindustrial economy-characterized by "ideopolises" organized around the production of ideas and services-on Democratic politics). *See* also HARDT & NEGRI, *Supra* note 60, at 409-11 (describing the "social worker" as the predominant constituency of labor power).

[750] SAMUEL BOWLES & HERBERT GINTIS, SCHOOLING IN CAPITALIST AMERICA: EDUCATIONAL REFORM AND THE CONTRADICTIONS OF ECONOMIC LIFE 253 (1976) ("[T]raditionally elite independent jobs-entrepreneurial, privileged white collar, professional, and technical occupations-are reduced to the condition of wage labor. No longer can professional and small-business people look confidently to a future of controlling their work processes, finding creative outlets in work, or holding decision-making power.").

[751] *See* BACHMANN, *Supra* note 2, at 46 n.31 (citing Marx, *Supra* note 100, at 338-39).

[752] *See* WINOGRAD & HAIS, *Supra* note 98, at 142-43 (citing research documenting the dramatic changes broadband access has on individual internet usage and using the communication service Skype as an example of how, thanks in part to broadband access, technological improvements have impacted communication abilities).

[753] *See Id.* at 119 (discussing the Democratic National Committee's efforts to mobilize voters through both "online interaction[s]" and "more traditional ways of organizing grassroots campaigns").

[754] *Id.* at 2-3.

[755] Rhoads, *Supra* note 130; Jake Sherman, *Conservatives Take a Page from Left's Online Playbook*, WALL ST. J., Aug. 19, 2009, at A4.

[756] *See* BACHMANN, *Supra* note 2, at 197 (attributing "disorganization in the ranks of the disenfranchised" to "identity politics").

[757] JACKSON LEARS, REBIRTH OF A NATION: THE MAKING OF MODERN AMERICA, 1877-1920, at 112-13, 153 (2009) (documenting the role racial and ethnic loyalties played in dividing socioeconomic classes when it came to labor issues at the end of the nineteenth century and radial agrarian politics in 1878). This list of characteristics can be extended, but one divisive economic issue must be noted: the differences between those on welfare and the working poor. While both are comparably powerless in relation to the means of production, differences between these constituencies have interfered with organizing efforts to unite them. Much of ACORN's history can be explained as attempts to appreciate this reality and overcome it. *See* GARY DELGADO, ORGANIZING THE MOVEMENT: THE ROOTS AND GROWTH OF ACORN 45-50 (1986).

[758] Charles M. Blow, Op-Ed., *Whose Country Is It?*, N.Y. TIMES, Mar. 27, 2010, at A19 (discussing Republican exploitation of the frustration and fears of the "disproportionately white, evangelical," and undereducated, in the context of support for health care reform being led by individuals who also happen to be female, Jewish, gay, or African-American).

[759] BACHMANN, *Supra* note 2, at 197-98.

[760] Culture may be defined as "socially transmitted behavior patterns, arts, beliefs, institutions, and all other products of human work and thought." THE AMERICAN HERITAGE DICTIONARY OF THE ENGLISH LANGUAGE, *Supra* note 35, at 454. Historian David Hackett Fischer uses the term "folkways" to describe culture, citing twenty-six empirical folkway indicators: speech, building, family, marriage, gender, sex, naming, childrearing, age, death, religion, magic, learning, literacy, food, dress, sport, work, time, wealth, inheritance, rank, association, order, power, and freedom. DAVID HACKETT FISCHER,

ALBION'S SEED: FOUR BRITISH FOLKWAYS IN AMERICA 11 n.10 (1989).

[761] *See, e.g.,* JOHN L. COMAROFF & JEAN COMAROFF, ETHNICITY, INC. (2009) (discussing the variable meanings, iterations, and uses of terms like ethnicity and cultural identity); JAMES DAVISON HUNTER, CULTURE WARS: THE STRUGGLE TO DEFINE AMERICA (1991) (identifying major issues of cultural disagreement in contemporary American society and analyzing the historical underpinnings and political consequences of these disputes); SAMUEL P. HUNTINGTON, THE CLASH OF CIVILIZATIONS AND THE REMAKING OF WORLD ORDER (1997) (categorizing the world's major cultures and exploring the potential for conflict generated by cultural differences); MICHAEL LIND, MADE IN TEXAS: GEORGE W. BUSH AND THE SOUTHERN TAKEOVER OF AMERICAN POLITICS (2003) (tracing the development of different cultural narratives in the state of Texas); CARL OGLESBY, THE YANKEE & COWBOY WAR: CONSPIRACIES FROM DALLAS TO WATERGATE (1976) (explaining how struggles between two different elite cultural groups, Northeastern liberal detentists, or Yankees, and Southwestern conservative militarists, or Cowboys, were manifested in the assassination of President Kennedy and the Watergate scandal); KEVIN PHILLIPS, THE COUSINS' WARS: RELIGION, POLITICS, AND THE TRIUMPH OF ANGLO-AMERICA (1999) (tracing the evolution of majority American culture, from British aristocratic roots to current democratic norms, as influenced by civil wars and political realignments); THOMAS SOWELL, BLACK REDNECKS AND WHITE LIBERALS (2005) (describing some of the characteristics unique to white Southern culture, traceable to British origins, and remarking on the continuing social and economic influence of these traditions on American blacks living in ghettoes). Cultural divisiveness is neither new, nor is it uniquely American. *See, e.g.,* FREDERICK BROWN, FOR THE SOUL OF FRANCE: CULTURE WARS IN THE AGE OF DREYFUS (2010) (highlighting cultural divides in nineteenth century France between scientific modernists and religious conservatives, a clash that came to the fore in the 1890s).

[762] FISCHER, *Supra* note 187, at 6, 785-88.

[763] *Id.* at 44-49.

[764] *See Id.* at 446-51, 601.

[765] *See Id.* at 495.

[766] *Id.* at 241-43.

[767] These areas (Wessex, Mercia, and Sussex) supported King John in the Magna Carta struggle, the Catholics during the Tudor Reformation, and King Charles during the English Revolution. *Id.* at 212-16.

[768] *Id.* at 398-401.

[769] *Id.*at 362.

[770] *Id.* at 623-32.

[771] *Id.* at 676.

[772] *Id.* at 740-41.

[773] *See Id.* at 814.

[774] Gender relations among the Puritans were marked by inequality in marriage but less so in religious settings, and laws protected women more so than in other regions. *See Id.* at 83-86. The Puritans also demonstrated a "zeal for learning and literacy." *Id.* at 132. Family structures among the Quakers were marked by a strong sense of egalitarianism, *Id.* at 483, and "[b]y and large they favored literacy and feared learning but were painfully ambivalent about both attainments," *Id.* at 531. By contrast, the Appalachian region was characterized by xenophobia, prejudice, violence, and cultural conservatism. *See Id.* at 65051. In Virginia, the colonial mood was "reinforced by the values of an English culture that tended to be profoundly conservative in every sense-elitist, hierarchical, and strenuously hostile to social change." *Id.* at 253.

[775] *See Id.* at 889-95 (observing persistence of cultural patterns by region and questioning factors that have contributed to this persistence).

[776] PHILLIPS, *Supra* note 188 (observing similar religious, ethno-cultural, and imperialist themes that trace through Anglo-American history and were solidified in the English Civil War, the American Revolutionary War, and the American Civil War).

[777] *See, e.g.,* LIND, *Supra* note 188 (detailing the origins of majority culture values in Texas, and the impact changing racial and ethnic demographics have had on the popularity of some of those historical trends); OGLESBY, *Supra* note 188, at 8 (calling "attention to the persistence of Civil War splits" in the political atmosphere of the United States during the 1960s and 1970s).

[778] FISCHER, *Supra* note 187, at 884-.87.

[779] Election results from 2008 show the greatest shifts towards Republican voting from Oklahoma through Tennessee into West Virginia, suggesting that Highlander culture was intensifying in its support for Republicans, while at the same time isolating itself from the rest of the country. *See* Adam Nossiter, *For South, a Waning Hold on National Politics,* N.Y. TIMES, Nov. 11, 2008, at Al.

[780] *See, e.g.,* PETER J. RICHERSON & ROBERT BOYD, NOT BY GENES ALONE: HOW CULTURE TRANSFORMED HUMAN EVOLUTION 1 (2005) ("The American South has long been more violent than the North. For example,

over the period 1865-1915, the homicide rate in the South was ten times the current rate for the whole United States, and twice the rate in our most violent cities. Modern homicide statistics tell the same story.").

781 *Id.* at 3.

782 *See* CHAISSON, *Supra* note 102, at 392 ("We are now in the midst of an ongoing debate concerning the relative importance of the gene and the environment…").

783 *See, e.g.,* ROBERT M. SAPOLSKY, MONKEYLUV: AND OTHER ESSAYS ON OUR LIVES AS ANIMALS 5 (2005) ("[I]mperceptibly subtle differences in environment can utterly change the effects of genes on behavior.").

784 *See generally* GREGORY COCHRAN & HENRY HARPENDING, THE 10,000 YEAR EXPLOSION: HOW CIVILIZATION ACCELERATED HUMAN EVOLUTION (2009).

785 BERREBY, *Supra* note 32, at 101. Another intermediate position holds that genes and environment necessarily interact to influence human behavior, rather than either factor governing primarily. *See* CHAISSON, *Supra* note 102, at 370 ("Part of our anatomy, abilities, attitudes, and desires, as well as our outlook on life and way of thinking, all derive to some extent from the genes of our ancestors, molded partly by the environments in which they lived."); RICHERSON & BOYD, *Supra* note 207, at 9 ("*Every bit* of the behavior…of every single organism living…results from the interaction of genetic information stored in the developing organism and the properties of its environment.").

786 After the appalling racism of the twentieth century it is hard not to embrace a generally plastic conception of humanity. However, some evidence can be cited to the contrary. *See, e.g.,* COCHRAN & HARPENDING, *Supra* note 211, at 187-224 (exploring the evolutionary origins of the fact that Ashkenazi Jews have the highest average IQ of any ethnic group). *See* also NOAM CHOMSKY, PROBLEMS OF KNOWLEDGE AND FREEDOM: THE RUSSELL LECTURES (2003) (pointing out that, as a political and philosophical matter, some genetic hardwiring is necessary for people to avoid being easy targets of manipulation).

787 COMAROFF & COMAROFF, *Supra* note 188, at 118-19. Despite (or perhaps because of) the long history of the corporate form shaping societies, the Comaroffs have a dour view of how the corporate form may soon construct national and individual identity. *See Id.* at 126-30.

788 GORDON BROWN TINDALL & DAVID EMORY SHI, 1 AMERICA: A NARRATIVE HISTORY 53-73 (5th ed. 1999).

789 KAREN ORDAHL KUPPERMAN, PROVIDENCE ISLAND, *1620-41:* THE

OTHER PURITAN COLONY (paperback ed. 1995).

[790] *See, e.g.,* JIM COLLINS, HOW THE MIGHTY FALL: AND WHY SOME COMPANIES NEVER GIVE IN (2009) (exploring the causes of the failure of "great" companies); HELGA DRUMMOND, INTRODUCTION TO ORGANIZATIONAL BEHAVIOR (2000) (exploring key theories of organizational behavior and their implications); HANDBOOK OF ORGANIZATIONAL CHANGE AND INNOVATION (Marshall Scott Poole & Andrew H. Van de Ven eds., 2004) (compiling social science research and theoretical perspectives on organizational change); DAVID SKEEL, ICARUS IN THE BOARDROOM: THE FUNDAMENTAL FLAWS IN CORPORATE AMERICA AND WHERE THEY COME FROM (2005) (describing corporate risk-taking, competition, and structure, and the balance of power between government regulators and corporate leaders).

[791] More than half the businesses started in the United States operate for five years or less. Scott A. Shane, NYTimes.com, You're the Boss Blog, Failure Is a Constant in Entrepreneurship (July 17, 2009), http://boss.blogs.nytimes.com/2009/07/15/failure-is-aconstant-in-entrepreneurship.

[792] Weber discusses these issues in terms of institutionalization of charisma, sect to church; the contrast between small group democracy and mass democracy; and the contrast between personality-based economic enterprise and bureaucratic capitalism. *See* MAX WEBER, THE PROTESTANT ETHIC AND THE SPIRIT OF CAPITALISM 145, 152, 254 (Talcott Parsons trans., Dover 2003) (1904-1905); MAX WEBER, SOCIOLOGICAL WRITINGS 88, 162 (Wolf V. Heydebrand ed., 1994).

[793] *See, e.g.,* JANA MATTHEWS, JEFF DENNIS & PETER ECONOMY, LESSONS FROM THE EDGE: SURVIVAL SKILLS FOR STARTING AND GROWING A COMPANY (2003) (collecting stories from entrepreneurs whose businesses faced failure and who found a way to nonetheless succeed); EDITH PENROSE, THE THEORY OF THE GROWTH OF THE FIRM (3d ed. 1995) (outlining a general theory of the growth of firms, in terms of increases in sales, profits, or size, as well as improvements in quality).

[794] While little has been written tracing the evolution of corporate organizations, two noteworthy exceptions are AMAR V. BHIDÉ, THE ORIGIN AND EVOLUTION OF NEW BUSINESSES (2000) (examining the origins of new businesses and the factors that lead some to succeed and others not to, and the economic and social contexts surrounding such organizations), and JAMES C. COLLINS & JERRY I. PORRAS, BUILT TO LAST: SUCCESSFUL HABITS OF VISIONARY COMPANIES (1994) (studying the qualities over time of

successful companies in comparison to similar companies with less success and setting forth principles for creating long-lasting, high quality organizations).

[795] *See* BACHMANN, *Supra* note 2, at 143 (arguing that the poor will only be able to lift themselves out of poverty and achieve social and political change through organizing). *See* also Smith, *Supra* note 47, at 169 ("The masters, being fewer in number, can combine much more easily.").

[796] *See, e.g.,* STEPHEN R. BLOCK, WHY NONPROFITS FAIL: OVERCOMING FOUNDER'S SYNDROME, FUNDPHOBIA, AND OTHER OBSTACLES TO SUCCESS 135-54 (2004) (discussing the problems associated with "founder's syndrome"-the entrenchment of a founder's powers and privileges). *See* also JEAN LIPMAN-BLUMEN, THE ALLURE OF TOXIC LEADERS: WHY WE FOLLOW DESTRUCTIVE BOSSES AND CORRUPT POLITICIANS-AND HOW WE CAN SURVIVE THEM (2005); Terry Leap, *Keys to Spotting a Flawed CEO-Before It's Too Late*, WALL ST. J., Dec. 1, 2007, at R3 (identifying "warning signs" and "measures...to reduce the likelihood of hiring a dysfunctional CEO"); Gary Wilson, How to Rein In the Imperial CEO, WALL ST. J., Jul. 9, 2008, at A15 (discussing problems with "[e]ntrenched management" and lack of accountability of "Imperial CEO[s]").

[797] *See* Stephanie Strom, *Funds Misappropriated at 2 Nonprofit Groups*, N.Y. TIMES, July 9,2008, at A21.

[798] Scott Shane, *Conservatives Draw Blood from Acorn, Favored Foe*, N.Y. TIMES, Sept. 16, 2009, at A14.

[799] Scott Shane, *A Political Gadfly Lampoons the Left via YouTube*, N.Y. TIMES, Sept. 19, 2009, at A9.

[800] As a result of the scandal, the Senate voted "to prohibit the Department of Housing and Urban Development from giving federal housing money to [ACORN]," and "the Census Bureau dropped Acorn as one of 80,000 national unpaid 'partners' helping promote the 2010 census." *Id.*

[801] Clark Hoyt, Op-Ed., *Tuning in Too Late*, N.Y. TIMES, Sept. 27, 2009, Week in Review Section, at 12.

[802] *See* BACHMANN, *Supra* note 2, at 45.

[803] For instance, the decoding of the human genome in 2000 was a major achievement with significant implications for the progress of evolutionary science. *See* Nicholas Wade, *Genetic Code of Human Life Is Cracked by Scientists*, N.Y. TIMES, June 27, 2000, at Al.

[804] *Cf.* Stuart Elliot, *Is the Ad a Success? The Brain Waves Tell All*, N.Y. TIMES, Mar. 31, 2008, at C7 (explaining how marketers have been able to use developments in

neuroscience to create more effective advertisements).

805 *See, e.g.*, Brooks, *Supra* note 14 (citing a neuropsychiatrist who "argues that of course culture and environment powerfully shape behavior, but brain structure and chemistry" play a critical role in accounting for generalized differences between the genders).

806 *See* J. CRAIG VENTER, A LIFE DECODED: MY GENOME: MY LIFE 136, 338 (2007) (finding that "up to forty-five thousand base pairs of genetic code [were] in [the author's] genome and in that of the chimp, but [did] not seem to be common in other people" and concluding that "the most accurate representation" of a human genome sequence requires analysis of some six billion base pairs of code). *Cf.* WILLIS H. JOHNSON, LOUIS E. DELANNEY, ELIOT C. WILLIAMS & THOMAS A. COLE, PRINCIPLES OF ZOOLOGY 324 (1969) (citing the grass frog, *Rana pipiens*, as one example of a "species that occup[ies] a very wide geographic range [such that] the subpopulations at the extremes of the range, when brought together, are not able to function as members of the same species").

807 *See, e.g.*, JÜRGEN HABERMAS, THE THEORY OF COMMUNICATIVE ACTION: REASON AND THE RATIONALIZATION OF SOCIETY (Thomas McCarthy trans., Beacon Press 1984) (1981) (discussing rational positions, ideally reached through discussion between parties enjoying comparable power).

808 Hitler's Third Reich provides a drastic example of this mode of organizing. For good histories of Hitler's Germany, *see generally* ALAN BULLOCK, HITLER: A STUDY IN TYRANNY (REV. ED. 1962); MICHAEL BURLEIGH, THE THIRD REICH: A NEW HISTORY (2000).

809 In particular, one group of self-consciously organized individuals played a key role in the founding of the United States: The Pilgrims of Plymouth Rock, who entered into the Mayflower Compact to "combine ourselves together into a civill [sic] body politick [sic], for our better ordering and preservation." THE MAYFLOWER COMPACT (1620), Reprinted in AMERICAN HISTORICAL DOCUMENTS 1000-1904, at 62 (Charles W. Eliot ed., 1910). In purposefully joining together to pursue a common aim, the Pilgrims illustrate the self-conscious end of the spectrum upon which organizing efforts may be situated.

810 Sartre described this type of organization as a "fused group," constituted by individuals induced into group consciousness through a common threat or through shared material circumstances. *See* JEAN PAUL SARTRE, CRITIQUE OF DIALECTICAL REASON 345- 404 (Alan Sheridan-Smith trans., Jonathan Rée ed., Verso 2004) (1960).

811 *See generally* GEORGE ORWELL, 1984 (1949) (imagining a society governed by

a totalitarian regime that ruled through fear and obscuration).

[812] Of course, the categories that can be used to divide-for example, differences based on religion, ethnicity, or language-are often the very same categories relied on to inspire group unity and loyalty. *See* BERREBY, *Supra* note 32 (discussing manifold sources for solidarity and hostility between humans).

[813] *See, e.g.*, DUNCAN K. FOLEY, ADAM'S FALLACY: A GUIDE TO ECONOMIC THEOLOGY (2006) (criticizing the classical concept of socially beneficial, self-interested, purely rational beings operating in the field of economics entirely separately from other arenas of human life and undermining the traditional view that economics can be separated out from political and social issues); Todd, *Supra* note 47, at 63 (critiquing "textbook economics").

[814] *See* TAYLOR, *Supra* note 68, at 17 ("[B]iologically we are feeling creatures that think."). *See* also ROBERT TRIVERS, NATURAL SELECTION AND SOCIAL THEORY 277 (2002) (observing that the brain does not register a nervous signal in consciousness until long after the signal has reached the brain).

[815] *See generally* DREW WESTEN, THE POLITICAL BRAIN: THE ROLE OF EMOTION IN DECIDING THE FATE OF THE NATION (2007) (arguing that emotional responses among voters play a larger role in politics than logical reasoning). Westen notes in the introduction, "This book is likely to be of particular interest to the 50 million Democratic voters who can't figure out why their party has lost so many elections despite polls showing that the average voter agrees with Democratic positions on most policy issues...." *Id.* at ix.

[816] For discussions on the degree to which real economists have begun to pay attention to some of these "irrational" phenomenon, *see generally* GEORGE A. AKERLOF & ROBERT J. SHILLER, ANIMAL SPIRITS: HOW HUMAN PSYCHOLOGY DRIVES THE ECONOMY, AND WHY IT MATTERS FOR GLOBAL CAPITALISM (2009); DAN ARIELY, PREDICTABLY IRRATIONAL: THE HIDDEN FORCES THAT SHAPE OUR DECISIONS (2008); FOLEY, *Supra* Note 240; JUSTIN FOX, THE MYTH OF THE RATIONAL MARKET: A HISTORY OF RISK, REWARD, AND DELUSION ON WALL STREET (2009); TIM HARFORD, THE UNDERCOVER ECONOMIST (2005); STEVEN D. LEVITT & STEPHEN J. DUBNER, FREAKONOMICS: A ROGUE ECONOMIST EXPLORES THE HIDDEN SIDE OF EVERYTHING (2005); RICHARD H. THALER & CASS R. SUNSTEIN, NUDGE: IMPROVING DECISIONS ABOUT HEALTH, WEALTH, AND HAPPINESS (2008).

[817] MARTIN LINDSTROM, BUYOLOGY: TRUTH AND LIES ABOUT WHY WE BUY 74-75 (2008). *See* also DONALD LORITZ, HOW THE BRAIN

EVOLVED LANGUAGE 156 (1999) (providing an example of priming in the context of word recognition). For example, one study demonstrated that "subjects recognize the word nurse more quickly after having first been 'primed' by hearing or seeing the word doctor." *Id.* at 168-69. One word recognition theory posits that this is so because recognition units are activated, or "fired," when a word is detected, "and the more they fired, the more easily they would fire the next time." *Id.* at 168.

[818] *See* LINDSTROM, *Supra* note 244, at 68-87 (tracing the history of the use of subliminal imaging, and its reported effects on everything from self-esteem to theft rates to the amount of money people are willing to pay for a beverage).

[819] *See Id.* at 74-75 (discussing the use of priming in political advertisements).

[820] "Philip Morris, for example, offers bar owners financial incentives to fill their venues with color schemes, specially designed furniture...and other subtle symbols that, when combined, convey the very essence of Marlboro...." *Id.* at 78-79. Consumers pick up on the similarities between the visual environment and the cigarette brand's packaging, which subconsciously triggers an urge to smoke that brand of cigarette. *See* also FARHAD MANJOO, TRUE ENOUGH: LEARNING TO LIVE IN A POST-FACT SOCIETY 74-80 (2008) (discussing the power of images, even fabricated or ambiguous ones, to influence or reinforce human perceptions); TRIVERS, *Supra* note 241, at 309-11 (discussing the importance of physical symmetry for mate selection among various animal species as well as humans); Murphet, *Supra* note 175, at 117 (discussing the impact that the modem deluge of visuals of commercialized and sexualized bodies has on self-image).

Anecdotes from the Reagan Administration illustrate the greater appreciation Republicans have shown for using visual images to trump language. *See* HEDRICK SMITH, THE POWER GAME: HOW WASHINGTON WORKS 420 (1988) ("You're always looking for a picture you don't ever have to explain. The picture tells the story regardless of what Ronald Reagan says.").

[821] While looking like a hippie may not be the issue today that it was for organizers in the 1970s, "looking like a lawyer" remains an issue for lawyers. *See* Christina Binkley, *Inside a Bastion of Old-School Power Attire*, WALL ST. J., Feb. 5, 2009, at D8 (observing that as the economy has slowed and job opportunities have become scarcer, "power dressing" has become more prominent at major law firms and business casual has declined). "Looking like a lawyer" may take on special significance when representing marginalized constituencies, a lesson 1960s civil rights lawyer Marian Wright Edelman learned when she first encountered rural Mississippi African Americans: "[They had] heard there was a Black lady lawyer in town...and...came to look for and at me. When they saw me in blue jeans and an

old sweatshirt, they were crestfallen. I never wore jeans in public again in Mississippi...." MARIAN WRIGHT EDELMAN, LANTERNS: A MEMOIR OF MENTORS 79 (1999).

822 DELGADO, *Supra* note 184, at 70.

823 SMITH, *Supra* note 47, at 169, 230.

824 GUTHRIE, *Supra* note 20, at 157, 255.

825 COHEN, *Supra* note 7.

826 *See* John Paul Newport, *Team USA's Management Victory*, WALL ST. J., Sept. 27, 2008, at W9 (discussing how team-building strategies were crucial to the American team's victory).

827 BERREBY, *Supra* note 32, at 219.

828 CAROLE JAHME, BEAUTY AND THE BEASTS: WOMAN, APE AND EVOLUTION 46 (2002).

829 GUTHRIE, *Supra* note 20, at 420.

830 *See* KURT VONNEGUT, PALM SUNDAY: AN AUTOBIOGRAPHICAL COLLAGE 180-81 (1981) ("Human beings are supposed to live in stable, like-minded, extended families of fifty people or more....[In the United States] we were agreeing, among other things, to do without such families. It is a painful, unhuman agreement to make. Emotionally, it is hideously expensive....Marriage is collapsing because our families are too small...Quantities of relatives of any sort are what we need."); Standish, *Supra* note 89.

831 GUTHRIE, *Supra* note 20, at 247, 308.

832 *See, e.g.*, CHUCK PETTIS, TECHNOBRANDS: HOW TO CREATE & USE "BRAND IDENTITY" TO MARKET, ADVERTISE & SELL TECHNOLOGY PRODUCTS 70-75 (1995) (describing the creation and success of the "Intel Inside" brand campaign, centered around the repetition and ubiquity of a simple visual image). A variation on this theme is typography, where the shapes of letters affect the ways in which messages are received. *See, e.g.*, Edward Rothstein, *Typography Fans Say Ikea Should Stick to Furniture*, N.Y. TIMES, Sept. 5, 2009, at C1 ("[A]dvertisers, logo designers, magazine and book publishers and catalog creators spend millions on fonts because they know the medium has a message.").

833 *See* LINDSTROM, *Supra* note 244, at 99 ("[A] lot of consumers have almost a religious sense of loyalty to their favorite brands and products.").

834 *See, e.g.*, FRANS DE WAAL, CHIMPANZEE POLITICS: POWER AND SEX AMONG APES 140 (rev. ed. 1998) (1982) (discussing the role of coalitions in challenges to alpha males).

835 JAHME, *Supra* note 255, at 156.

836 DE WAAL, *Supra* note 261, at 12.

837 JAHME, *Supra* note 255, at 299, 361; De Waal, *Supra* note 261, at 10-11, 17.

838 *See, e.g.,* BERREBY, *Supra* note 32, at 211 (describing the views of social Darwinist William Graham Sumner).

839 *See Supra* Part III.D.1.

840 *See* AYN RAND, THE VIRTUE OF SELFISHNESS: A NEW CONCEPT OF EGOISM (1964) (articulating a moral system that values acting in one's own self-interest). *See* also KURT VONNEGUT, GOD BLESS YOU, MR. ROSEWATER: OR PEARLS BEFORE SWINE 52-53 (1965) ("Enlightened Self-interest gives them [mental processes] a flag, which they adore on sight. It is essentially the black and white Jolly Roger, with these words written beneath the skull and crossbones, 'The hell with you, Jack, I've got mine!'").

841 *See, e.g.,* CHAISSON, *Supra* note 102, at 392 ("Competition is not the sole driving force in evolution; cooperation is also a factor....."); Trivers, *Supra* note 241, at 3-55 (discussing reciprocal altruism- "I'll scratch your back if you scratch mine"- from an evolutionary perspective). Nor are humans unique in this respect. *See, e.g.,* Gautam Naik, *Deep Inside Bacteria, a Germ of Human Personality-Scientists Hope to Fight Infections by Blocking the Social Creatures' Ability to Sense When They Have Sufficient Numbers to Attack*, WALL ST. J., Sept. 8, 2009, at A18 (observing that bacteria display social behaviors).

842 *See* TRIVERS, *Supra* note 241, at 3-55.

843 *See* GUTHRIE, *Supra* note 20, at 216, 256. The complexity of having to cooperate and interact socially with other members of one's species also may have led to an increase in brain size and neural complexity. *Id.* at 218-19.

844 FRANS DE WAAL, THE AGE OF EMPATHY: NATURE'S LESSONS FOR A KINDER SOCIETY 70 (2009). While several hypotheses were presented for the rats' reactions, including fear for their own well-being or distraction, de Waal argues that the rats responded out of "an innate emotional response" to the pain of their fellow rats. *Id.* "One rat's distress may simply distress another." *Id.*

845 *Id.* at 75.

846 *Id.* at 187.

847 *Id.* at 33.

848 GUTHRIE, *Supra* note 20, at 256, 422. For additional discussion of how modem human behavior evolved in pre-modern times, *see* S. BOYD EATON, MARJORIE SHOSTAK & MELVIN KONNER, THE PALEOLITHIC

PRESCRIPTION (1988) (arguing that people today are still very similar to Paleolithic hunter-gatherers, and that health and quality of life will be improved by following a diet and exercise routine emulating the Paleolithic lifestyle).

[849] BARACK OBAMA, DREAMS FROM MY FATHER: A STORY OF RACE AND INHERITANCE 437 (Three Rivers Press rev. ed. 2004) (1995).

[850] *See* BACHMANN, *Supra* note 2, at 39. Many skeptical of the efficacy of social change lawyers have derived this conclusion from the belief that courts are not the best institutions from which to achieve social change. *See* GERALD N. ROSENBERG, THE HOLLOW HOPE: CAN COURTS BRING ABOUT SOCIAL CHANGE? (2d ed. 2008) (presenting competing views of the institutional abilities of courts, examining the conditions under which courts may bring about significant social reforms, and concluding that ultimately courts are rarely effective at producing such reforms).

The President may share a similar perspective. *See* Jodi Kantor, *As a Professor, a Pragmatist About the Supreme Court*, N.Y. TIMES, May 3, 2009, at A1 ("Former students and colleagues describe Mr. Obama as a minimalist (skeptical of court-led efforts at social change) ...").

[851] BACHMANN, *Supra* note 2, at 64.

[852] For a description of the kind of direct-action activity characteristic of ACORN's work during this period, *see* Delgado, *Supra* note 184, at 71-73. This sort of activity is fairly straightforward, and much of it can be done without significant legal training.

[853] These organizations include ACORN Housing Corporation, Inc.; ACORN Community Land Association, Inc.; and United Labor Organizations. United Labor Organizations was begun as an independent labor union in New Orleans and eventually bifurcated into two locals of the Service Employees International Union (SEIU). One was Local 100 in New Orleans (whose charter was revoked in 2009). The other was Local 880, based in Chicago, which grew into SEIU Health Care Illinois and Indiana.

[854] For example, the Labor Management Relations (Taft-Hartley) Act, first passed in 1947, established legal requirements with which labor unions had to comply. *See* Labor Management Relations Act, 1947, Pub. L. 80-101, 61 Stat. 136 (codified as amended in scattered sections of U.S.C.). The passage of the Labor-Management Reporting and Disclosure (Landrum-Griffin) Act created a complex system of regulations and reporting requirements for labor unions to follow. *See* Labor-Management Reporting and Disclosure Act of 1959, Pub. L. 86-257, 73 Stat. 519 (codified as amended in scattered sections of U.S.C.). For an informative discussion on the history of labor relations and the influence of judicial decisions in shaping

class struggle in the United States, *see* Karl E. Klare, *Judicial Deradicalization of the Wagner Act and the Origins of Modern Legal Consciousness*, 1937-1941, 62 MINN. L. REV. 265 (1978).

[855] My initial conclusion was that this could be explained by capital's fear, if not panic, when faced with organized labor. Labor union history shows that one way the state tries to control insurgent movements is to legalize them and then contain and trap them in a welter of regulations. *See* Klare, *Supra* note 281; Ken Silverstein, *Labor's Last Stand: The Corporate Campaign to Kill the Employee Free Choice Act*, HARPER'S MAG., July 2009, at 38.

[856] *See Supra* Part II.C.

[857] *See, e.g.*, BACHMANN, *Supra* note 2, at 206 (citing GINSBERG & SHEFTER, *Supra* note 126, at 18, 21-22, 46, 66, 86, 191) (positing theories as to why neither major political party has engaged in massive voter mobilization since the nineteenth century).

[858] *See, e.g.*, Patricia Lopez, *Ritchie Is Sued over Voter-Registration Records*, STAR TRIBUNE (Minneapolis, Minn.), May 29, 2009, at 2B (describing suit brought by conservative advocacy group and Republican legislators over discrepancy between vote totals from canvassing boards and number of registered voters). The number of election related lawsuits has risen dramatically in recent years. *See* Marcia Coyle, Nat'l Law Journal, *Election Law Litigation Has Doubled Since 2000*, Law.Com, Feb. 19, 2009, http://www.law.com/jsp/article.jsp?id=1202428407304 ("The amount of election law litigation has more than doubled nationwide since the hotly contested 2000 presidential election, and more of that litigation is being fought in federal courts.... In the pre-2000 period, the country averaged 94 election law cases per year; the post-2000 average is 237."). Of course, not all of these are examples of conservatives seeking to restrict the franchise; in several instances, progressive activists have successfully used litigation to expand voting rights. *See* Stephanie Simon, *Latino Activists Seize on Texas Ruling to Boost Voting Power*, WALL ST. J., July 25, 2009, at A3 (reporting a recent ruling that "offers a road map for activists" who "plan to press politicians to give Latino residents more influence" when making redistricting decisions).

[859] *E.g.*, Gary Fineout, *Overhaul of Florida Voting Rules Is Proposed*, N.Y. TIMES, Apr. 16, 2009, at A21 (describing changes proposed by Republican lawmakers in Florida that would impose additional requirements on voters). For a broader discussion on the consequences of restrictive voting rules, *see* Editorial, *The Acorn Story*, N.Y. TIMES, Oct. 17, 2008, at A32 (observing that "one-third of eligible voters are not registered," largely due to "overly restrictive registration rules"); Ian Urbina, *Hurdles to Voting Persisted in 2008*, N.Y. TIMES, Mar. 11, 2009, at A 18 (reporting that

several million voters failed to vote in the presidential election of 2008 "because they encountered registration problems or failed to receive absentee ballots," and many additional voters "were 'discouraged' from voting due to administrative hassles, like long lines and voter identification requirements").

[860] *See, e.g.*, Thomas Basile, *Inventing the "Right to Vote"* in Crawford v. Marion County Election Board, *128 S. ct. 1610 (2008)*, 32 HARV. J.L. & PUB. POL'Y 431. (2009) (arguing that the Equal Protection Clause likely did not create a fundamental right to vote).

[861] *See, e.g.*, John Schwartz, U.S. *Judge Opposes Republicans on Elections*, N.Y. TIMES, Dec. 3, 2009, at A26 (describing continuing enforcement of court's injunction of GOP tactics linked to suppression of voting by racial minorities).

[862] While poor whites may have shared more interests with poor blacks than with wealthy whites during and immediately following Reconstruction, race was used to divide socioeconomic classes and prevent the lower classes from uniting against entrenched interests. *See generally* WILLIAM IVY HAIR, BOURBONISM AND AGRARIAN PROTEST: LOUISIANA POLITICS *1877-1900* (1969) (describing race relations in Louisiana following Reconstruction and the obstacles that impeded the populist movement's attempt to break down racial barriers); ROGER W. SHUGG, ORIGINS OF CLASS STRUGGLE IN LOUISIANA (1939) (documenting the use of race to divide groups with common class interests).

[863] *See* TODD, *Supra* note 47, at 17 ("In developed countries a new class is emerging that comprises roughly 20 percent of the population in terms of sheer numbers but controls about half of each nation's wealth. This new class has more and more trouble putting up with the constraint of universal suffrage."). Implicit in Todd's remarks is that certain developments in the most contemporary "modes of production" of wealthier nations are giving rise to an ideology and practice of neo-mandarinism, a term coined by Noam Chomsky to describe a capitalist order governed by a cultivated but ruthless elite. *See* NOAM CHOMSKY, AMERICAN POWER AND THE NEW MANDARINS (1967). China may now embody this order in its purest form. *See* Slavoj Zizdek, *20 Years of Collapse*, N.Y. TIMES, Nov. 9, 2009, at A23 (raising the possibility that political democracy could impede economic growth, and citing China's "authoritarian capitalism" as potentially "more efficient, more profitable, than…liberal capitalism"). Russia appears to be taking note. *See* Clifford J. Levy, *In Chinese Communist Party, Russia's Rulers See a Role Model for Governing*, N.Y. TIMES, Oct. 18, 2009, at A6 ("What [Russian leaders] admire, it seems, is the Chinese ability to use a one-party system to keep tight control over the country while still driving significant economic growth."). Of course, as Todd points out, softer versions are arising in the West in France, the

United Kingdom, and the United States. *See* TODD, *Supra* note 47, at 17-19. Commentators in these countries have voiced their concern. *See, e.g.*, BOURDIEU, *Supra* note 16, at 33 (critiquing an arrogant ruling class that is characterized by "very high cultural capital" and subscribes to a "racism of intelligence"); Walter Benn Michaels, *What Matters*, LONDON REV. BOOKS, Aug. 27, 2009, at 11, 11 ("[A] diversified elite is not made any the less elite by its diversity and, as a response to the demand for equality, far from being left-wing politics, it is right-wing politics."). In the United States, Obama and his administration illustrate one version of this phenomenon: senior members of the administration and high-ranking appointees were drawn from "Washington insiders" with elite educations and backgrounds. David Brooks, Op-Ed., *The Insider's Crusade*, N.Y. TIMES, Nov. 21, 2008, at A35 (identifying the elite universities attended by many senior members of the administration and concluding that "[e]ven more than past administrations, this will be a valedictocracy-rule by those who graduate first in their high school classes"). *See* also Thomas L. Friedman, Op-Ed., *Our One-Party Democracy*, N.Y. TIMES, Sept. 9, 2009, at A29.

[864] *See* Daniel Patrick Moynihan, *The Professionalization of Reform*, in THE GREAT SOCIETY READER: THE FAILURE OF AMERICAN LIBERALISM 459, 470 (Marvin E. Gettleman & David Mermelstein eds., 1967) (observing the increase in the number of professionals and professions, and that "an enormous number [of professionals are] involved in various aspects of social welfare and reform").

[865] *See* Elinor Graham, *The Politics of Poverty*, in THE GREAT SOCIETY READER, *Supra* note 291, at 213, 217 ("[T]he social-service orientation of the War on Poverty...provides a legitimate outlet for the energies of a group that poses a greater threat to the political system and moral fabric of the society than the inadequately educated poor who are the official objects of aid.").

[866] PHILLIPS, *Supra* note 109, at 41. Teles points to this example to demonstrate the difficulties outsiders may face when attempting to challenge entrenched interests. TELES, *Supra* note 86, at 16.

[867] *See* BACHMANN, *Supra* note 2, at 42-43 (noting ACORN's preference for community participation and limited resort to litigation).

[868] *See, e.g.*, Katherine R. Kruse, *Fortress in the Sand: The Plural Values of Client-Centered Representation*, 12 CLINICAL L. REV. 369 (2006) (discussing the development of client-centered lawyering and the inherent tension between a client-centered approach and the traditional autonomy accorded lawyers' professional decision making abilities).

[869] *See* ERIC HOBSBAWM, THE AGE OF CAPITAL: 1848-75, at 21 (Vintage Books 1996) (1975) (observing that in the mid-1800s, bourgeois society was

incapable of "provid[ing] enough posts of adequate status for the educated").

[870] MOYNIHAN, *Supra* note 291, at 470.

[871] *See* BOWLES & GINTIS, *Supra* note 177, at 253 ("[T]raditionally elite…jobs…are reduced to the condition of wage labor. No longer can professional and small-business people look confidently to a future of controlling their work processes, finding creative outlets in work, or holding decision-making power.").

[872] Rama Lakshmi, *U.S. Legal Work Booms in India: New Outsourcing Industry Is Growing 60 Percent Annually*, WASH. POST, May 11, 2008, at A20; Niraj Sheth & Nathan Koppel, *With Times Tight, Even Lawyers Get Outsourced*, WALL ST. J., Nov. 26, 2008, at Bl. Of course, this observation may not discourage the young reader from a career in law, as it is not clear how much autonomy and fulfillment are provided in other jobs generated by capitalism. *See* BOWLES & GINTIS, *Supra* note 177, at 253.

[873] Even large law firms are being forced to switch from hourly billing to flat fee contracts, potentially reducing profits. Nathan Koppel & Ashby Jones, *"Billable Hour" Under Attack*, WALL ST. J., Aug. 24, 2009, at Al. Law students are finding it hard to get jobs at these firms, even as they drown in debt from student loans. Gerry Shih, *Downturn Dims Prospects Even at Top Law Schools*, N.Y. TIMES, Aug. 26, 2009, at Bl.

[874] *See* BACHMANN, *Supra* note 2, at 168.

[875] 42 U.S.C. 1988(b) (2006).

[876] *See* BACHMANN, *Supra* note 2, at 203-04 & n.17.

[877] *See* CHRISTOPHER H. JOHNSON, MAURICE SUGAR: LAW, LABOR, AND THE LEFT IN DETROIT, 1912-1950, at 13-14 (1988) (describing some of Sugar's accomplishments with the Detroit labor movement and his impact on the relationship of law to labor).

[878] *See Id.* at 47-54 (noting the difficulty Sugar had finding employment after graduation from law school and the dearth of lawyers devoted to labor cases).

[879] *Id.* at 295-98.

[880] *See* ARTHUR KINOY, RIGHTS ON TRIAL: THE ODYSSEY OF A PEOPLE'S LAWYER 83-90 (1983) (describing the motivations of Kinoy and his partners in starting their firm, some of their early work, and some of the questions they had to confront in attempting to serve as progressive lawyers).

[881] William J. Brennan, Jr., State *Constitutions and the Protection of Individual Rights*, 90 HARV. L. REV. 489, 491 (1977) (observing that, under the Supreme Court's Fourteenth Amendment jurisprudence, there had been a "legal revolution which…brought federal law to the fore").

882 *See generally* JOHN J. DINAN, KEEPING THE PEOPLE'S LIBERTIES: LEGISLATORS, CITIZENS, AND JUDGES AS GUARDIANS OF RIGHTS (1998) (examining the role played by state institutions in protecting individual rights).

883 *See generally* BRENNAN, *Supra* note 308 (observing the ability of state courts to use federal constitutional decisions to expand the protections granted under state constitutions).

884 *See* e.g., Vanessa Fuhrmans, *UnitedHealth Settles Class Actions*, WALL ST. J., Jan. 16, 2009, at B3 (describing a settlement agreement in several class actions brought against a major insurer on claims of systemic underpayment, reached after the state attorney general's office investigated payment practices); Adi Ignatius, *Wall Street's Top Cop*, TIME, Dec. 30, 2002, at 64, 66 (documenting New York State Attorney General Eliot Spitzer's record prosecuting fraudulent corporations, "organized crime, gun manufacturers, air polluters, [and] Korean grocers who don't pay minimum wage"). *See* also Damien Paletta & Brett Kendall, *Supreme Court: The Term Ends: States Get More Power to Challenge National Banks*, WALL ST. J., June 30, 2009, at A4 (reporting a Supreme Court decision that will enable state attorneys general to sue national banks in certain cases under state laws).

885 *See Supra* notes 308-11 and accompanying text.

886 *See* David M. Halbfinger, *A Small Party Pushes to Be a Statewide Force*, N.Y. TIMES, Oct. 31, 2008, at A25 (describing the Working Families Party's statewide electoral success and its support for certain Democratic candidates in exchange for increasing the influence of the Working Family Party's platform). *See* also Raymond Hernandez, *Region's House Democrats Facing Pressure on Health Care Overhaul*, N.Y. TIMES, Nov. 23, 2009, at A21 (observing the "growing clout of the Working Families Party" in the context of the debate on national health care reform).

887 "Fusion" is shorthand for an electoral system that allows one candidate's name to appear on the ballot line of more than one party, and voters for a single candidate endorsed by multiple parties are "fused." *See* Peter H. Argersinger, *"A Place on the Ballot": Fusion Politics and Antifusion Laws*, 85 AM. HIST. REV. 287, 288 (1980) (defining "fusion" as "the electoral support of a single set of candidates by two or more parties"). The practical effect of fusion is to make minor parties relevant in a political system dominated by two major parties: when a minor party can put a major party candidate forward on its ballot line, it may be able to attract enough votes to qualify for a spot on the ballot (as many state balloting rules make parties eligible for a place on the ballot if they obtained sufficient electoral support in the previous election). STEVE COBBLE, CTR. FOR A NEW DEMOCRACY, A REPORT ON STATE FUSION LAWS 2 (1992) (on file with author). Once the

minor party qualifies for a place on the ballot, it can run other candidates that have not been approved by the major parties. Additionally, if a major party candidate is elected with significant support from the minor party, that candidate has a greater incentive to respond to the minor party's agenda than if that candidate had been elected solely with major party support. *See* Halbfinger, *Supra* note 313 ("Victory would mean a chance to demand that newly empowered-and deeply indebted-Democratic lawmakers press the [Working Families Party's] liberal agenda...."). Fusion can make life complicated for major parties, often pushing them from the center towards the right or the left. Cobble, *supra*, at 2. Thus in most states, the majority parties have passed legislation making fusion illegal, on the grounds that it is too complicated and interferes with the state's "interest in protecting the integrity, fairness, and efficiency of their ballots and election processes." Timmons v. Twin Cities Area New Party, 520 U.S. 351, 364 (1996). Proponents of fusion argue that fusion promotes democratic participation and the right to associate. The Supreme Court resolved this argument in *Timmons*, holding that fusion was a matter for state resolution and not a constitutional right. 520 U.S. 351.

[888] *See* BACHMANN, *Supra* note 2, at 158-61. I describe the "ideology of expertise" as the concept that, as a result of the increasing complexity of modern society, "ordinary" people need experts (professionals) to solve their problems for them. But the professionalization of many of these fields may have been a response to the need for more upper-middle-class employment opportunities, rather than any actual need for greater expertise. *See Supra* Part IV.B,

[889] *See* DUXBURY, *Supra* note 71, at 14-17. Contrary to this belief in the science of law, law involves more practical experience than "scientific" expertise, as exemplified by the lack of previous judicial experience among members of the Supreme Court. *See* HENRY J. ABRAHAM, JUSTICES, PRESIDENTS, & SENATORS: A HISTORY OF THE U.S. SUPREME COURT APPOINTMENTS FROM WASHINGTON TO BUSH II 40 (5th ed. 2008) ("Among the justices who had served on the Court by 2007, only 26 had had ten or more years of experiences on any tribunal-federal or state-and 38 had had no judicial experience at all...[M]any of the most illustrious members of the Court were judicially inexperienced."). More recently, the Chairman of the Senate Judiciary Committee expressed the hope to see "some more people outside the judicial monastery" on the Supreme Court. Sewell Chan, *Democrat Predicts Speedy Court Confirmation. Republicans Sound Note of Caution*, N.Y. TIMES, Apr. 12, 2010, at A18.

[890] *See generally* LUCAS A. POWELL, JR., THE SUPREME COURT AND THE AMERICAN ELITE, 1789-2008 (2009) (arguing that, because the justices on the Supreme Court come from the class of professional elites, their perspectives-and

thus their decisions-are sympathetic to and supportive of entrenched political interests).

[891] *See* John W. Dean, *The New Nattering Nabobs of Negativism Are Gunning for Obama's Judicial Nominees: A Republican Strategy That We Must All Hope Fails*, FindLaw, Apr. 17, 2009, http://writ.news.findlaw.com/dean/20090417.html (observing that the last five Republican presidents "are responsible for over 58 percent of the federal judiciary").

[892] Compare the current situation to the political climate of 1801, when the newly-elected President Jefferson observed that the defeated Federalists "'have retired into the Judiciary as a stronghold...and from that battery all the works of Republicanism are to be beaten down and erased.'" RICHARD E. ELLIS, THE JEFFERSONIAN CRISIS: COURTS AND POLITICS IN THE YOUNG REPUBLIC 44 (1971) (quoting Letter from Thomas Jefferson to John Dickinson (Dec. 18, 1801)) (alteration in original).

[893] *See, e.g.*, Max M. Schanzenbach & Emerson H. Tiller, *Reviewing the Sentencing Guidelines: Judicial Politics, Empirical Evidence, and Reform*, 75 U. CHI. L. REV. 715 (2008) (observing that the length of sentences ordered in criminal cases and departures from sentencing guidelines are affected by judges' ideological preferences, measured by the party of the appointing president and by the degree of alignment between the sentencing judge and the reviewing circuit court).

[894] Inspiration may be drawn from the Republican response in the 1800s: "The Republicans...began impeachment proceedings against a notorious Federalist judge...and then moved against Supreme Court Justice Samuel Chase who had howled against the Jefferson's [sic] 'mobocracy.' This impeachment effort failed, but Chase watched his mouth ever after." STEVE BACHMANN, CONSTITUTION FOR BEGINNERS 67 (1987). *See* also ELLIS, *Supra* note 319, at 96-107 (recounting Justice Chase's impeachment trial); TINDALL & SHI, *Supra* note 215, at 375-76 (describing the impeachment proceedings against Justice Chase). The Republicans in the twentieth century (including Gerald Ford) were happy to follow the example of their nineteenth century namesakes. *See* WILLIAM O. DOUGLAS, THE COURT YEARS, 1939-1975, at 359 (1981). *Cf.* JEFFERY TOOBIN, A VAST CONSPIRACY: THE REAL STORY OF THE SEX SCANDAL THAT NEARLY BROUGHT DOWN A PRESIDENT (1999) (examining in detail the impeachment of President Bill Clinton).

[895] *See Supra* notes 30-32 and accompanying text.

[896] As per Proust:

This work of the artist, this struggle to discern beneath matter, beneath experience, beneath words, something that is different from them, is a process exactly the reverse of that which, in those everyday lives which we live with our gaze averted from ourselves, is at every moment being accomplished by vanity and passion and the intellect, and habit too, when they smother our true impressions, so as entirely to conceal them from us, beneath a whole heap of verbal concepts and practical goals which we falsely call life.... Our vanity, our passions, our spirit of imitation, our abstract intelligence, our habits have long been at work, and it is the task of art to undo this work of theirs.

MARCEL PROUST, TIME REGAINED, IN SEARCH OF LOST TIME VI 299-300 (Terence Kilmartin & Andreas Mayor trans., D.J. Enright ed., Modern Library 1999) (1927).

There may be some evolutionary explanation for Proust's position: it seems that language replaced grooming as a means to social solidarity amongst our primate forebears. *See* ROBIN DUNBAR, GROOMING, GOSSIP, AND THE EVOLUTION OF LANGUAGE (1996) (observing that most human communication is centered around social information, and comparing language-based communications to the more physical communication of primates). In other words, as the effectiveness and breadth of human communication evolved, physical intimacy was suppressed. Human efficacy increased at the price of intimacy; the price for logos was eros.

[897] DELGADO, *Supra* note 184, at 88.

[898] *See, e.g.*, ORWELL, *Supra* note 238.

[899] *See* BAUDRILLARD, *Supra* note 11, at 25 (positing that culture "clones us" and negates innate differences among people).

[900] This point has been acknowledged by an array of political commentators under a number of concepts. *See, e.g.*, ANTONIO GRAMSCI, THE MODERN PRINCE AND OTHER WRITINGS (Louis Marks trans., 1957) (discussing the concept of hegemony); LAWRENCE TRIBE, AMERICAN CONSTITUTIONAL LAW 785-89 (2d ed. 1988) (arguing that the right to privacy established in the First Amendment is paramount, because discussion is only valuable when the individuals involved have been able to shape their own thoughts, free from the coercive influence of the government); FRIEDRICH ENGELS, LETTERS ON HISTORICAL MATERIALISM, IN BASIC WRITINGS ON POLITICS AND PHILOSOPHY, *Supra* note 16, at 395, 408 (discussing the concept of "false consciousness" and its vulnerability to "misunderstandings and distortions"); George Orwell, *Politics and the English Language*, in ORWELL: IN FRONT OF YOUR NOSE, 1945-1950, at 127, 127 (Sonia Orwell & Ian Angus, eds., Nonpareil 2000) (1968) (remarking on the decline of language, which "must

ultimately have political and economic causes").

901 HANS MAGNUS ENZENSBERGER, THE INDUSTRIALIZATION OF THE MIND, IN CRITICAL ESSAYS 3, 11 (Reinhold Grimm & Bruce Armstrong eds., 1982) ("The self-appointed elites who run modern societies must try to control people's minds…The few cannot go on accumulating wealth unless they accumulate the power to manipulate the minds of the many. To expropriate manpower they have to expropriate the brain.").

902 *See* STEVE BACHMANN, EXTREME PROUST: PHILOSOPHY OF THE "MADELEINE MOMENT" 129 (2007) ("The point of art is to assist us past cliché; but again, art can reinforce and create cliché….').

903 TELES, *Supra* note 86, at 135-80.

904 *Id.* at 16.

905 *Id.* at 12.

906 *Id.* at 140.

907 *See, e.g., Id.* at 158-60 (describing the prominent role Federalist Society leaders played in advising the Bush White House on judicial appointments).

908 *See Id.* at 181-82 ("For a good deal of the period [before the Federalist Society's prominence) the question that loomed over law and economics [the main legal perspective advanced by the Society] was not whether it was right or wrong, but whether it was worthy of being considered at all….Today, law and economics is dominant in private law and plays an important role in much of the rest of legal education.").

909 *See Supra* note 93 and accompanying text.

910 *See* RICH, *Supra* note 79.

911 *See* Charlie Savage, *Liberal Legal Group Is Following New Administration's Path to Power*, N.Y. TIMES, Dec. 11, 2008, at A30 ("[T]he American Constitution Society, founded in 2001 to be a liberal counterweight to the conservative Federalist Society, is rising to power….[T]he society's affiliates are already well positioned to shape legal policy, hiring decisions and judicial nominations for years to come.").

912 *See, e.g.,* Peter Lattman, WSJ.com, Law Blog, Lawyers in the U.S. Senate Quiz: The Answers (Sept. 5, 2007), http://blogs.wsj.comnaw/2007/09/05/lawyers-in-the-us-senatequiz-the-answers/ (noting that sixty percent of Senators hold law degrees, and a large number of those practiced before entering politics). According to the American Bar Association (the ABA), there are 1,143,358 lawyers in the United States as of December 2006, or less than one percent of the population, and yet the ABA reports that the 110th Congress had 174 attorneys in House of Representatives, or forty percent of 535 seats. *Id.*

[913] *See Supra* notes 119-34 and accompanying text.

[914] One could see the high rates of incarceration in the United States as evidence of the lack of freedom in this country. *See, e.g.*, David Cole, *Can Our Shameful Prisons Be Reformed?*, N.Y. REV. BOOKS Nov. 19, 2009, at 41 (describing troubling trends in the high rates of incarceration, including dramatic racial differences and the consequences of the War on Drugs); David Runciman, *How Messy It All Is*, LONDON REV. BOOKS, Oct. 22, 2009, at 3, 3 (observing that a graph comparing American prison rates to those of other developed countries must "be recorded on a log scale, because otherwise the US would be off the chart, even off the page").

[915] *See, e.g.*, John Lanchester, *Bankocracy*, London Rev. Books, Nov. 5, 2009, at 35. In discussing the American financial system following the 2008 subprime mortgage crash, Lanchester suggests: "[P]erhaps we should try and think of a name for the new economic system, which certainly isn't capitalism: that, remember, is all about 'creative destruction', and the freedom to fail. That's exactly what we don't have." *Id.* at 36.

[916] *See Supra* notes 47, 52-53 and accompanying text.

[917] *See Supra* notes 268-71 and accompanying text.

[918] *Id.*

[919] *See* generally BACHMANN, *Supra* note 329; ABRAHAM H. MASLOW, THE FARTHER REACHES OF HUMAN NATURE (Arkana 1993) (1971) (discussing the biological settings required for the actualization of humans).

[920] U.S. CONST. pmbl. ("We the People of the United States, in Order to form a more perfect Union, establish Justice, insure domestic Tranquility, provide for the common defence [sic], promote the general Welfare, and secure the Blessings of Liberty to ourselves and our Posterity, do ordain and establish this Constitution for the United States of America."). For a report card as of 1987, *see* BACHMANN, *Supra* note 321, at 154.

[921] *See* ADORNO, *Supra* note 17, at 365-66 (asserting that philosophy has "slipped into material questions of existence" and describing vividly the sensations of the physical world).

[922] *See* TELES, *Supra* note 86, at 179 (identifying the Federalist Society, composed of legal elites, as the most successful "case of conservative mobilization outside of economic and foreign policy, with the exception of welfare reform").

[923] *See Supra* note 119.

[924] TELES, *Supra* note 86, at 196.

[925] *Id.* at 181-219.

[926] *See Id.* at 9 (observing that "nonelectoral dimensions of party activity have become increasingly important" in this "era of electoral displacement").

[927] *See, e.g., Id.* at 158-60 (describing the prominent role Federalist Society leaders played in advising the Bush White House on judicial appointments).

[928] OBAMA, *Supra* note 276, at 437.

[929] SAMUEL BECKETT, *WORSTWARD HO* 7 (1983).

[930] E.P. THOMPSON: THE POVERTY OF THEORY & OTHER ESSAYS 42 (1978).

[931] NEIL YOUNG & CRAZY HORSE, RUST NEVER SLEEPS (Reprise Records 1979). *See* also BERTOLT BRECHT, WAR PRIMER *81* (John Willet trans. & ed., Libris 1998) (1955) (featuring a picture of Adolf Hitler) ("That's how the world was going to be run! /.../ (In case you think the battle has been won)- / The womb is fertile from which that crept.").

[932] *See, e.g.,* PHILIP JENKINS, DECADE OF NIGHTMARES: THE END OF THE SIXTIES AND THE MAKING OF EIGHTIES AMERICA (2006) (documenting the advances in gender and racial equality that marked the 1960s and their impact on American society); MARK HAMILTON LYTLE, AMERICA'S UNCIVIL WARS: THE SIXTIES ERA FROM ELVIS TO THE FALL OF RICHARD NIXON (2006) (describing the upheaval along racial, gender, class, and other lines during the 1960s).

[933] *See* Richard J. Evans, *Cite Ourselves!,* LONDON REV. BOOKS, Dec. 3, 2009, at 12 (describing the development of a school of thought by French historians during the 1960s).

[934] While history has irrevocably changed, during the resurrection of the conservative movement that began in the 1980s, conservative historians began trying to minimize the importance and efficacy of previous social change organizing. For example, mainstream works concluded that the revolutions in France and Britain were tawdry and unnecessary. *See* e.g., SIMON SCHAMA, CITIZENS: A CHRONICLE OF THE FRENCH REVOLUTION (1989); Mark Kishlansky, *Mighty Causes,* LONDON REV. BOOKS, June 11, 2009, at 31 (reviewing BLAIR WORDEN, THE ENGLISH CIVIL WARS: 1640-1660 (2010)). Thus, the efforts to achieve present victories must not ignore the power of future historians to rewrite today's events.

[935] Some instances of new interpretations of history made more possible and credible by the 1960S include, e.g., JOHN DOMINIC CROSSAN, THE HISTORICAL JESUS: THE LIFE OF A MEDITERRANEAN JEWISH PEASANT (1991) (exploring the life of Jesus from a historical and anthropological

perspective); EUGENE D. GENOVESE, THE WORLD THE SLAVEHOLDERS MADE: TWO ESSAYS IN INTERPRETATION (1969) (tracing the conflicting tendencies of slave regimes); EDWARD W. SAID, ORIENTALISM (1978) (presenting a study of Orientalism).

www.ingramcontent.com/pod-product-compliance
Lightning Source LLC
Chambersburg PA
CBHW051435250726
48655CB00001B/66